Trading
Risk

Founded in 1807, John Wiley & Sons is the oldest independent publishing company in the United States. With offices in North America, Europe, Australia, and Asia, Wiley is globally committed to developing and marketing print and electronic products and services for our customers' professional and personal knowledge and understanding.

The Wiley Trading series features books by traders who have survived the market's ever-changing temperament and have prospered—some by reinventing systems, others by getting back to basics. Whether a novice trader, professional, or somewhere in-between, these books will provide the advice and strategies needed to prosper today and well into the future.

For a list of available titles, visit our web site at www.WileyFinance.com.

Trading Risk

Enhanced Profitability through Risk Control

KENNETH L. GRANT

WILEY

John Wiley & Sons, Inc.

To Nina,
for how could I possibly name anyone else?

Contents

Preface

*Make voyages. Attempt them. There's
nothing else.*
                        —Tennessee Williams
                        Camino Real

You are interested in making money in the markets, or you would not
have selected this book from the millions of other choices—from,
say, Thomas Wolfe to Tom Wolfe. If you're going to forsake the sub-
lime in favor of the pedestrian, then certainly you expect to be paid for the
sacrifice. And who am I to blame you? The truth is, I'd like to get paid, too.

I'm here to tell you that our common objective demands more of us
than simply making the right trades. Every single successful trader I know
employs effective risk management as a part of his or her working program. Of course, I am biased on this subject because risk management is
my career—a profession that has rendered me neither fabulously
wealthy nor immensely popular with my colleagues, but at least perpetually employed.

Not that I set out with any direct intention to become a risk manager.
In fact, it would be more accurate to say that I simply stumbled into it.
Prior to this watershed event, I would have best described myself as someone loitering at the intersection between the financial and the academic
worlds, looking for something to at least partially cover, if not justify, the
financial toll visited on my parents as the result of their willingness to sub-
sidize my two master's degrees. Then, perhaps by fate, the futures markets
beckoned. My uncle and his partners were looking for quantitative
methodologies to estimate what they might lose if things went awry among
the team of traders whose Chicago Board of Trade bond pit activity they
were staking. This was back in the mid-1980s, when no one spent much
time thinking about risk management and, therefore, no one I spoke to had
much of a clue as to how I should begin this task.

I managed to muddle through, however, and did it well enough to
convince the Chicago Mercantile Exchange (the Merc) to entrust me with
the responsibility of building a risk management practice within the bow-
els of its clearinghouse: the central risk-processing unit for that vast and

complex market mechanism. By this time, the field of risk management had evolved to the point that when I told people that this was what I did for a living, the comment was occasionally received with something other than a blank stare. We spent a good amount of time and resources thinking, talking, and engaging in much hand wringing on risk management—and ultimately to good effect, I think. What is more, the stakes were high. Given the impact of the 1987 crash on the Merc's financial system, it was pretty clear that in the future it would have to have a pretty good handle on who was risking what in its markets, and with what resources behind them. Still, I won't lie: There was much trial and error and many mistakes made before we ever began to get it right.

Since that time, I have more or less made a career out of convincing others that if risk management was their objective, I was their guy. My first such "patient" was Société Générale, the venerable French bank, where I gained the enormous advantage of applying the discipline to a multiproduct, multicurrency environment. This was certainly interesting and challenging, for a while; but cursed wanderlust eventually overtook me again. Only this time, I really fixed things for myself, landing in what can only be described as the Dodge City of risk management jurisdictions—the hedge fund industry. Here, as elsewhere, when I arrived, there were nearly no rules; so I had to make up my own. Now the place is a bit more civilized; but what is perhaps even more surprising is that the topic of hedge fund risk management has held my attention for the better part of a decade. Part of the reason for this is that I've had the honor to manage risk for some of the world's finest traders, including Steve Cohen and Paul Tudor Jones, and have managed to survive such wide-ranging crises as the emerging markets meltdown of 1997, the collapse of Long-Term Capital Management (everyone's favorite hedge fund till the winds blew ill there), the September 11 attacks, the fraud-related collapse of Enron and WorldCom, and a host of others too pedestrian to name in this space.

Along the way, it is good that I've learned what I think are some valuable lessons. And what's even better (at least from an expository perspective) is that these lessons are remarkably consistent with one another and draw from a surprisingly small set of themes — themes that will form the framework for the core arguments I will put forward in this book. And while it would be silly to reveal all of them in the preface, I can at least begin to make the case as to why I believe so strongly in these materials.

As alluded to earlier, wherever I've gone in the world of risk management, from trading pits to hedge funds to banks, I have noted that the best traders and investors (and I've worked with both the best and the worst) are all, first and foremost, great managers of portfolio risk. I believe that this is more than mere coincidence, that, in fact, there is a positively Darwinian dynamic at play here. Making money in the markets is very difficult. No one does it all the time. Because great traders are seldom out of the market for extended periods, it follows that when they are not making money, they are actually losing it. Success, therefore, demands that they control their downside during periods of suboptimal performance.

I hope to convince you that my experience is not an isolated phenomenon and that risk management is not only useful but, in fact, essential. Even if you have the market insights and instincts of George Soros or Warren Buffett, your fate as an investor may very well ride on your ability and willingness to practice sound risk management. To be successful in the markets means having a clear understanding of the risks that are inherent in trading/investing profiles so as not to be surprised when bad things happen (and they will). Armed with this understanding, as I've been telling people for years, it becomes possible to actually control these exposures—at least most of the time, which, in my estimation, is a whole lot better than never.

The hard fact is that most people underestimate the control they wield over their exposure profiles, and this, sadly, applies pretty uniformly among amateurs and professionals. I can't tell you how many times I've heard seasoned professionals express surprise at having lost $X in the markets, even though the likelihood of their losing $X was entirely foreseeable. Then they'll go out and lose $X again (or $2X, or $nX, or even X^n) and be surprised yet again, until the entire cycle degenerates into madness and insolvency.

Whether you are an individual trader or an investor who lost a bundle on the tech bust or a professional who bought the debt of one of the high-profile companies (e.g., Enron or WorldCom) that went belly-up as a result of the fraudulent activities of corporate insiders, it is entirely likely that you believe your misfortune was due to an ill wind—a virtual hurricane, a perfect storm—over which you had no control and couldn't possibly have seen coming. In my experience, this is seldom an accurate characterization of matters. More often than not, when looking back on a difficult period in the markets, you will see that (1) there was a wealth of information available to estimate potential loss, and (2) this information could have been used to size exposures in a way that would have rendered even the worst-case scenarios entirely manageable.

Thus, we are not typically the victims of "Mother Nature" or other unseen forces; rather, we are often our own greatest oppressors. My business is to study market patterns to measure their attendant impact on portfolio exposures. And I can tell you for sure that, regardless of your place in the market pecking order, if you spend five minutes a week looking at simple statistics available online from any e-broker or professional data service (such as Bloomberg), you afford yourself the opportunity to gain a very clear understanding of the type of losses you are likely to incur when the markets take a turn against you. It is then in your power to adjust the risk downward if you don't like the digits that such a review produces.

Of course, adopting this sort of approach isn't necessarily conducive to the maximization of returns during periods of peak market opportunity. Quite to the contrary; it is designed to reign investors in at points when their enthusiasm might otherwise reach an apex. It may even cause you to curse your fates when it seems as though everyone else is riding a gravy train that left you at the station. But if you make capital preservation one of your main objectives and institute a simple program to achieve this outcome, not only will you not lose in the (not even very) long run, but you will see sustained and consistent enhancement of your overall financial well-being. Capital preservation during difficult periods pays off in the form of having the ability to put more capital at risk when trends become more favorable. Risk management is not just about not losing money; it is about preserving your capital in a way that will increase profits over the course of your investment career.

This book, then, will show you how to implement a risk management program and how to stick to it. I promise that you won't regret it. The idea will be to create a system that will protect your capital and grow your returns. We will not be focusing on what markets you should trade or which specific financial instruments you should use or what trades you should put on once you have made these decisions for yourself. In these areas, you're pretty much on your own. Our work together will largely be confined to creating a tool kit that will help you understand the statistical characteristics of your portfolio and to defining ways to use these statistics to effect portfolio decision making that is consistent with your financial objectives and associated constraints.

You can think of this book as a practical guide to the art and science of risk management. I hope that once we're through, you'll agree with me that this is a unique perspective on this topic, primarily because of its direct focus on how to actually *devise and execute* a risk management strategy for your portfolio. It's not that we will ignore entirely the concept of risk *estimation*, which, near as I can tell, is the all-encompassing obsession of the risk management literature published thus far. No, we won't forsake these mysteries; rather, we will reduce them to the simplest mathematical forms possible, such that they are both understandable and applicable to the practical situations you will face as a portfolio manager. Perhaps more important, we will use risk estimation merely as the starting point for our risk management program, rather than as an end in itself. We will focus most of our time on discussing how to use these and other tools to deal effectively with such real-life portfolio management problems as

- Determining the levels of exposure most consistent with our objectives, in light of our constraints.
- Identifying alternatives for risk adjustment whenever exposures fall outside of these ranges.
- Anticipating and correcting for internal and external factors that create incentives for portfolio managers to take action that works against their interest from a risk management and capital preservation perspective.

Trust me, brothers and sisters, your success in risk management (and, I would argue, in portfolio management as a whole) turns much more on these matters than it does on selecting the right betas for your stock portfolio or the appropriate model for pricing your options. I have learned this the hard way, in extraordinarily aggressive risk-taking environments, across as diverse a set of market conditions as anyone could reasonably expect to experience over an entire career. I feel that these experiences are both unique and instructive and that they have given me insights worth sharing.

So I'm excited about the prospects for success in this little joint venture of ours, and I hope you are, too. If it works, you'll come away from the experience with a handful of simple guidelines that will save you a fortune in times of duress and, as a result (so I would argue), make you a fortune over the course of your investing career. Along the way, I'll share some of my goofier experiences and give you some insight into rock and roll—a topic on which I have even more to say than I do about risk management. But rest assured that throughout, we'll keep our eyes on the prize: establishing a simple, workable risk management program that is consistent with your objectives and that allocates your scarce, risk-taking resources efficiently across the full range of triumphant and tragic conditions you will experience as an investor.

What do you say? Let's get started.

KENNETH L. GRANT

New York, New York
July 2004

Acknowledgments

This book, nearly five years in the making, draws both directly and indirectly on my experiences in risk management over the past couple of decades. As such, I want to express my heartfelt appreciation to everyone I worked with over this time period, for all of their instruction and for a million smiles (and a few tears). I am particularly indebted to several of my bosses and closest colleagues, among them my uncle Ron Manaster (who gave me my start in the business); John Davidson, Kate Meyer, and Phupinder Gill (my bosses and colleagues at the Chicago Mercantile Exchange, who gave me my first big break); Pierre Schroeder (my supervisor at Société Générale, and one of the most outstanding professionals I ever encountered); Dr. Ari Kiev (who planted the writing seed in my brain); John Macfarlane (my manager at Tudor, who helped me really frame much of the philosophy embedded in this book); and, of course, the illustrious chairmen and senior management of SAC Capital and Tudor Investments. In addition, I gratefully acknowledge specific assistance on this project from individuals including John Higgins, David Hwang, Chris Meier, and others, who know who they are but whom, for various reasons, I won't name specifically. Each lent a significant hand to the process at critical stages; and, had they not been there to provide a helping hand, I believe it would not be an exaggeration to say that the book might not have been completed. I'd also like to thank my editor, Pamela van Giessen, who hung in there over the past half decade through many fits and starts and whose patience and guidance were a driving force in bringing these materials into publication.

Finally, and at the risk of descending beyond the point of utter sentimentality, I want to thank my wife, Deanna, and my children, Brianna and Alex, for making the journey a joyous and worthwhile one and for forcing me from time to time to be at my best, whether I wanted to be or not.

Sincere apologies (and thanks) to anyone I've forgotten. My memory is not what it used to be.

K. L. G.

CHAPTER 1

The Risk Management Investment

*Once a jolly swagman camped by a billabong,
under the shade of a coolibah tree, and he sang as
he watched and waited 'til his billy boiled, you'll
come a-waltzing Matilda with me.*

*Waltzing Matilda, waltzing Matilda, you'll come a
waltzing Matilda with me. And he sang as he
watched and waited 'til his billy boiled, you'll
come a-waltzing Matilda with me.*

—"Banjo" (A.B.) Paterson
"Waltzing Matilda"

In the words of a famous and well-compensated but (perhaps understandably) anonymous economist, "market prices tend to fluctuate." I know this to be the case, for I have witnessed such fluctuation firsthand. Perhaps you have, too. Furthermore, I think we can agree that this, on balance, is a good thing. It's certainly beneficial to my business, and I believe it is to yours, as well. However, I don't pretend that this little bit of philosophy will offer much comfort to you when said price movement adversely affects your portfolio—particularly if, as often is the case, the movement is significant and abrupt and occurs without warning. Still, I encourage you to bear in mind the big picture the next time your favorite stock preannounces bad earnings. And also, come to think of it, do the same thing when your other favorite stock preannounces a *good* number, because you are much more likely to attribute this to your own shrewdness than you are to a lucky roll of the dice.

The truth is that market risk, like the very oxygen that we breathe, remains ubiquitous, necessary, and (oftentimes) unnoticed in the world of portfolio management affairs. Our mission, whether or not we choose to accept it, will be to manage this risk. If we do this job well, it's a fair bet we will be rewarded; if not, we are highly likely to suffer a penalty. Daily I hear from the traders I manage, "Don't worry, Ken, of course we will manage the risk. After all, we're *professionals.*" Fine. Good. Perfect. Only there's one problem: Risk management *costs money* (or were you under the impression that I do this for my health?). Risk management verily hovers over the portfolio management process, reminding you of its presence and making demands at the most inopportune times. During periods of healthy performance, its unrelenting protocols nag at you in a very bothersome manner. When performance suffers, the steps you neglect to take in its name often fall under the heading of "too little too late."

Like highly personal physical exams my fellow baby boomers have the honor of receiving on an annual basis, risk management is a costly, often unpleasant (not only for the recipient, but also, I assure you, for the practitioner) exercise that, if performed regularly, can help prevent nefarious outcomes. My doctor, who is nothing if not a salesman, encourages me to view these procedures as an "investment" (or did he say "intervention"?). That the exercise costs me (in addition to a modest loss of dignity) nothing more than a nominal co-payment is an indication that my insurance company agrees with this characterization. Lying on the examiner's slab last year, eagerly anticipating our annual bonding ritual, the parallels between what lay in store for me and the services I perform on a professional basis really hit home.

And so it is partly as a tribute to my doctor that I call this chapter with which we'll begin "The Risk Management Investment." Risk management *is* an investment; and the more you think of it in these terms, the better off you'll be. As with any investment, it requires the allocation of scarce resources, for which it is reasonable to expect a return. I'm biased, but I believe that a well-conceived and efficiently executed investment in a risk management program ought to generate as healthy and steady a return as anything that's likely to make its way into your portfolio. And I heartily recommend that the next time the invisible hand of risk management finds its way into your nether regions, just do like I do: Close your eyes, repeat over and over again "It's an investment," and wait for the returns to come rolling in.

The Risk Management Investment will insinuate itself into your otherwise tranquil portfolio management existence in myriad ways. For example, you're almost certainly going to have to map your returns through a series of risk metrics that offer perspectives that differ materially from the ways in which you might otherwise view your overall performance. If you are a professional money manager, this measurement system is likely to be designed by others and will invariably, from time to time, yield results that seem counterintuitive. Indeed, as we will discuss later, your employing institution may have viewpoints on how to best measure and control risk that may differ from yours and may impose constraints on you that actually interfere with your ability to efficiently manage portfolio exposure as you see it—even when you are operating with the purest of risk management intentions.

The mapping of your portfolio into risk estimation mechanisms is also likely to require some computing power, data inputs, and other resources for which the providers tend to charge a fee. Either you or someone you pay is going to have to understand this output, at least at its most superficial level. If this person does happen to be you, the time and energy that you apply to these activities will come at the expense of other uses you might have in mind for these most precious of your resources.

However, all of these commitments are minor when compared to this most important, capital-intensive element of the risk management investment process: its impact on your portfolio management decision making. Specifically, *your success from a risk management perspective will be determined by your willingness and ability to effectively adjust your portfolio in ways that serve the objective of risk control and capital preservation and that will, at times, run counter to the actions you would take if you were not constrained by a finite capacity to sustain losses.* These adjustments, to be sure, will occasionally cost you money, but I'm confident that not making them will cost you much, much more.

My guess is that just about everyone who has read this far agrees with this general premise. However, we will be seeking more than moral victories from here on. Specifically, now that we've agreed that a solid, comprehensive, and consistently applied risk management program is a good idea, we will devote the balance of our time together developing such a program, the objective of which will be to provide you with the means to

- Establish rational and effective risk parameters for your account.
- Measure your exposures against these parameters.
- Identify the various alternatives in the marketplace to adjust your exposures, should you deem it advisable to do so.
- Pinpoint the specific situations that call for such adjustment, as well as the psychological and market-based obstacles that might interfere with your ability and/or willingness to make such adjustments—even when they are critical to your financial well-being.

As part of this process, we will develop a statistical tool kit, which will provide a simple, quantitative framework for both risk management and performance assessment. Certainly, this tool kit will not make us omniscient: We won't be able to predict with precision exactly what will happen to a portfolio every single time it is subject to market events—any more than a heart surgeon can forecast the precise sequence of events that take place each time he or she opens up someone's chest. In both situations, there is an ability to estimate a range of outcomes, along with associated probabilities, given a careful reading of internal and external conditions. Moreover, in either case, while the outcome of any single intervention (into the portfolio or the chest) cannot be engineered with certainty, it's a fair bet that practitioners who use available empirical information as the basis for decision making will achieve favorable outcomes more often than those who don't. Over time and across situations, more heart patients survive and, in a similar fashion, more market portfolios are rendered much healthier—each by using techniques of simple statistical estimation that are based on inputs derived from empirical data.

However, while no one dares to describe the field of medicine (or any other biological discipline) as falling outside of the realm of science just because outcomes can't be predicted with certainty, people often wrinkle their noses at the suggestion that trading and risk management be given the same designation. In my estimation, both are *life sciences*, driven by factors that lend themselves to *prediction* that falls short of *certainty*. Moreover, if we don't accept that we can learn a great deal from certain patterns that tend to repeat themselves, in trading and risk management as in medicine and biology, then I would argue that we have no business whatsoever risking capital in the markets. From this perspective alone, unless you are committed to the use of available information inputs as the basis for a scientifically driven approach to portfolio management, there's not much point in wasting your time with these materials. On the one hand, if you don't see the opportunity—in fact, the need—to establish as clinical a trading environment as nature will allow, then your time will be wasted here. On the other hand, if you do choose to seek a statistical advantage through a sustained commitment to a rational and dynamic evaluation of both the market environment and the behavioral characteristics of your portfolio, then I'd say there's cause for heady optimism. Your powers of intervention through observation-based decision making, should you be shrewd enough to use them, can open windows of profitability that are not only sustainable but also scalable.

The keys to success in the effort are, in my view:

1. Identification of a rational set of return objectives, combined with an unfettered commitment to adhere to the essential constraints that apply to your investment program.

2. Ability to estimate portfolio exposures, for the most part on the basis of simple, historical statistics.

3. Understanding of the tools available to adjust these exposures.

4. Capacity for identifying situations where exposure adjustments are necessary (i.e., when risk profiles don't jibe with the aforementioned objectives and constraints).

5. Commitment to make such adjustments consistently and irrespective of the temptations that invariably exist to the contrary.

As we will see, risk management is much less about estimating and much more about doing—a subtle distinction that, sadly, is often overlooked by professional risk practitioners, as well as by those whose portfolios they impact.

The risk management investment takes several forms: These will include time, effort, and maybe some outlays for systems if your portfolio is sufficiently complex as to require the application of mathematical models to understand the pricing dynamics of instruments that you are trading. Most important, adherence to a sound risk management doctrine will routinely compel you to make trades and to assume portfolio profiles other than those that would precisely apply if risk management were not a consideration. Specifically, if you act as you ought, you will oftentimes find yourself unable to put as much capital at risk as you might like when great trading/investment opportunities present themselves. Similarly (though perhaps not as often), it may make sense to apply an excessive amount of capital at a trade about which you are less than thrilled—again, in the name of risk management.

The outlays imposed on those who choose to practice sound risk management therefore take the form of direct expenditures and opportunity costs. It should not surprise you that I will be encouraging you to view these "sacrifices" as investments rather than as expenses, for reasons that are implied in the title of this chapter and that comprise the core premise of this exercise.

Many of these concepts were well established long before that fateful day when I ventured into the field of risk management; but at least from where I stand, the process of applying them cohesively to the practice of portfolio management has been painfully slow to take hold. Most of my work over the years has thus involved the application of simple statistical principals to a practical risk-taking setting. Throughout the evolution of these efforts, I have attempted, at least nominally, to apply the scientific method (OGHET—Observe, Generalize, Hypothesize, Experiment, Theorize—to those who remember their school days) and would summarize the conclusions that I have drawn in the process in the following manner:

- There is a bona fide science that underlies the activities of trading, investment, and portfolio management.

- The various components of this science can be isolated and evaluated in terms of their impact on financial performance.
- Using an extremely simple set of statistical and arithmetic tools, it is possible to evaluate which elements of a given portfolio management process are working efficiently and which are not.
- In turn, by making these quantitative comparisons across periods of time and intervals of varying success, it is possible to gain insights into the specific elements of the process that are underperforming in periods of performance difficulty versus those that are working when things are going right.
- Although it is not always possible to correct problems without generating other inefficiencies in the portfolio management process, it is extremely useful to understand these undercurrents, such that traders can harness their strengths and minimize their weaknesses in the most effective manner available.
- The methodology is also very useful in determining which types of market conditions work most directly in portfolio managers' favor and which work against them. In turn, this knowledge offers the opportunity to more efficiently match resource allocation to associated opportunity in the marketplace.
- When and where a portfolio manager finds areas for potential improvement, the same simple set of statistical tools that is useful in identifying problem areas can also be applied to attack the problems in a controlled manner.

This book and the risk management strategy I will outline simply build on these themes. We begin by discussing a process of identifying and living by a set of core objectives that will serve as the macrolevel measuring sticks of your success and/or failure. Here, you need to think very carefully about your options because, as I will argue when we get to it, there are multiple core objectives that rational investors can set for themselves, each based on a combination of market and personal factors and each implying a slightly different approach to portfolio management.

Once we have established the applicable objectives for performance analysis, we begin to build the statistical tool kit, which is designed to describe your trading portfolio from a quantitative perspective. The first element of this is what is commonly referred to as *profit/loss (P/L) time series analysis*, through which we will put your profitability patterns across time under a microscope—much in the same way that you would look at the technical patterns on the chart of your favorite security. Note that in order to achieve a practical understanding of time series analysis, it is necessary to grasp a small number of bedrock statistical concepts, most notably *mean, standard deviation,* and *correlation.* Each, in my opinion, is conceptually simple and easy to calculate. Taken individually and as a group, they can offer insights into everything from the way markets behave to the relative merits of trading strategies that hope to capitalize on this market behavior.

It is likely that you will have encountered these concepts elsewhere, perhaps in your academic training; and I believe they are useful tools for anyone wishing to better understand portfolio management and its various subcomponents. I encourage you, if necessary, to review your understanding of them, as they are easy to master; and very little else in the bothersome area of statistics is needed to perform the type of targeted performance measurement that is the centerpiece of this book.

Through P/L time series analysis, we will discuss ways to measure your returns not just in terms of dollars invested, but also as a function of the amount of risk you are taking. We will also explore a methodology for setting your exposures to levels that will allow you to reach your objectives, while at the same time enabling you to ensure that under most market conditions you do not lose more than the amount you have predetermined to be your maximum threshold for economic reversal. Separately, I will cover the topic of *correlation analysis*, focusing on ways to measure and interpret the implications of similarities between your performance and external factors, such as the performance of the market as a whole, as well as internal factors, such as how actively you are trading, how much you are investing, and so on.

With the P/L time series tool kit available to help you identify and evaluate your performance in a much more scientific manner, I then describe a range of alternatives at your disposal that allow you to modify some pattern you have determined is counterproductive to your overall portfolio objectives (or making inefficient use of scarce portfolio management resources, such as risk capital). In addition, I discuss ways to use the same tool kit that identifies problem areas to evaluate the effectiveness of any corrective action you choose to take. Again, these methodologies won't be of any help in determining what trades to do when you are somehow operating outside zones of effectiveness. Instead, they will give you the means to identify and evaluate your alternatives in such a way that, I believe, best suits the very personal nature of the portfolio management process.

The final pieces of the statistical methodology I present are those that characterize your performance not across time but on an individual transaction level. By simply aggregating information that you have stored on individual transactions, you can do everything from figuring out how often you are right on a trade versus how often you are wrong, to determining how long you are holding each position and how this impacts profitability. Beyond this, I cover such topics as identifying and analyzing performance in individual securities, in sectors or market segments, in sides of the market (long versus short), and in amount of capital deployed in individual trades.

Trust me on this one—there's a treasure trove of useful information here. What is more (and you'll find me annoyingly repetitive on this topic), by frequently performing these same statistical reviews—across different time intervals and periods of varying performance—you stand to achieve a much clearer understanding of the impact of external factors (e.g., the market environment) and internal considerations (e.g., the individual components of your decision making) on your prospects for achieving your goals and living within your constraints. In turn, the routine performance of statistical analysis across periods of relative success will allow you, should you so choose (and I think you should), to match up your market activity with the conditions and the modes of operation that are most conducive to your success. This alone won't ensure glory or even consistent profitability, but it will give you a heck of an edge over your peers and other market participants who don't heed these metrics and, as a result, risk squandering at least a portion of their scarce investment resources in ways that are almost certainly counterproductive—given their goals and constraints.

We don't want to overstate the case here. While the analytical approach I will recommend *ought* to be useful to just about everybody, it is wrong to think that it offers a precise road map for improved performance. In my experience, there are very few unambiguous diagnoses and even fewer unilaterally beneficial remedies that emanate from the regimens prescribed in these pages. In fact (as we will discuss in detail later), there is a significant risk of taking too literal an interpretation of the analytical output and reacting to it in ways that will actually impede your path to optimal performance. For example, the numbers may indicate very clearly that the longer you hold on to individual positions, the better the result. However, if you respond to this input by simply lengthening your holding periods on every trade you do, taking little or no heed as to how this adjustment might impact other elements of your portfolio decision-making process, it's a fair bet not only that will you not experience improvement, but also that you will lose in terms of both money and aggravation. It pains me to offer this disclaimer, but in the name of public service, I believe I am obliged to do so. Put it this way: If I had discovered any reliable statistical methodology that offered simple, unambiguous remedies for the scourge of portfolio management underperformance, (1) I'd be even more fabulously wealthy than I already am, and (2) I'd need to have my head examined if I even considered the possibility of sharing these results in written form for the royalty on the price of a book.

Know instead that the secrets to deriving full benefit from this magic can be found in the subtler shades of your market experience. These secrets take the form of putting your capital to work when its prospects for yielding some benefit are high; of avoiding the repetition of identifiable mistakes; and of relying on those formidable but elusive twin pillars of the temple of gracious living, patience and discipline, when the likely short-term benefits for such reliance are neither comfortable nor gratifying.

"To thine own self be true," said Polonius to Laertes, in Shakespeare's *Hamlet*; and even though both were ultimately dispatched by the capricious blade of the Mad Dane, I think this advice was worthy of a loving father to his son. Brutal internal honesty is about as adaptive a trait for market participants as I can think of; and, for reasons that should be clear by now, *honesty* will be a major theme of this document. With this in mind, and before we start with the gory but necessary details of portfolio analysis, I'd like to share some high-level qualitative observations that I believe are perfectly in keeping with the spirit of both what I've written thus far and what those steadfast enough to forge ahead will read in subsequent chapters:

Have a Plan and Stick to It.   Prior to engaging in market activity, it is important to take a careful study of everything from your objectives, to the resources you have at your disposal, to the market inefficiencies you are trying to exploit. Unfortunately, my experience in these matters is that even among professional money managers, this type of planning is the exception rather than the norm.

Fight for Every Fraction of a Point in Trade Execution.   Often-times, even the best portfolio managers are focused more on the quality of their trading ideas than on the execution of the strategies. This is a critical mistake. Great ideas are easy to squander, and great follow-through always pays off. By carefully engineering your points of initiation and liquidation, you will experience significant positive differentiation of revenues, relative to a strategy that doesn't feature this level of diligence—no matter how great or lousy your ideas are.

Don't Do a Trade Unless It Is Tied to a Predetermined Target Price and Stop.   As part of the process of both position selection and executions management, you should always adhere to a prespecified price range, on both the upside and the downside, that serves as a prerequisite for keeping the position open. This means that if the market you are trading either reaches your target or violates your stop/loss level, you must liquidate the position. If you still feel you are correctly positioned in this particular instrument, then get out and reinitiate the position with new target/stop parameters. If you do this, you are shaping your own destiny on every trade. If you don't, then there's no limit to how much money you can theoretically lose on a given transaction. Sooner or later, some combination of trades will blow you up.

Don't Operate outside Your Limits or Other Constraints.
Whether you are trading for yourself or earning your keep managing other
people's money, you should have a series of limits in place that govern your
portfolio management activities. These limits will invariably prevent you
from constructing your ideal portfolio from time to time, so adhering to
them will routinely imply trade-offs between what you feel is warranted
based on market opportunity and what I argue is best for your long-term
well-being as a portfolio manager. You will provide your own counsel in
these instances, but I urge you to allow risk-control considerations to carry
the day. Although you may be correct in your assessment of what's going
to happen in the markets at any given time, your risk parameters are based
on more static considerations that are likely to be less influenced by wishful thinking (e.g., by personal financial constraints or by the risk-appetite
constraints of external capital providers).

If you live within these parameters (assuming they are set rationally),
you may give up some upside in selected situations, but you gain the considerable benefit of control. By contrast, if you violate them routinely,
someday you are almost certainly going to be wrong, and in a big way
(to paraphrase Blondie, "One way or another, it's gonna getcha getcha
getcha"). I have seen even the most highly regarded traders in the world
end their careers rather meekly because of this unfortunate reality.

Compare and Contrast Periods of Relative Success. Among the
most important methodologies for portfolio diagnosis that I will describe
in this book is that of comparing individual portfolio decision-making elements in periods of strong success against those in intervals of frustration.
For example, you may want to compare such factors as your correlations
to market benchmarks, or trading winning percentages across these inter-
ludes of diverging fortune, in order to see if they are markedly different.
As we will discuss in great detail, this won't necessarily give you an
answer key as to what will work in the future, but it will certainly offer
insights that may help you apply your capital and other scarce resources
more efficiently.

Try New Things. Markets, by their very nature, are in a constant state
of flux. One reason for this is that any strategy yielding above-average
risk-adjusted return (which we will define in painful detail later) is, by the
unshakable laws of human nature, under a sustained threat by other market participants seeking to correct this "inefficiency." Indeed, as any close
observer will tell you, the rate of change is increasing at an increasing
rate. This means that there is a limited shelf life for nearly any highly successful market approach. Ultimately, I believe that almost any strategy
either will require significant tweaking or will be periodically subject to

diminished returns over what constitutes a very real but little understood business cycle that exists for market participation of all kinds.

As a result, only those who are willing to perpetually adapt to change have the opportunity to succeed consistently at trading and investment over a lifetime. In addition to encouraging you to be proactive in the adaptation of your strategies, I will show you ways to use a statistical tool kit to establish a framework to ensure that your forays into uncharted waters are undertaken as controlled experiments, such that the likelihood of their success can be maximized, with minimal damage if things go wrong.

Take More Risk When You Are Up and Less When You Are Down. The Children of Israel didn't receive this commandment from Moses on the mountaintop, but I'm pretty sure that it was in the first draft of the tablets. Rumor has it that the Almighty, in his infinite wisdom, removed it as part of the punishment for that idol-worshiping romp in the desert (as led by Edward G. Robinson in the Cecil B. DeMille vehicle). It thus falls upon mere mortals such as myself to lead the faithful out of the wilderness of setting risk levels that don't include recent performance as a key decision factor.

The practice of sizing your risk on the basis of recent P/L performance is perhaps the most important rule for success that I've encountered in the markets. However, even if you buy into the concept, you will find it among the most difficult of conventions to follow (ranking, by some accounts, on a par with that one about thy neighbor's wife). This is particularly true when you are losing money, as there is a natural urge to increase exposures during difficult periods in the hopes of minimizing the time period of underperformance. Your instincts will tell you to load up and make it all back as quickly as possible—and your instincts couldn't be more wrong. For enlightened portfolio managers who wish to have long careers, the price of a P/L setback is measured not in the dollars needed to recover but in the time necessary to make those dollars.

By contrast, those who choose to increase their exposures after a difficult interval may see this strategy pay off once, twice, or even several times; but ultimately, it is a ticket to disaster where they will bomb out—perhaps in spectacular fashion. A mentor of mine, and one of the true pioneers of modern-day portfolio management (okay, it's Paul Tudor Jones), is fond of saying that sooner or later, we all go to the trader graveyard. In my experience, this does not actually have to be the case. I believe that if you cut losses during periods of performance difficulty, you can, in fact, trade into a state of immortality.

In addition to arguing the merits of setting your exposures as a positive function of performance, I will discuss simple statistical tools that will enable you to operate at exposure levels that will help you to stay in the game indefinitely, no matter how badly you may suck at reading the markets.

HEY, JOE, WHERE ARE YOU GOING WITH THE RISK IN YOUR BOOK?

Listen, Joe, I need to speak to you about your portfolio. I've been watching you closely over the past few weeks (of course, as your risk manager, this is my job). I know your performance has been a bit disappointing, but I want you to know I'm not particularly troubled about that. You've been through this before, and I'm confident that you'll pull through quite nicely, as you always have in the past. However, I do sense a certain anxiety on your part; and I won't lie to you, this concerns me a great deal. I know it's getting later in the year, and you're anxious to reverse your performance so you can get paid. I also sense, and correct me if I'm wrong here, that you're sniffing big opportunities in your space. Bottom line: My instincts tell me that you're debating whether now wouldn't be a perfect time to increase your risk profile.

What's that? Did I hear you say you want to take a shot here? Of course, you do! After all, we're looking at a world-class market opportunity, are we not? You've done your homework, and you couldn't possibly be wrong, could you? Besides, you're tired of losing money, and I don't blame you one bit for this. To put it bluntly, your recent performance has sucked, and the only rational answer is to trade bigger. There's certainly no portfolio management problem I've ever encountered that couldn't be solved by simply trading in bigger sizes, and God Almighty didn't breathe life into us just to trade for chump change. Once you've nailed your big trade, a lot of things are going to change for the better. You'll be nicely profitable, and you'll be in a great position to move forward in the markets in a very disciplined manner. All you really need to do is to get this next one right, and everything else will fall into place.

But what if you're not right? Trust me here, you'll have bigger problems than you are anticipating at the moment—so big, in fact, that I strongly suspect the upside is not worth the downside. For one thing, you'll have lost a good deal of money—in the process further exhausting your risk capital at a most inopportune time. What's more, it will be difficult, without great effort, to rationalize away the following unpleasant realities: (1) Your thoughts about what constitutes a high-conviction trading opportunity are somewhat less than infallible; and (2) you've failed pretty unambiguously at the challenge of capital preservation—at a point when capital preservation was a particularly important objective. At that point, your capital reserve and confidence will be at an ebb; and what might be worse, I will be looking more fervently over your shoulder than ever before.

You now have the opportunity to play your big idea in smaller size. If you do this, no matter what happens, you will experience a palatable range of outcomes. Assuming you nail the trade, you should still make money (just not as much as if you had played it in large size). If the markets go against you, the financial damage will be minimal. Either way, you will gain the confidence that emanates from a sound and consistently applied risk management program. All of this could be yours by simply setting aside some of your remaining capital for a rainy day (sort of like an investment, if you catch the drift) and sacrificing some potential upside on a single set of high-conviction market ideas. At the end of the day, you'll probably end up ignoring my advice and, if things go wrong, just blaming the risk manager. Why not? Everyone else does. But for your own welfare, I urge you to take a good look in the mirror and ask yourself whether you might've had just the teeniest hand in creating your own misery from this sorry episode.

Always Save a Healthy Amount of Risk Capital for "Special Situations." Although the act of playing your best ideas at smaller sizes during a period of suboptimal performance is a prime example of the Risk Management Investment at work, you may be surprised to read that it does not always represent the best use of your risk management resources. I must point out that the mark of portfolio managers who have truly mastered these concepts is their ability to nearly *always* have an abundant reserve of risk capital available for high-conviction market opportunities. Specifically, *by practicing relentless risk management throughout all phases of a trading cycle, they avoid suffering precipitous drops in their risk-taking capacity and are therefore poised to take advantage of unique opportunities, whenever they present themselves.* This means setting aside a portion of their profits on all of their winning trades, as opposed to always and immediately redeploying these winnings in the market. It means cutting losing trades before their impact extends beyond that of mere annoyance. It means being patient about recovering losses after a bad spell, and it means exercising restraint and discipline at all times. This is what great traders do.

By contrast, mediocre traders often find themselves on a treadmill, where they've repeatedly squandered their risk capital on substandard ideas—a problem that they frequently exacerbate by pressing their bets at the wrong time. Then, when really good ideas do formulate in their brains, they have neither the means to put the trades on in respectable size nor the staying power to hold the trades long enough for the sequence that they envision to play itself out. After the fact, they curse their luck and blame sinister outside forces for their inability to make any money, the accuracy of their predictions notwithstanding.

I'm here to tell you that there's very little luck involved in these situations; that there are indeed outside forces at play; and that you are not wrong to believe there is a systemic conspiracy seeking to ensure that when your market prospects are at their greatest, your ability to capitalize on them is maximally constrained. This is true because portfolio managers as well as those who monitor their risk tend to operate with something of a herd mentality. Traders often have similar thoughts about market opportunity and routinely put on the same types of bets at similar times. In turn, risk managers (a breed not typically distinguished by their propensity for original thought) tend to impose similar types of constraints on portfolio managers, who therefore tend to effect risk reduction, at the same time and in a homogeneous fashion. Many, many times this means selling at or near the absolute lows or covering short positions at the top of their ranges. These risk-reducing trades often leave pricing inefficiencies in their wake, and those who have carefully preserved capital (i.e., those who are *invested* in risk management) frequently find themselves in an ideal position to capitalize. So when your risk management system tells you to sell your longs or cover your shorts, it is no accident that you may be making the former trades at the lows and the latter ones at the highs. And rest assured that the windfall you may be handing to the person sitting on the other side of the trade is likely the result of superior risk management on his or her part.

Examples of this "group-act" occur just about every day, embedded in market events both large and small. Consider the 1987 crash: Consensus was pretty bullish back then; and speaking for my fellow geezers everywhere who remember this event, the timing took everyone more or less by surprise. Anyone who was aggressively long got carried out; and for much of that day, there were no buyers anywhere (the New York Stock Exchange specialists showed themselves to be especially gallant by not answering phones and hiding under desks). So most who were forced to sell did so at or near the absolute lows. By contrast, some market participants were aggressively short, and they received a very fortunate windfall. Here's hoping they put some of that away for a rainy day.

Others—those who managed its risk very carefully, trading both sides of the market and maintaining a healthy reserve of risk capital for all contingencies—had a world-class opportunity when the market restabilized by staging an impressive four-month rally from its early December low. From there, as everyone knows, the markets were off to the races for more than the next decade. By carefully contrasting the outcomes that befell the heathens with those of the risk management faithful, one notices an acute dichotomy. With regard to the former, not only did they probably lose their shirts during the crash, but they also missed a chance to load up early into a market that increased fivefold over the next decade. By contrast, those who minimized their damage in 1987 had investing power aplenty to catch the wave.

There are a whole bunch of scenarios like this, playing themselves out in events dramatic and mundane. Success can be defined in terms of having the capital to risk when risk is worth taking, or at least of having the sense not to take big risks when you can't afford to be wrong.

Make Sure You're Taking Enough Risk to Justify Your Trading.
There are also situations when the Risk Management Investment actually dictates the need to assume higher levels of exposures than those you are predisposed to take. And while these are perhaps less intuitive, the impact is often no less dramatic and, as such, they bear mention. One such situation occurs when the portfolio manager is operating at levels of exposure so low he or she can't possibly hope to meet return objectives. This manager may believe that he or she is being prudent, but I would quarrel with this characterization—particularly for professional money managers, a group who in my experience quite often run into this problem. You are not going to endear yourself to your capital providers by using up their financial and perhaps trading infrastructure resources in efforts that can't hope to produce the desired level of performance. For many of those to whom this applies, their risk-taking deficiency may render it impossible for them to even cover associated infrastructure costs. And I have witnessed enough of these scenarios to know with certainty that this is a condition that cannot last for long. Either risk taking increases, or the individual in question gets fired. It's as simple as that.

Over the longer term, successful portfolio managers also need to set aside some risk capital for developmental purposes, and this too can be thought of as a Risk Management Investment. Markets are always changing, and the methods that are working for you now are unlikely to sustain you in your purpose over an investing lifetime. It is therefore prudent not only to carefully note the changes you are observing, but also to use a portion of your accumulated risk capital to test new hypotheses and ultimately to develop new strategies. In later chapters, we'll discuss ways to establish clinical parameters for these developmental efforts, including timing, such that they become unlikely to cost you anything more than you are willing to expend on them, as well as methodologies for analyzing the prospects for success of these new approaches in a manner liberated from the natural forces of subjectivity.

Pay Very Close Heed to Events "at the Margin." One of the few truly useful concepts that the field of economics offers is that decision making at the margin of behavior is a key driver of economic outcomes. Examples of this are everywhere. Businesses produce up to the point where marginal revenue equals marginal cost. Consumers consume up to the point where marginal utility and cost intersect. Because of these realities, if you want to understand the economics of any situation, it pays to pay attention to activity at the margin.

How does this apply to portfolio management? In trading, success or failure is decided, more often than not, by behavior at the margin. If on each transaction you strive to save yourself a few pennies on commission, achieve a tick or two better on each execution, manage your risk to slightly more precise parameters, and conduct that extra little bit of research, you will achieve a dramatic, positive impact on your performance. I promise that, depending on where you are in your P/L cycle, this will turn good periods into great ones, mediocre periods into respectable ones, and otherwise catastrophic intervals into ones where the consequences are acceptable. Managing these types of performance metrics is hard work, but it is not nearly as difficult as losing lots of money or simply treading water. What is more, you'll never maximize your returns unless you factor these components in. Improving performance at the margins of your trading activity will be a main theme of this book.

Do Not Become Overreliant on Other Market Participants for Comfort or Assistance. Blanche DuBois would not have lasted through the first scene of *A Wall Street Car Named Desire* because depending on the kindness of strangers is the practical equivalent of financial suicide (except for me—I am your friend).

Don't Do It (Just) for the Money. Word up, brothers and sisters, if you're going to be in the markets, y'all ought to try to have some fun along the way. No field of human activity is more competitive; and in light of this, I believe that success requires not just ability but desire as well. More power to those who can get juiced by nothing else than the relentless pursuit of the dead prez. But in my experience, those who operate entirely from this perspective will not only run out of steam eventually but will also fail to capture some fundamental elements of the experience: the joy, the pride, the buzz.

Why the joy? Wherefore the pride? Whither the buzz? Because you are playing one of the greatest games known to mankind. Because, as Teddy Roosevelt said, "In the arena," and not a "timid soul who knew neither victory nor defeat." Because your successes and failures will be very much of your own making. Because without traders like you, willing to risk capital in your belief about the value of economic assets, the world would have a much poorer notion of what those assets were worth. Because the markets you trade are critical to a process that builds roads and factories and hospitals around the world. Because if you weren't there to help efficiently price capital assets, money would flow to the wrong economic projects, and we'd all be worse off as a result. Because no one really knows for sure what will happen over the next five minutes, much less the next five years. Because the band is playing and your feet should be tapping. Can you hear the beat? I can.

STRAY CAT BLUES

Brian was a very successful portfolio manager at a highly respected financial institution. Several years ago, he found himself in a career-defining crisis, triggered by a widely publicized global market disruption. Up till that time, he had put together an amazing track record, over many years and across an impressively broad set of market conditions. Not only had he done very nicely in his own right, but he had become something of an industry unto himself, with literally dozens (if not hundreds) of stakeholders leaning on him for a portion of their well-being. True to his nature, Brian bore all of this with modest good spirit. When the crisis began to unfold, he was in the midst of yet another record year; but as fortune would have it, his portfolio was caught in the crossfire of a hurricane that nearly engulfed the global financial marketplace.

Because he had unique market insight, he not only saw the unfolding storm threatening in its extreme formative stages but also recognized its potential magnitude before almost any of his competitors. At the first true warning signs, he started a massive liquidation, exhorting his colleagues to do the same—all well before the contagion expressed itself in the form of a full-blown market panic. The liquidation was a very expensive process and eradicated considerable portions of his profitability. His notions of a record year gone (at least at that moment), he focused exclusively on the objective of capital preservation. Most everyone around him was disappointed with his actions. Few had sympathy, and some of his closest supporters told him to go to the devil. "What's the matter with the boy?" they said "Is he checking out for sure? Is he gonna close the door on me?" Then the crisis began to unfold in earnest, and this, of course, afforded him a measure of vindication. However, as often is the case in market disruption, the real damage occurred in intermittent phases. After the initial crisis, there was a period of calm, which nearly everyone (with the notable exception of Brian) took as a signal of a complete return to normal market conditions.

All through the calm period, Brian continued to liquidate his portfolio, letting most of his hard-won profits bleed away in the process. Some of his colleagues tried to be aggressive in the markets and encouraged him to do the same, but Brian didn't listen to any of them. Every day, he came in and reduced his position size as much as he could—given the liquidity of the markets. Then the second critical market disruption hit. By this time, Brian was nearly flat. Meanwhile, many of his competitors were in free-fall liquidation mode in markets for which there were simply no takers for the other side of these trades. Several of his comrades blew their careers during this period. Some lost nearly all (and nearly all lost some) of their capital. Brian emerged, in the aftermath, with a healthy level of profitability still intact and ample risk capital to carry on the fight.

A story like this we would typically end right here, but Brian wasn't done —far from it, in fact. Though still up for the year, wherever he saw red, he was determined to paint it black. He was way down from his highs, and he was determined to operate at modest risk levels until he'd recovered these losses. The process took months; and at various turns, Brian resisted the temptation to return to aggressive or even normal risk levels. He simply wasn't going to risk another drawdown at that critical juncture. Sure, there were market opportunities; but he knew that if he got very aggressive there and happened to be wrong about his ideas, he'd be back down near his lows, and he was simply unwilling to put himself in that position.

After several months, he'd made it all back and was ready to attack wherever and whenever it made sense to do so. As the fates dictated, there were abundant opportunities for much of the rest of that year, and Brian ended up beating his record after all. Clearly, he had understood the value of the Risk Management Investment.

Brian is invisible now; he's got no secrets to conceal. Rumor has it though that he's got his trading Jones back, but I personally doubt he ever lost it. In fact, if you listen closely, you can hear the clip-clap of his feet on the stairs.

I'd like to conclude this chapter my stating my belief that on the whole, Risk Management is a demanding but benevolent mistress who can and will cause all kinds of annoyances (or worse) if she is treated with benign (or, for that matter, malignant) neglect. For the most part, her demands will be reasonable; but if you don't attend to her wishes routinely, she won't be there for you when you need her most. At that point, you'll discover charms that you hardly noticed when she was hovering about you, begging for your attention. Strive to keep her satisfied while doing so is a matter of convenience and not absolute necessity. You'll find her a stalwart companion. Remember, she has your best interest at heart. Make her your regular dance partner; but be careful as to the style of music you select. She will tolerate Rap but tires quickly of it. She is leery of Hip-Hop, Grunge, New Wave, and other faddish genres; and she altogether eschews Punk. She's Never Been to Spain, but she kinda likes the music.

Above all, she loves the waltz, with its graceful, flowing lines; and she won't insist on leading—unless you utterly botch the job on your own. And no matter how clumsy you are, try not to step on her toes.

CHAPTER 2

Setting Performance Objectives

Joy is at the end of hoping,
Happiness is there some days,
Jesus told me I'm a spaceman,
and I believe in every word he says.

—Shawn Phillips

So what is it that you're trying to accomplish in the markets anyway? Have you given it much thought? Perhaps you should, and maybe I can help frame the question. For rhetorical purposes, we'll continue to assume that your goals have something vaguely to do with making money; but now's the time to move beyond glib generalities. Remember, we're talking about *investment* here, which implies the allocation of scarce resources—by which I mean resources that I'm assuming you can't afford to squander. Further, because the *risk management* elements of investment add an additional layer of complexity to what is already a complicated process, establishing methods to evaluate performance becomes an even more critical prerequisite to success.

On the one hand, we know that our goal setting must extend beyond a general commitment to trade profitably. On the other hand, we've got enough inputs (or will have, within a couple of chapters) to create, if we were so disposed, a mosaic of objectives of self-defeating complexity.

Recall, if you will (and for those who haven't encountered it, I suggest you amend this error quickly), the Byrds song "Chestnut Mare." In it, the singer talks about catching a horse, but not just any horse, one that he himself could befriend for life. This is one way of thinking about the task of setting your portfolio management objectives.

What kind of horse are you going to catch (if you can)? If you are like me, you'll agree that the question is an important one that should take into account all contributing factors.

Let's start by identifying the following critical constraints:

- Market conditions are both dynamic and unpredictable. Sometimes they're good and sometimes they're bad; and it's very difficult to know one from the other—at least until after the fact. Conditions also change rapidly and without warning.
- Market participants have finite resources, most notably those associated with time and the ability to sustain losses.

Given, then, that you are operating with limited resources in a universe where the quality of the environment is difficult to measure and constantly shifting, I believe that your goal setting must take into account a number of possible outcomes. At one end of the spectrum, there's certainly nothing wrong with thinking expansively, and I'd be the last to argue against setting ambitious objectives simply because difficult obstacles may stand in the way of your attaining them. However, part of your planning should also reflect the fact that the markets themselves may limit your upside and that no set of objectives would be complete if they fail to contemplate capital preservation under difficult if not disastrous circumstances.

To reinforce these points, I recommend the setting of not one but three sets of objectives:

1. *Optimal Target Return.*   This is the amount of profit that you are shooting for if everything (i.e., external market conditions and internal account management) goes right. Your profit figure should typically be high enough that you will have to stretch your skills to reach it, but not so high as to be inherently self-defeating.

   "Too low they build, who build beneath the stars," said the English poet Edward Young in *Night Thoughts*. I'm not sure that this is always true for the science of portfolio management and trading; but then again, maybe I've been on the risk management side of the business for too long.

2. *Nominal Target Return.*   This figure should be fixed at the amount of revenues that you feel confident you can achieve under almost all market circumstances and below which you will acknowledge that something may have gone wrong with your plan, thereby allowing for subsequent critical analysis.

3. *Stop-Out Level.*   Perhaps the most important parameter of all, this figure is the amount of loss at which you commit to a complete

liquidation of your portfolio—and is a figure that you must commit not to exceed.

Because these objectives will serve as critical benchmarks, not only in judging overall performance but also in terms of evaluating the efficiency with which you are managing your resources, I discuss each in further detail.

OPTIMAL TARGET RETURN

Another righteous English poet, Robert Browning, said (in *Andrea Del Sarto*), "Ah, but a man's reach should exceed his grasp, or what's a heaven for?" Each year (or other applicable period of your own choosing), it's almost certainly a good idea to set a performance goal that is sufficiently aggressive as to represent a major accomplishment if you are able to achieve it. While this might raise a few eyebrows among my brethren at the Temple of the Risk Averse, I am willing to accept their derision because I feel that the setting of an Optimal Target Return is an ideal start-ing point for the formation of a plan of attack for any upcoming trading cycle.

If you're going to be at your best in this difficult project, it's pretty important for you to challenge yourself. You really have no choice but to try to become better at this game, as you are not likely to remain at the same level of investment competency for very long. By definition, either your skill set is improving or it is eroding. If you want to succeed, you must continually push yourself.

Even if you are making more money than you ever imagined and/or have accumulated more capital than you can envision spending, if you wish to continue on in the business of trading, it will be necessary to *reach* for performance objectives that are beyond your *grasp*, if nothing else as a means of ensuring that you don't fall into a comfort zone that may be harmful to your longevity in the markets.

How does the setting of an ambitious performance objective help ensure that your trading skills continue to improve, as opposed to erode? Among other factors, the mere process of setting the high target will force you, if you are not given to introspection, to carefully examine every aspect of your trading in order to identify potential areas of improvement. In particular, if you are comfortable that in a given cycle you are likely to make $X and then set your target level of return to, say, between 125 per-cent and 150 percent of $X, you will simply not have any alternative other than to take a look at every individual associated subprocess in order to find sources of potential efficiency improvement and scalability.

Indeed, while the market superstars I have known are as diverse a group as the United Nations General Assembly, they all have in common the setting of aggressive performance goals. At least once a year (more frequently if necessary), they use the exercise of setting the optimal target return to undertake a full-scale evaluation of their programs and to make whatever changes they deem necessary to help them achieve their lofty objectives. Again, the underlying objective here is to continue your professional growth so as not to fall into a trap of stagnation that can lead to regressive behavior and deteriorating performance.

How does this reengineering process occur? What forms can it assume? Obviously, this will vary from situation to situation. Following is a list of four analytical steps that you might begin to take, which may provide great insights into the best means of achieving goals that you may believe are currently outside your grasp.

1. *Critical Self-Assessment of Performance during Previous Cycle.* The first step in the evaluation process should be a review of your performance over the recent past. Here, you should begin by looking at everything that touches your trading/investing process, from the quality of market opportunities to the physical environment in which you are operating. How were the markets last year? Were you satisfied with your performance in light of these conditions? Which opportunities did you make the most of and which did you miss? What component of your performance can you honestly attribute to good luck, to bad luck? Given all of this, what would you have done differently?

2. *Review of Current Conditions.* The next step is to take a very close look at the current characteristics of your trading environment. Here again it is important to evaluate both market-based factors and situation-specific factors. Note that the purpose in doing so is to create an objective and realistic backdrop for your strategic market initiatives, not to force yourself to generate a "market call." If your market call is good enough, you will need little in the way of trading technique in order to be successful; and you will not find very much in this book or any other trading manual that would create much of an additional impact. Most of us are weak in this area, and we know it; so it's important to develop as careful an understanding of the prevailing conditions as is practical.

   Focus here on qualitative factors. Are the markets trending or choppy? What types of participants are increasing their activities? What types are reducing capital usage or bailing out altogether? How is all of this impacting the market's liquidity and volatility? Answer these questions as objectively as possible. Now, try to assess how the associated answers are likely to present themselves—in the form of opportunities and obstacles to optimal performance.

It is also important to review the more immediate external factors associated with your trading. How comfortable are you in your physical trading environment? How is your relationship with those immediately around you and with your supervisor or capital provider? What are the best and the worst elements of this setting, in terms of associated prospects for maximizing your performance?

3. *Formulating an Action Plan.*   Once you have completed the review of recent performance and current external environment, you are in a very strong position to figure out the adjustments necessary for you to operate on the higher plateau that the optimal target return concept demands. If all is going well, the key factor here might be an increase of your trading size, intensity level, and/or support resources. If, however, you have experienced a recent history of trading at levels below your optimal expectations, other more rudimentary changes may be in order. For example, you may have to commit to structural changes in your trading behavior (a concept we will discuss in further detail), to a rethinking of your day-to-day operating modes, or to other similar adjustments. Maybe you are simply not working hard enough. Maybe you're overdoing it. Whatever the case may be, it will be up to you to identify the opportunities for improved performance, to formulate a plan, and to put it into action.

Finally, with respect to optimal target return, I should mention that in some cases this figure may justifiably be set at levels below historical performance. This would be particularly true in cases where recent returns have been suboptimal and/or erratic or where a trader's market environment has changed sufficiently to warrant a downgrade of expectations. The point is to identify a performance target level that will take you out of the zone of comfort and into that of challenge and to build your trading program around this objective.

4. *Masters and Their Master Plans.*   I've actually been amazed at the effort that I've seen superstar traders put into this goal-setting business. After awhile, it started to make more and more sense. Most of them are introspective by nature and are always tinkering with various aspects of their portfolio approach. However, these efforts are minor compared to the all-encompassing, top-to-bottom analysis that takes place in very solemn fashion for nearly all of these guys at the end of each year. While this analysis is typically very scientific, the goal-setting part of it is often not. For one thing, the figures they set tend to be positively astronomical. For another, the actual numbers at which they arrive have a ritualistic quality to them that varies in its origin from one to the next. One guy might like nice round figures, so his

targets always have multiple zeros at the end. Another trader I've observed adds the amount he'd like to give to charity (increasing each year at an increasing rate) to the amount he anticipates his wife will spend (rate of acceleration even higher still) to determine the amount he needs to make. Sometimes, if he meets or exceeds his revenue pace, he has been known to prod his wife to spend even more so the bar can be set even higher.

Once the superstars have the appropriate number in mind, they have to figure out how to get there, and this involves focusing on questions like: How good are markets likely to be next year, opportunity-wise? Where are these opportunities likely to be? How do I need to change my trading style to capture them? What adjustments do I need in terms of my support resources? What trading sizes will work best in these markets? How can I adjust my work habits to help achieve my goals?

I've seen this analysis process yield amazing results, even when the trader in question, as often happens, failed to reach his or her target returns at the end of the period. It's taken me awhile, but I'm now convinced that the exercise is a worthwhile one.

It all kind of reminds me of what I believe artists must do to sustain their relevance. Whether it be Bowie and Iggy Pop migrating to Berlin in the mid-1970s to record astonishing albums behind the Iron Curtain, or John Lennon breaking up the Beatles at their creative peak, or Vincent van Gogh abandoning the comfort of his artist's community in Paris only to burn his brains out with badly made absinthe in the bleeding hot sun of Arles, intellectual excellence can only be achieved through continuous evolution. Guard against getting too comfortable in the markets; like the wilderness itself, the creed of "adapt or die" prevails.

NOMINAL TARGET RETURN

As important as it is to set an optimal target return, it is equally important to set a minimum performance target that represents the lower bound of acceptability. In this case, instead of targeting a performance objective that is geared toward challenge and development, you want to set a figure that is at a level entirely within your comfort zone. The main reason for this is that I want you to think of the nominal target return as a benchmark, which, if you fail to reach it, will cause you to acknowledge that some element of your portfolio strategy is not working. In turn, this will force you to review your entire portfolio management environment, this time with an eye toward either fixing what's broke or scaling back your expectations, or some combination of the two.

For certain professional traders (particularly those operating in formal financial institutions), this figure might be tied to your budget revenues, though I am hesitant to be too formulaic in this regard as the relationship between budget revenues and nominal targets will vary from situation to situation. In some cases, trading managers will take the incredibly scientific approach of setting their budget revenues at an arbitrary but significant percentage above last year's performance, oftentimes without giving due consideration (or, for that matter, consideration of any kind) to any obstacles that may render such an objective unrealistic or even irresponsible. In other cases, management may set the budget bar too low, preferring the somewhat illusory comfort of knowing that they will meet or exceed this target under all but the worst foreseeable market conditions. In any event, while you certainly will want to be mindful of the budgetary process in establishing your nominal targets, you should not allow the (potentially irrational) budgetary process of your firm to interfere with the process of carefully and objectively determining your nominal profit/loss (P/L) target.

If you are operating outside the framework of a professional trading organization, you will have more freedom to establish a rational lower-bound return target. However, I encourage all free agents to go through the process in a fairly rigorous fashion nevertheless. While it will be tempting to tie this figure to such nonmarket factors as meeting minimum spendable income levels, I suggest that you instead orient the goal entirely toward issues that pertain directly to your trading. Make a realistic assessment of all aspects of your portfolio management environment, including the markets, your modes of execution, and financial constraints. Then ask yourself the following question: "Operating within the conditions/constraints that I currently face, what is the minimum performance that I would consider satisfactory?" Understand that if you don't reach this threshold, certain adjustments are in order. It's halftime, you're down by 10, and your matchup zone just ain't working. Number 43 is lighting you up. If you're going to win the game, you better try a box-and-one.

By doing this, you stand to accomplish a number of objectives. First, the review process will force you toward the types of sound trading habits that we will continue to stress as the difference between success and failure in many circumstances. In addition, by committing to realistic minimal return objectives, you will impose a level of objectivity on your trading that I believe separates the highly successful traders from the rest of the crowd. Absent this kind of thought process, it will be easy for you to evaluate any suboptimal interval of performance, identify some related external factors as the source of your trouble, and happily forgive yourself any transgressions that you may have contributed to the breakdown. However, if you rise above this kind of wishful thinking, you will place yourself in a position of control that, as I have seen time and time again, articulates itself in the form of a fatter bottom line.

Finally, this type of analysis will be invaluable to the health and well-being of anyone whose best trading strategy is to get out of the markets altogether (and, sadly, there are many of us out there). If you are consistently failing to meet what you have objectively set as minimally acceptable return goals, it becomes relatively easy to start to quantify the cost of continuing on, as measured in terms of mental/physical health, lost opportunity to devote your energies more effectively elsewhere, actual financial expense, and so on, and to walk away when these costs become prohibitive. Conversely, I find that those without a formal program of this type run the risk of falling into a pattern of perpetuated failure until the cold, hard realities of the financial marketplace take the timing of the exit decision out of their hands.

STOP-OUT LEVEL

In addition to casting our sights to the heavens, Browning also warns us about "hearts, how shall I say, too soon made glad" stating (in *My Last Duchess*), "I gave commands; Then all smiles stopped together."[1] Recalling this, our task of establishing performance parameters simply cannot be considered complete until we address the issue of maximum tolerable loss. The hard fact is that this is the most important performance parameter of them all, and one that all portfolio managers ignore at their peril.

Think of it in this way: The business of trading is rooted in the trade-offs between risk and reward. From this perspective, it is perhaps not an exaggeration to characterize *risk* as "the currency of trading." And what is risk other than the propensity for a given situation to generate negative outcomes? Each trading account has (explicitly or implicitly) a finite amount of this currency, and it is vital to manage portfolio affairs in such a way that respects this resource constraint. Moreover, while the amount of risk that a given trader can responsibly assume has absolute boundaries (expressed, typically, in financial terms), within these boundaries, it is usually within the control of the individual to set his or her individual risk tolerance at levels that are likely to reach these boundaries or to exceed

---

[1]Browning, in addition to being righteous, was quite prolific.

them by some measure, or to fall somewhere within them. The efficient use of economic stop-outs involves setting your loss-assumption tolerance at manageable levels that will afford you much greater control over the broad and diverse set of circumstances that you are likely to confront over the course of your trading career.

Of course, the specific level of acceptable maximum loss will vary, in both absolute and percentage terms, from account to account, depending on such factors as the professional nature of your trading activities, the source of your funding, and the volatility characteristics of the markets in which you operate. For starters, virtually all professional traders being funded by financial institutions will be assigned such a "risk capital" number, which should be subject to negotiation on a year-to-year basis. I encourage you to negotiate this parameter aggressively, bearing in mind that while other limits may be imposed on you (e.g., cash/working capital constraints and position-size restrictions), it is the amount of loss your funding institution is willing to underwrite that will determine, more than any other single factor, your money-making capacity.

Well-run trading businesses with enlightened risk management structures may offer rationally constructed risk-capital allocations based on such factors as historical performance, market liquidity characteristics, and internal rate of return targets (both raw and risk-adjusted). However, my experience is that such well-ordered policy structures are the exception. More often than not, the risk-capital/stop-out levels that are imposed on you will bear only incidental resemblance to the underlying economics of your trading environment. For example, many levels will be based on elaborate stress tests, using historical, worst-case scenarios as the basis for setting loss limits. In addition to the sheer divergence from market realities that is implicit in this approach, such methodologies often miss the more subtle components of exposure that may cause more actual revenue damage than that caused by events that have a statistical probability of recurrence, say, once in a century.

Under these circumstances, you may find yourself in the frustrating situation of having to manage to limit structures that significantly diminish your ability to deliver risk-adjusted return and, in some cases, may actually provide incentive to make suboptimal risk-reward decisions. This is indeed unfortunate, and any associated frustration you feel is certainly justified. However, it would be a serious mistake to allow this to interfere with creating the most efficient portfolio parameters that you can possibly devise, given the constraints you face. I encourage you to create your own risk model and to identify a worst-case acceptable-loss level that would work best for your specific situation, absent the institutional guidelines imposed on you. Of course, since you won't be able to avoid the institutional limits, your own rules will have to devise a system that will give you what you need but keep you out of trouble with your management. If you can thread this needle, you stand the best chance of identifying the most favorable trading program available to you, given those elements of your environment that are beyond your power to control.

RISK CONTROL FROM A CONTINENTAL PERSPECTIVE (PART 1)

Let's not pretend that a topic such as risk management is exempt from biases emanating from non-economic issues, ranging from internal/enterprise factors to deeply embedded elements of culture. For example, a bank's policies are almost sure to differ from those of, say, a hedge fund. Further, a European entity is going to look at the subject differently than a U.S. firm would. Because these points are important, I have framed a hypothetical sequence from the perspective of a French bank, which bears only incidental resemblance to my actual experiences in the French banking system, because I believe that it offers some interesting insights into the manner in which risk judgments can be driven by a multitude of factors, some of which may not jibe with the critical objective of generating returns while preserving capital.

The first thing you need to know about the French, as they will be only too glad to tell you, is that their country boasts some of the greatest mathematicians in modern history—from Descartes to Fermat. In part for this reason, they take great and justifiable pride in their ability to apply quantitative models to financial problem solving, as produced almost exclusively by the best and the brightest of engineers from its leading polytechnical institute (itself the academic home to the crème de la crème of quantitative practitioners).

It is possible under these circumstances to create risk models that fail to simulate forests due to overabundance of trees. Consider, if you will, a hypothetical limit-setting methodology used by one French trading institution that was thought to convey such a market advantage that the company in question was afraid to provide details of the models to anyone—including those whose job it was to implement the system and monitor associated compliance. In our hypothetical example, the methodology, software, and support systems were officially assigned the title of *Douce Machine* (Soft Machine) in a tribute to both the William Boroughs novel and the *avant garde* British rock band that took its name (most of the risk dudes in this bank, and even some of its senior management, were righteously erudite). Then came the hard part: actually putting to good use a system whose components weren't well understood by anyone operating under its guidelines. This was a painful process for all and, as I understand it, remains painful to this day. At one point, some insiders weren't quite sure if its architects themselves understood what they had built; but they quickly dismissed this suspicion on the basis that its designers were, after all, polytechnicians and were thus incapable of human failings of this kind. They ended up concluding that there was simply too much at stake in terms of proprietary intellectual capital to clue in the nonnative employees of the firm as to what they were trying to accomplish and how they were trying to accomplish it.

It was very interesting to watch what happened from there. The best traders and trading groups established their own risk criteria in a manner that harmonized the *Douce Machine* with pricing patterns that were actually occurring in the marketplace. Those that couldn't pull off this trick were always frustrated, and often unprofitable. They would routinely blow limits on positions they swore were risk-neutral and often had to liquidate under conditions of market duress. When many of these individuals and groups found other means of employment, the brilliance of *Projet Boitte Noire* finally revealed itself. It was one of the greatest trading-desk headcount-reduction programs ever implemented.

For institutional traders fortunate enough to operate under more rational risk management regimes, it is nevertheless useful to go through the exercise of identifying a maximum tolerable loss that works best for you, which oftentimes may be less than the actual risk-taking capacity allocated to you by your funding organization. One way of doing this is to set stop-out levels for shorter time increments than those set by your funding institution. For example, your primary risk guideline might be a liquidation trigger at, say, down 15% of your working capital, as reset on an annual basis. You may find it most effective to translate this into a self-imposed 1% stop-out level each month. This will place you well within the parameters set by the organization and might offer you additional peace of mind, in the sense that you have set aside a risk capital reserve, which will hopefully accumulate over time and reduce the likelihood of a firm-imposed liquidation.

The task of setting the stop-out threshold if you are funding your own portfolio is one with characteristics that are very different from those set for an institutional portfolio. Ideally, you will also set this figure on the basis of a thorough review of your market environment, and within boundaries that don't approach constraints such as the amount of wealth you possess or (worse yet) the sum of your wealth and your borrowing capacity. Instead, you should risk only *discretionary* capital, that is, those financial resources at your disposal that you can afford to lose without significant sacrifice to the critical elements of your lifestyle or long-term financial well-being (mortgage, tuition, car payment, retirement nest egg, etc.).

In fact, other than as part of an efficiently adapted wealth-management program, I can think of no good reason to ever put core personal financial resources at risk in the marketplace. I do, however, know of a number of bad reasons, and the first that comes to mind is because you are convinced of the success of your trading model. If your system is that good, then I would argue that time is on your side. Stick with smaller bets, and let your transaction size accumulate, along with your profits. If you can't afford to wait, it must only mean that you don't expect the opportunities you are seeing to recur (in which case, I question why you are making such a commitment to trading in the first place); that you have access to information that may be illegal to use in the markets; or that you are trading from a position of financial disadvantage, which is a likely recipe for disaster in almost all circumstances.

In addition to staying within a loss threshold that will keep you out of the poorhouse (and, perhaps, also the bighouse, when the feds find out; or the doghouse, when your spouse catches on), there are a number of factors that you should consider in setting your maximum-loss threshold. In particular, I recommend sitting down and performing the same type of review of markets, trading modes, and so on, that a professional institutional trader conducts. Have market conditions improved or worsened? How much time and energy can you devote to trading? Are you set up to maximize information flow and execution efficiency? Once you have answered these questions and applied them through the filter of your risk tolerance, the final piece of the puzzle will in most cases reside in your psyche. You should set your stop-out level at a figure that is large enough for you to feel that you have given your trading a fair shot but that falls short of the point where reaching it becomes demoralizing or debilitating.

Whatever figure you finally identify as your largest acceptable loss, the most important thing is to live within this limit and to commit to a full-scale portfolio liquidation if you are unable to prevent this outcome. Over the course of a given negative trading cycle—particularly for those who have self-imposed limits—there will often be temptation to point toward specific sets of unique external factors (a market crash, a divorce, negative vibes from your astrologer) and to adjust your stop-out level downward.

Please resist this temptation. I find that 90% or more of the time the external factors you believe are at the root of your problems may very well represent a partial cause, but rarely do they tell the complete story. Things seldom turn themselves around without fairly dramatic actions in these circumstances, and by far your best bet is to simply step aside and shift those energies that you were applying to the markets toward an objective assessment of what went wrong.

One of the most acute dangers associated with increasing your stop-out level during a rough period is that, once having done so, the next thought that will invariably enter your mind will be to increase your day-to-day risk levels—perhaps by ratcheting up the size of your trades, expanding your loss-taking capacity on individual transactions, and other similar tactics. Once this has occurred, you have effectively removed a critical and in some cases final element of risk control. Your increased risk taking is intertwined with impatience, with a desire to make back all that you have lost in a brief time period. It's like a swimmer who gets caught in an outward tide, abandons the steady pace that would actually move him closer to safety, and instead wastes his much-needed energy on mad, frenzied strokes toward the shoreline. The effort in both cases is futile.

For professional/institutional traders who increase risk after a large drawdown, all I can say is, "Shame on you." You're playing with fire, and I can all but assure you that everyone, with the possible exception of yourself, knows it. This biggest element of the danger you're creating is that your desire to quickly make back your losses in almost all cases runs in direct conflict with the best interests of the owners of your portfolio. From their point of view, you now represent someone who (1) is not going to get paid unless fortunes take a dramatic turn for the better; (2) may view his or her job to be in jeopardy; and, as a result, (3) is no worse off (and may in fact be better off) taking even bigger risks than the ones that helped dig the hole in the first place. For most institutions, you are not their sole source of trading revenue, and every new dollar of loss is an additional burden to them. They may, as a result, act much more decisively to cut off your funding supply than might be hoped for if you demonstrate a clear commitment to operate within your loss limits.

For these reasons, one of my core risk management concepts is the need to set your risk levels as a function of your P/L performance. This means that the time to increase your market exposure is after you have accumulated some positive returns for the cycle. The more important converse is that it is critical that you reduce your exposure in periods of negative performance. My decades-long experience in the field of risk management tells me that no risk-control concept is more important. For reasons stated earlier and for others discussed throughout this book, trading accounts that don't learn to operate at lower levels of risk—both during and immediately after significant drawdowns—eventually trade themselves out of existence. This may not happen the first time, or the second time, or the third. However, statistically speaking, your blowout is a virtual inevitability; it's simply a matter of time.

Conversely, if you can learn to manage your risk as a function of your performance for the period, you stand every chance of withstanding the slings and arrows of outrageous market fortune and of being around with risk capital to burn when markets take a turn for the better (which I'm pretty sure they will). However, actually doing this is more difficult than it

sounds, first and foremost because it often has important financial implications. By committing to play small until you make back what you have
lost, you implicitly submit to an investment of time, perhaps a considerable
amount of time, depending on factors such as market conditions and the
depth of the hole you've dug for yourself, which will be hard to endure in
a number of ways. First, whether you trade for your own account or manage money for some other entity, the time and energy you spend recouping
your losses will inevitably divert resources away from generating the
income that presumably is the main objective of your trading program. On
a related note, such a program will force you either to miss certain of your
best market opportunities or, at best, to capture them at lower orders of
magnitude, relative to what would be possible under your normal risk-taking capacity.

Second, you should be aware that this process is often worse from a
psychological perspective than it is as measured in terms of economics. I
can't begin to tell you how many traders whine to me that they are missing
opportunities of a lifetime because they occurred during a period where
preceding losses had constrained risk-taking capacity. Take it from me;
this is mostly in your mind. If you stick to your program, you may live to
enjoy many, many more once-in-a-lifetime opportunities. If you break the
rules you have set for yourself, these opportunities may never come your
way again.

Finally, I want to make clear that hitting your stop-out level—particularly if you have followed some of the good disciplines I have recommended—needn't mean that your trading career is over. It does, however,
mean that you must close out all open positions in your portfolio and
reassess your situation. Do so as quickly, as efficiently, and as profitably as
you can—a task that will have been rendered much easier if you have followed the risk-reduction advice presented here. Once this process is complete, take some time off—at least a week, but longer if it feels right. The
first thing you should do is get as far away from the markets and from trading as you possibly can. Go on a trip, preferably out of the country (or at
least out of the time zone). Train for a marathon and then run in it. Get your
band back together and record some new tracks. Just do something that is
not trade related.

THE BEACH

In Pete Townsend / The Who's "Quadrophenia," the last, desperate flip-out
of the main character takes place on the beach: a place of sanctuary for
this troubled soul, tragic ending notwithstanding. In the business of

trading, we like to send people to the beach at an earlier stage of a cycle of dementia. If the trip is executed in a timely and efficient manner, the results can be just as dramatic and entirely more positive.

What exactly is implied, in trader parlance, by the term "going to the beach"? Stated simply, it describes a process whereby, in the wake of a string of losses, a given portfolio manager liquidates his or her portfolio and walks away from the markets for a time. Specific application varies here, but the rule of thumb is that the more significant the portfolio event, the longer and more "market remote" the trip to the beach should be. Oftentimes, a trader will suffer a temporary and entirely identifiable breakdown in decision making, which doesn't carry career-threatening P/L consequences but which may have more significant implications until the trader can straighten himself or herself out. In these cases, I have found that a couple of weeks off, with the trader completely unburdened from the responsibility of portfolio management, can work wonders. Under a more acute set of loss circumstances, mostly involving loss levels that threaten the existing trading franchise, it may be necessary for the individual in question to hit the beach for a period of up to several months.

The idea, in any event, is to come back with a fresh outlook on the markets. Sometimes this works; sometimes it doesn't. In the case of Jimmy, the Who's multipersonalitied protagonist, he ended up stranded, on a rock, in the rain, wasted and without sanctuary, presumably forever. Still, on the whole, I don't think that the beach is the worst place in the world for traders to visit now and again. Just remember to bring your sunblock and maybe an umbrella (just in case).

Let's look at a case study of a trader who needed a trip to the beach in the worst way and didn't get one—until . . . the high tide nearly washed him away.

SQUEEZING O.J.

I know a guy who clawed his way out of the back office of a major trading firm and onto to the trading desk through a combination of talent, diligence, persistence, and good fortune. This doesn't happen very often; and as a result, everyone—most notably the colleagues he left behind in operations—was rooting for him. He happened to trade agricultural commodities, including such arcane products as orange juice (OJ). He also happened to be black. I only mention this because I've decided to call him O.J. here. For a time, he put up some Heisman-like numbers—albeit on small size—in his trading account. He had a keen eye for spotting the parts of the market that were moving, which is essential for someone who trades actively. Surrounded by a group of very clever and more seasoned market participants and operating in a space that was, during his good years, very active, O.J. caught the eye of the entire management team, who thought of him as having real potential.

But O.J. had big plans and already thought of himself as a Hall of Famer. At the tail end of a two-year successful run, he demanded a huge increase in capital, going so far as to propose a contractual schedule, which would increase the money he was managing 10-fold in a matter of months, and presented it to his management as something of an ultimatum. Alas, several members of his company's management team were agnostic on his trading skills. In particular, they felt he was much more the beneficiary of good markets and proximity to talented portfolio managers than he was an architect of his own success. They determined that his ambitions were significantly ahead of his development schedule and left his capital right where it was.

This threw O.J. into a rage. Perhaps understandably (though, I can assure you, incorrectly), he felt there was an element of prejudice in the decision-making process. And, as often occurs in situations like this, his deteriorating mental state coincided with something of a sea change in his markets. Just at a point when his motivations shifted away from profitability and toward a desire to show the firm that they were wrong, the strategy on which he relied most strongly began to lose its effectiveness. On second thought, this is much too polite a characterization: O.J.'s trades started to suck lemons.

It didn't take long before O.J.'s market struggles and personal unhappiness began to wreak havoc with his decision making. This breakdown took several forms. First, he started to double down on positions working against him. Then, as risk management issues started to take a higher priority, he transferred almost his entire portfolio into long options strategies, thinking this was the best way to limit his exposures. Soon, he began complaining that the options were throwing off losses that were inconsistent with the manner in which risks were represented in the trading systems—systems that during his success met his needs to his full satisfaction. When he tried to hedge out his options-based exposures, it only exacerbated his losses.

With the benefit of 20/20 hindsight, it is easy to see that this would have been a perfect moment for a trip to the beach. When his management suggested this to him, he reacted badly. No, he said, he was determined to trade his way out of his problems. He further indicated that he had spent a great deal of time and energy analyzing his problems and, based on this analysis, was convinced not only that the hard times were behind him, but also that a wealth of market opportunities just on the horizon made this the worst possible time to liquidate his portfolio. Not wanting to undermine his confidence unduly, his management reluctantly went along with the plan.

As O.J's losses deepened, so did his conviction as to the correctness of his core ideas. To control risks, he liquidated all but a couple of commodity futures positions that represented the centerpieces of his market viewpoint:

short positions in winter wheat and orange juice. Other markets were actually acting much more favorably for his strategy, but he didn't care. He was sure wheat and OJ were going to break and looked to this happy event as one that would not only bail out his P/L, but also provide him with sweet vindication. And you know what? These markets indeed started to break. Exhausted but confident, O.J. took a week off.

The coupe de grace came toward the end of this holiday, just as the OJ contract headed into its delivery cycle. First came the news, in the form of a sternly worded letter from the New York Orange Juice Exchange, that the firm had exceeded speculative delivery limits for its lead-month orange juice contract. You see, as most agricultural futures contracts are liquidated before they become deliverable, the exchanges allow traders to hold much bigger position sizes prior to the point when delivery occurs than they do after the process of physical transfer has begun. Professional traders know this and have an obligation to adjust their positions accordingly. O.J.'s failure to make this adjustment was therefore a very amateurish error on his part. Moreover, it was a major embarrassment to the firm, which was a significant sponsor of the Orange Juice Exchange and which had, up to that point, an unblemished record of compliance with agricultural delivery procedures.

However, the biggest impact of this mistake was not the public relations problem, but a direct, market-based one. Deliverable positions are published to market participants, and everyone could see that someone was out there, obligated to make delivery on a whole lot of orange juice. Insiders knew that deliverable supplies were tight. At the risk of heaping one bad pun upon another, *O.J. was about to be squeezed.*

Speculative buyers smelled blood in the water and bid up the price of delivery-month OJ like it was a cure for male-pattern baldness. At this point, O.J. and his firm had two choices: either buy back those futures contracts in a hurry, or start squeezing oranges itself. Problem was, there were almost no sellers in the futures market. O.J. (whose holiday, it must be told, ended early and abruptly) was able to buy his way out of his position only at much higher prices and after a prolonged and agonizing fortnight that comprised the entire delivery cycle. When the dust had settled, he had lost nearly everything he had made in the markets during his magnificent earlier two-year run.

O.J. is out of the markets now. Rumor has it, he devotes most of his time to golf.

Once you are back from the beach, take a cold hard look at what went wrong. Start with a review of the metrics presented in this book: Are your losses based on correlations to underlying markets that went against you or on poor selection decisions? Did the losses occur in a handful of unfortunate trades, or are they spread widely across your account? How do the losses distribute themselves over time? In what ways are the numbers you generate different from those tied to your profitable intervals? Do your best to answer each of these and related questions as objectively as possible.

Now go speak to people whom you trust within your market sector. What is their view of what went wrong? Do they feel that your problem is correctable, or should you go on to something else?

Note that it may be useful to put all of this down in writing and submit your synopsis to an outside party for review. However, whether you choose to make this a formal process, if you take the time and the effort to go through this exercise, you will place yourself in the best possible position to objectively assess your situation and to formulate your best strategy for attacking the markets in the future.

If you are hip to the "Chestnut Mare," you already know that the hero did catch his horse but was only able to ride it for a short while. I always thought it significant that he fell off after seeing what turned out to be his reflection in the water.

Nevertheless, I think on the whole that he found the experience satisfactory and went on to write one righteous song about it. And, as he says, he'll be back—and so should you. Be smart the next time around, and use whatever lessons you can from previous experience. This ought to point you toward a simple trading program that features moderate risk levels and will allow you to reorient yourself toward the market in a way that maximizes your prospects for success. Even if the answer you come up with is that you want to suspend your trading indefinitely (and often this is a very viable alternative), you will save yourself a great deal of pain and aggravation if you've followed the steps set forth in this chapter, relative to an approach where you simply dive back in, experience either the favor or the wrath of the markets, and never contemplate the reasons why.

CHAPTER 3

Understanding the Profit/Loss Patterns over Time

We will be geared toward the average, rather than the exceptional.

—Gerald "Little Milton" Bostock
(aka Ian Anderson)
"Thick as a Brick"

By now, you have established two critical components of an informed performance management effort: You've (1) picked one or more time intervals for evaluation and (2) set some rational series of performance objectives. Without going any further down the analytical path, you are now ahead of many of your peers because you are in a position to measure your results in ways that are consistent with your environments and constraints. It's now time to take the next step and perform a statistical evaluation of your returns, which, if executed in an efficient manner, will provide critical insights into the true characteristics of your success (or lack thereof) and which will be crucial to your efforts to achieve maximum returns over an extended time horizon and across the full range of market conditions.

These statistics will not provide you with perfect insight into the dynamics of your portfolio. Rather, they will offer you clues as to the combinations of dependent and independent variables that are tied most closely to your relative success. Moreover, there is considerable hazard in taking too literal an interpretation of the statistics you calculate. For example, you may find yourself negatively correlated with a benchmark index, such as the Standard & Poor's (S&P) 500, and form the logical hypothesis that you are making most of your money on the short side. In fact, as we will see, it is entirely possible to be negatively correlated with the S&P 500 without ever having sold short a single security over the period of analysis.

You must therefore gird yourself against the temptation to undertake aggressive modifications of your trading behavior on the basis of a direct interpretation of a single statistic or even a combination of quantitative indicators. Trading is a very complex process that involves many interdependencies that do not lend themselves to evaluation on an isolated, case-by-case basis. Indeed, by changing individual aspects of your trading behavior, you are likely to impact several other aspects in such a way that is far from guaranteed to generate a net benefit.

Instead, you should use these statistics as a general diagnostic in your portfolio management tool kit, which, like various doctor's tools (stethoscope, thermometer, blood pressure cuff, etc.) will give you more concrete indications about what's going on in your portfolio than you could possibly identify through pure qualitative observation. In going down this path, we may find areas for potential improvement; but we won't respond with any rash adjustments because changing one factor can have unintended consequences, upsetting a hard-won, delicate balance that is the hallmark of most successful portfolios and doing more overall harm than good. As a result, we're going to be careful before drawing any conclusions that actually imply the need for intervention; and if we do decide to change things, it is going to be based on controlled experiments, using finite amounts of capital, and on an evaluation of results that draws from the same statistical tool kit that we used to identify the problems in the first place.

Hopefully, this sounds encouraging. But I urge you to withhold final judgment until we begin to address specific trading patterns and associated response alternatives. In the meantime, we can start by defining the types of statistical information that are useful in obtaining a better understanding of those characteristics of your portfolio that may be having the greatest impact on your performance.

One last point before we begin: Some of the stuff contained in this next section is positively trivial for anyone with even a rudimentary understanding of mathematics and statistics. If this applies to you, you won't learn much here and may wonder why it is included in a book geared to people who may use these tools routinely in their day-to-day activities. However, in my experience, I've run into enough people who don't have a firm understanding of this material (both personal account traders and professionals) that I decided to err on the side of overexplanation. To those who do know this material, a quick review certainly won't hurt before we get to the really good stuff.

AND NOW TO STATISTICS, BUT FIRST A WORD (OR MORE) ABOUT TIME SERIES CONSTRUCTION

In order to effectively evaluate your performance, it is going to be necessary to establish a benchmark unit block for this analysis. Here, there are several alternatives, but the first and perhaps the most important of these is *time*. In fact, I'd go so far as to say that without looking at your performance in "time series" units, your chances of deriving much benefit from these materials is severely diminished. Understanding the ins and outs of time series analysis is so important that, as boring as it may be, we have to cover it first (if only to get it out of the way). If you are familiar with this territory, feel free to skip; but think carefully before you just blow past it, as it may ultimately be worthy of your attention.

Time is one of the most critical scarce resources that comprise the Risk Management Investment (in some ways, it's the most important), and the manner in which your market performance distributes itself across time is, therefore, an essential framework through which to evaluate your success.

In framing our time series analysis, we'll focus on two different and important questions: (1) What is an appropriate *span* of time over which to evaluate your performance? (2) What *unit* of time represents the most appropriate data point? Here, I will argue that there are a number of alternative time spans that you should analyze and that the time *span* (as well as availability) of data should determine the *unit* size. By comparing and contrasting your performance over different time spans, you stand to gain significant insights into what is driving its underlying account economics.

In order to define the analytical problem with maximum precision, we must first make the distinction between the two measures:

1. *Time Unit (or Increment):* The size of a given profit/loss (P/L) observation, as measured in increments of time. This figure can typically be expressed in increments as small as one day or as large as a year, with each having different analytical implications, as defined in later chapters. Although it is theoretically possible to measure time in units much smaller than a single day, for reasons explained later we find that there may be hazard in doing so, most notably the potential mismatches in the manner in which certain securities are priced intraday.

2. *Time Span (or Interval):* The entire period of evaluation, comprised of individual time units, across which we wish to calculate basic information. Typical time spans can range from one week to a year, again with different implications in each case.

The decision I ask you to consider, therefore, is which *time units* to review over what *time spans*. It may be useful to think of your alternatives in this regard as being summarized in the following matrix:

Time Span → Time Unit ↓	Weekly	Monthly	Quarterly	Annual
Daily				
Weekly				
Monthly				
Quarterly				
Annual				

Now let's look at the implications of each alternative in terms of its implications for time series analysis.

Time Units

Daily.   This is the level of P/L unit analysis that I believe offers the most comprehensive set of information, largely because it is the most granular. For any given *time span*, a daily P/L series will yield the largest number of observations, which in turn will offer the highest level of *statistical significance*. Though more robust definitions are certainly available, it may be useful to think of *statistical significance* as the presence of a sufficient number of data points to ensure the stability of a given statistical calculation. This concept, which is critical to the objective of maximizing the interpretation accuracy of the data I will ask you to analyze, is addressed in detail in the body of the text. I recommend that, if at all possible, traders build and maintain a time series of their daily market performance. This data will serve as the primary building block in determining such critical statistical benchmarks as correlations to outside markets, P/L volatility, and drawdown characteristics.

For some traders operating in certain markets, it may be difficult or even impossible to calculate daily return statistics. Apart from other obstacles, such as availability and accuracy of data, the instruments they are trading may simply not price every day. However, I encourage portfolio managers to strive as best they can under these circumstances to *estimate* the impact of market changes on their overall P/L on a daily basis. This figure should, at minimum, tie back to the weekly or monthly data that should be at their disposal and will serve as a useful proxy to daily P/L, wherever such information is otherwise unavailable.

Weekly. If daily P/L observation information is unavailable for whatever reason, weekly data is the next best proxy, again for reasons of granularity and statistical significance. Note that for some portfolios, under some conditions, the analysis tied to weekly P/L streams may provide a more accurate illustration of performance dynamics than daily data will. Examples of this include international traders/markets, whose day-to-day correlations may span multiple time zones and, therefore, not lend themselves to accurate daily analysis; and portfolios where pricing dynamics are not best fit into single-day increments (e.g., those with a large component of interest rate carry, such as repo-financed bond transactions).

Monthly. This is probably the largest acceptable minimum time unit that can be applied to our analytical tool kit. Stated another way, if you can't at least get monthly data on your performance, very little use can be made of any of the statistics. Moreover, I would have to seriously question the ability of traders to perform the type of risk management necessary to achieve rational financial goals typically associated with trading and investing if information is not available on, at minimum, a monthly basis. However, this is almost never a problem, as monthly data should be available for virtually every type of trading program out there.

Monthly data have drawbacks in terms of both granularity and statistical significance, but they can be useful nevertheless from a number of perspectives. Over extended periods of time, they will provide insights into longer-term performance patterns that are difficult to discern with daily or weekly information. This is particularly true for complex portfolios, where it may not be practical to synchronize performance data on a more frequent basis. Moreover, because many investment portfolios (particularly hedge funds and Commodity Trading Advisors) report results on a monthly basis, monthly data can be a useful means of benchmarking your performance against other professional traders.

I would suggest that even if you are able to put together daily or weekly performance results, you should create and analyze your monthly time series as well. In doing so, you are likely to find different and interesting patterns in this "higher aggregation level data" that are potentially important to the full understanding of your portfolio management dynamics. For example, you might find your monthly performance highly correlated to the monthly returns of a benchmark such as the S&P 500 but much less correlated or not at all with respect to daily data. If you take the further step of asking yourself what this might mean—what combination of external conditions and internal decision making might generate such a pattern—you might come up with a number of plausible explanations. Perhaps, as was the case for most of the past two decades, the market is simply rallying while you are making your money on the short side of the market. This would suggest that the daily, low-correlation numbers were probably telling the more accurate story. By examining these types of hypotheses (as well as any number of equally plausible explanations you might find), you stand to learn something about your trading that you didn't already know, and that fact can only be beneficial.

Quarterly.   As we move down the scale of broader time units, we continue to face issues of granularity and statistical significance. However, I submit that it is important to aggregate your data into quarterly results so as to identify seasonal patterns, those tied to equity earnings cycles, and so on.

Annual.   No matter what the smallest time unit is that you are able to accumulate, it is important to aggregate this information into an annual return profile. In some respects, this will be your most critical time unit benchmark, representing among other things the time interval across which you expect to get paid, the best time unit against which to compare your performance against external benchmarks, and so on.

Intraday.   As indicated previously, it may in some cases be possible to track your P/L performance on an intraday basis. Absent issues tied to the accuracy of associated data, this type of analysis can be useful in helping traders identify the manner in which their trading activity generates P/L across the daily market cycle. However, I caution against allocating significant resources to the task of logging your intraday performance, as, for all but the most liquid markets, it is likely to be difficult to create a precise picture of what you have made or lost at various points within a given day. For this reason and others, I recommend undertaking such an exercise only for traders with extremely advanced pricing systems and operating in the most liquid, actively traded markets.

Now let's review how we can examine information from these P/L time units across larger time spans.

Time Spans

As you may surmise, the availability and decisions you make regarding *time units* will drive your selection of time spans:

Weekly.   First, at the risk of stating the obvious, we can only begin to examine weekly time spans using daily data, which gives us at most five observatzions– well below the threshold needed to perform meaningful statistical evaluation. Nevertheless, I am all in favor of traders looking at weekly patterns of P/L data because they may provide many insights into the qualitative aspects patterns of their performance. Specifically, using this data, we can begin to question such matters as whether trading programs are more successful on certain days of the week than others. Beyond this, if we start comparing weekly groups of daily performance statistics against one another, we can begin to see patterns of what successful trading cycles look like, as compared to more problematic ones. Are gains concentrated in one or two days, while losses tend to extend out across larger time periods? Is the opposite true? What might all of this mean for improving the success of your trading performance? A qualitative weekly analysis might begin to provide just these types of insights.

Second, because certain market events tend to play themselves out across a period roughly spanning a given week, the analysis of a P/L pattern over this time frame might provide significant insight into the relative success a trader is achieving in capturing market volatility opportunities. Examples of this type of dynamic abound, including weeks of busy earnings releases for equities and multiday treasury auctions for fixed income. In each case that may be relevant to your trading, I suggest that you maintain detailed records of the economic events that will impact your portfolio and track your performance across the relevant multiday period. Then compare and contrast similar economic intervals with respect to performance. Does your portfolio perform better when new economic information is moving the markets, or worse? Why might this be the case?

The same approach may be applied to market-moving events that are not tied to planned economic releases. You could compare and contrast your performance on, say, the week that WorldCom defaulted on its debt to your P/L in the October crashes. Have you done well during periods of unanticipated market volatility, or poorly? What could you have legitimately done differently to improve your result? These types of analyses can best be conducted by tracking weekly performance against a cross-referenced list of economic activity.

Monthly.   The 20 observations of daily trading P/L that comprise a typical month begin to form a data set across which we can perform some meaningful statistical analysis, including mean, volatility, and correlation statistics, which will be discussed in the next chapter. In addition, a qualitative review of monthly performance data will provide further insights regarding your relative level of success with respect to capitalizing on specific market inefficiencies. Of course, the market cycle of economic information that comprises a month differs from the weekly cycle we just reviewed and will include, among other things, an entire round of government data releases. As was the case with weekly analysis, one possible approach would be to generally catalogue some key economic statistics that characterize a given month and to start to compare and contrast your performance across months that have similar types of economic activity. Do they represent a pattern?

Finally, monthly data is probably the smallest time span against which you should compare your performance relative to the goals you have established for yourself, which will be discussed in greater detail later. However, to give you some foreshadowing of how monthly data can help you manage your performance against targets, you should keep in mind that there are only 12 monthly chances to meet annual goals. So while one observation below the target is certainly acceptable and in most cases unavoidable, a sequence of, say, three or four such outcomes should cause you to reevaluate both your performance and your objectives in ways that I will describe in further detail in later chapters.

Quarterly.   By the time you have gathered a quarter's worth of daily information, you will be in an excellent position to perform statistical analysis with confidence that the numbers you generate will be both stable and statistically significant. Moreover, a quarter's worth of economic activity begins to offer meaningful information of overall anticipated performance across the spans for which professional traders are typically paid for their performance (i.e., one year). It therefore is not too early here, in addition to the standard volatility information I will discuss later in this chapter, to begin to benchmark your returns against those of relevant market indexes, against the returns of professional portfolio managers whom you'd like to emulate, and, again, against the targets you have established for yourself.

From a qualitative perspective, one quarter of economic activity begins to tell the story of an entire year (which, of course, is one reason why it is the unit of time over which investors most thoroughly analyze the earnings performance of corporations). In evaluating your performance over this time span, you will want to ask yourself generally whether market conditions were poor or favorable and to critically evaluate your performance against this backdrop.

Annual.   Perhaps it is not surprising that I would argue that the annual time span is probably the most important window for analysis, offering ample data to ensure statistical significance along with an entire cycle of economic activity against which to evaluate your relative performance. Moreover, most professional traders are paid on some sort of annual cycle, so it is imperative to view performance in annualized terms. Here, as elsewhere, there is a large opportunity to view things through both a qualitative and a quantitative filter. With regard to the former, the more questions you ask yourself the better. Was it a good year or a bad year for your markets? How would you evaluate your overall compensation in light of these conditions? How did you perform as compared to your peers? What was your best decision over the course of the trading year? What was your worst decision? What were the associated impacts of these? Where do you go from here?

A thorough and objective qualitative evaluation of your performance on an annualized time span is a critical component of your planning for the next year. Here, the process needs to start a bit before year-end, as you move from asking and answering the hard questions into a mode where you begin to carefully and honestly examine the manner in which you plan to attack the markets over the next 12 months. If things are going extremely well, this process might center on fixing the appropriate set of objectives for the next annual cycle. However, for the majority of traders, a great deal more should be involved. In particular, I recommend that even the most successful traders take the time to evaluate such critical but often deemphasized elements of trading as cost structures and capital investments, technology platforms, and execution and clearing relationships.

Whether you are pleased or (to whatever degree) disappointed with your performance the preceding year, you should focus this analysis on setting your objectives going forward, and I will discuss this at greater length in the coming chapters. As a general guideline, if your evaluation leads you to objectively conclude that your performance was satisfactory or better (and you have reason to believe that favorable conditions in your markets will persist), it might be time to focus on the scalability of your portfolio. The good times won't last forever (they never do), so it's important to try to make as much as possible when you're getting things right. Conversely, if you have fallen short of expectations, you must examine your overall business strategy and infrastructure so as to ensure that there is nothing inrooted in these basics that is at the source of your problems.

For professional traders working for financial institutions, the process of evaluating your infrastructure will often be imposed on you formally through that organization's budgetary/performance review cycle. As painful as it may be, it is a good thing, and I strongly recommend that traders take the opportunity to use this exercise as an opportunity to undertake the more personalized evaluation of the administrative sides of your portfolio as described earlier.

Finally, as I will discuss later, there will come a point in many traders' career cycles where they must reevaluate their entire approach to the markets, including, perhaps, what they are trading and who is funding them. The best time to undertake such an analysis is at the end of an annual trading interval. This is true most notably because it coincides with many of the most important structural elements of the trading calendar, including those associated with compensation, budgets, and the setting of objectives. It is obviously easier both to address these issues at year-end and to effect any changes that are needed at that time than it is at midyear, where there may not be sufficient data to make such a determination and when embedded financial/contractual issues may render them more diffi-cult to resolve.

The point here is to ensure that no matter what the circumstances are under which you participate in the markets, you should establish routine intervals for evaluation of your performance. While there may be signifi-cant benefit to undertaking a multifaceted approach to this task and per-forming the evaluation across multiple time spans, it is essential to commit to some program of this kind. For most traders, the ideal program may involve a review of daily data, over both an annual and a monthly/quarterly time span.

YOU'VE GOT A FRIEND

You've got a friend, and I'll call him Keith. He's a bit of a renaissance man, careerwise, having undertaken roles as varied as burger flipper, pig raiser, and world-class money manager. He gets paid a percentage of the profits in this latest (most lucrative) gig each December 31. This means that he doesn't get paid in April and he doesn't get paid in June. If he hasn't covered his nut (and then some, I daresay), he still doesn't get paid come December 31 if his returns for the year come to zero. His mission? Have as much greenery as possible on his books at precisely eight hours before the ball drops and the corks start popping. He knows it and acts accordingly. To him, good months and good quarters are only valuable if they add up to good years.

I also have a friend (unlikely as that may seem). Call him Mo. Someday, he's going to be a big Hollywood producer. He already has a half dozen (somewhat misunderstood) alternative films to his credit. One of these days, any one of his projects could launch him into the bright lights. In the meantime, to meet his expenses, he straps himself each morning into a workstation at the local ISCALP electronic trading complex in a major East Coast city. Mo, as it turns out, is a very good trader; some might even say he's a better trader than producer. However, for those who know and love him (and I feel fortunate to count myself among this number), he has the soul of an artist.

ISCALP puts up the capital and pays 50% of the profits on a monthly basis. This works out well for Mo because, as I mentioned, he has bills to pay; and typically the big ones (rent, car payment, health club membership) come due on a monthly basis as well. Mo focuses his attention on maximizing his profits each month. This helps him manage his risk, keep creditors at bay, and maintain the schedule flexibility he needs to be able to drop everything when he receives word (and the phone call is expected at any time) that Dreamworks has decided to provide funding for his bold but underdeveloped concept for a musical adaptation of Adam Smith's *The Wealth of Nations*, featuring his self-penned (soon to be) smash hit, "I Wanna Hold Your (Invisible) Hand."

In addition, I have a relative in this game, who I also consider a friend. Her name is Barbara. She's raised a whole passel of kids and grandkids and is the chief financial officer of the family business. We don't see eye-to-eye on every issue, but she has a better outlook on life than just about anybody I know. Improbably, she is also a very good trader. She has bought and sold stock, profitably, for several decades, across all types of market conditions; and it has provided a steady source of supplemental income for her and her brood. She trades part-time and tends to evaluate her performance not across units of time, but rather across results thresholds. For example, she might try to trade her way to a couple of thousand dollars profit to finance a trip to Europe that she is planning this summer.

She knows that I don't think people should set return targets on the basis of personal financial need (in fact, it's a perfect example of the type of thing we differ on); but she is very disciplined about identifying her targets, the amount she is willing to risk, and the time horizon that is most consistent with the realization of her objectives. She has demonstrated an uncanny market feel. Her market-based successes are a marvel to me and serve as a constant reminder that a disciplined adherence to a methodology of any kind is better than no methodology at all. There are many, many days when I feel tempted to give her all my money to manage.

All three of these friends have successfully incorporated the concept of time into their trading and investing framework—albeit in widely divergent ways. Ultimately, this will be your challenge as well.

Now that we have discussed the various alternatives, let's take another look at the time unit/time span matrix, to see what inferences we can draw as to what works best:

Time Span → / Time Unit ↓	Weekly	Monthly	Quarterly	Annual
Daily				
Weekly				
Monthly				
Quarterly				
Annual				

Key:
| Important |
| Interesting |
| Marginal |
| Not Usable |

I reckon that's about all I have to say about time series construction, and no doubt we're all glad to get it out of the way. Now let's start seeing how it can be applied to some useful analytical purposes.

Graphical Representation of Daily P/L

The first type of data analysis I recommend is a graph of daily performance across the relevant time span. Ideally, the graph will feature a continuous line, representing your cumulative P/L, and a series of individual bars, reflecting individual daily performance, as is indicated in Figures 3.1 and 3.2. However, these graphs can be broken out separately if this is easier for the user to create or evaluate.

These graphs allow sharp-eyed observers to quickly obtain numerous useful insights into portfolio performance over the period in question. First, as with any chart, we hope that the general trend is upward. Second,

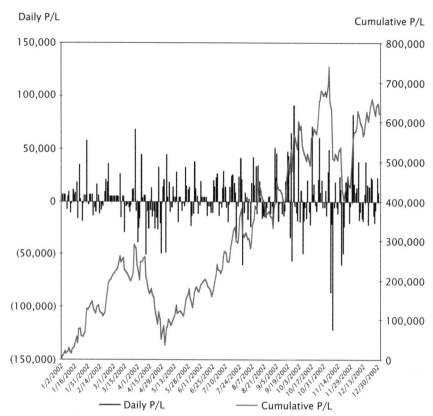

FIGURE 3.1 Prototype volatility for successful account. Note that in a combined graph such as this one, it is necessary to establish two different vertical scales: one for the daily P/L observations and another (presumably higher) for the cumulative performance. This is easily done in either Microsoft Excel or other spreadsheet programs.

we can immediately identify any periods of difficulty, assess their magnitude relative to overall performance, and use this as the basis for additional analysis. We can also tell a great deal about how the individuals in question manage risk, whether they respond to periods of adversity by preserving capital or whether their reactions show undue impatience, as manifested in spiraling increases in volatility patterns. Third, we can assess whether the overall pattern is reflective of the smooth upward arch that represents the ideal in this business or whether the P/L path is one with many peaks and valleys, which indicates that the portfolio, whatever its overall performance, was one with material levels of market risk.

Take a good look at these graphs—they speak volumes about the trade-offs between risk and return. Pay particularly close attention to

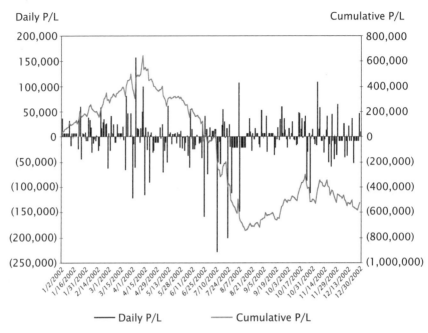

Daily P/L   Cumulative P/L

——— Daily P/L   ——— Cumulative P/L

FIGURE 3.2   Prototype volatility for troubled account.

"drawdowns." Mark the dates, and try to reverse engineer what went wrong. Were market conditions atrocious? Was your specific performance below expectations? Perhaps some combination of the two? Conversely (and as we will discuss later), it may be that your drawdown occurred as part of a process of scaling into your most profitable positions, at such time as these positions were moving against you. If so, my guess is that you can feel pretty good about things, as you most likely made a fortune.

It is also quite instructive, I find, to compare the time periods associated with a given drawdown with the corresponding *recovery period* (i.e., the time period that is involved in recouping all of your drawdown-related losses). Note that duration of these periods may exceed the time periods associated with the corresponding downdrafts (which are unavoidable for most mere mortals) by significant amounts (i.e., twice as long or more); and this is why it is important to exert as much control over their magnitude as is humanly possible.

Figures 3.1 and 3.2 are simplified illustrations of these phenomena at work. In Figure 3.1, the account in question demonstrates a healthy volatility pattern, under which the drawdowns that do take place occur at the ends of intervals of strong performance and are of magnitudes that reduce but do not exhaust the P/L reserve established during the run-up. As performance begins to turn negative, the portfolio manager in question demonstrates the ability to reduce P/L volatility until such time as he begins to enjoy a turnaround, at which point he feels comfortable once again in increasing his exposures. A pattern such as this one, in my experience, can generate profitable, scalable returns over an extended time period; and if this trader can continue to exercise the basic discipline of risk management, I am confident in his ability to continue to operate successfully.

Contrast this to the story told by Figure 3.2. In addition to the fact that the general trend is negative, there is discernable effort to tie the level of volatility to performance success. As events continue to worsen, volatility (as depicted by the vertical bars) remains constant or even increases. Eventually, the portfolio shifts into risk-reduction mode, but by then it is too late. The opportunity to recoup losses and to reach new plateaus of profitability has been severely compromised, if not lost altogether.

For my tastes, there's simply nothing in the entire tool kit that is as useful as these graphs. Once you get comfortable reading them, you can pretty much see what's going on in a portfolio in a heartbeat. What is more, if you are oriented toward technical analysis, you can apply the same methodologies to the review of these diagrams as you use in looking at stock or commodities charts. To reinforce this point, think of the two portfolios represented as individual securities. In the case of the first, performance fluctuates; but every time it suffers, there is a nice basing pattern that forms —each time at levels comfortably within the established range. The trend over the entire period is upward, and it looks like this trend will continue.

Now take another look at the other portfolio. Here, the trend is downward, and performance is deteriorating at what looks like an increasing rate. If this portfolio were a stock, it would be one of the last ones in the world you would want to own. In fact, as any chartist would be happy to tell you, the only possible trade here is to be short.

Histogram of P/L Observations

Another visual tool that is well worth a thousand statistics is the graphic presentation of returns in the form of a *P/L histogram*. The creation of a histogram involves grouping individual P/L observations into size categories and identifying the number of observations within each increment. The ranges of these increments can be expressed in terms of dollars or percentages. When the histogram is plotted in bar chart form, it provides an illustrative description of your P/L.

Consider Figure 3.3, the histogram associated with the portfolio first introduced to us in Figure 3.1: If you tilt your head at a 45-degree angle and kind of squint out of your left eye, you can see what looks a little bit like a

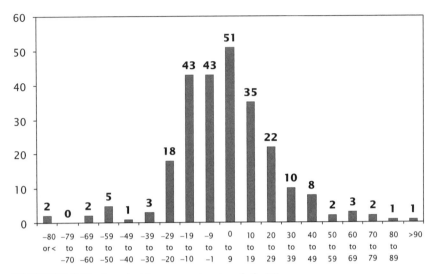

FIGURE 3.3   Sample histogram showing daily P/L.

bell shape, with most observations centered around the mean and decreasing numbers of data points situated within the outer brackets. This, as we will discuss shortly, is very typical for P/L distributions and other random data sets—a fact that, as we will also cover, is more important than perhaps it ought to be. You will also notice that there are more observations at the extreme ends of the distribution than might be entirely intuitive; but this too, as we will review, is to be expected.

The graph of the histogram offers an immediate visual image as to the manner in which portfolio returns distribute themselves, but it also provides the basis for meaningful further analysis. In particular, take a close look at the observations in both tails of the distribution. Try to draw comparisons here. Are the big gains part of the same market sequence, or do they at least occur during markets with similar characteristics? Are they tied to the same financial instruments? If they are, is it because these instruments are inherently volatile, because you traded them during a particularly volatile period, because of position sizing, or some combination thereof? Once you have taken the effort to fully reconstruct the portfolio/market characteristics associated with your extreme observations, it is useful to attempt to reengineer associated trading decisions as well. For the negative observations, were there any mistakes you made that were objectively avoidable? Similarly, for those days of extreme profitability, did you do everything in your power to maximize on this favorable trend?

Other questions of a similar nature should come to you also—a process you should nurture. Do your best to answer the questions. You may learn something in the process.

Finally, if you find that over extended periods of time you continue to experience larger numbers of negative extreme data points than are consistent with a bell-curve distribution, you must take the time to examine these dynamics and to form a plan for effective management of associated exposures. Absent a fundamental flaw in the way you are approaching risk management, excessive losses are more than likely due to the presence of some kurtosis (i.e., overabundance of extreme observations) in the underlying markets that you are trading. Many markets are characterized by kurtosis—particularly over very long time horizons—most notably global equities and most emerging markets. Test this hypothesis for your markets, if you can, by plotting the distribution of daily returns for the securities in which you are most active. Do they lend themselves to occasional abrupt departures from normal pricing patterns? If so, it will be important to size your associated position taking in a manner that accounts appropriately for the additional exposure.

In any event, if extreme negative-return events continue to persist, it will be necessary for you to reduce your risk profile relative to what would be acceptable if your portfolio had the similar risk characteristics, without the excessive presence of negative outliers. While it will require considerable amounts of discipline to do so, the payoff will come in the form of dampening the magnitude and associated impact of the worst points in your trading cycle.

STATISTICS

We could spend a month drawing pictures and interpreting them for fun and profit. Certainly Dr. Freud would endorse this approach, and it might even pay us over the long run. But now, having put off the matter longer than I had intended, I find I must revert to the numeric. Statistics I have promised, and statistics I will deliver.

A Tribute to Sir Isaac Newton

To fortify us in this exceedingly daunting enterprise, I will call on the spirit of Sir Isaac Newton. It seems to me that Newton would have made a great trader; history tells us he had all of the tools. He spent his early days observing certain patterns of motion in the universe, generalized them into a theory that is certainly the basis for all modern physics, and invented the mathematical science of calculus as a means of explaining his theories.[1] As the world eventually found out, this latter discovery was not only perfectly applicable to the description of the physical universe, but also proved itself to be enormously handy in modeling the social sciences, most notably (at least for our purposes) economics.

Rumor has it that before they hoisted him up to his final resting place in Westminster Abbey, he amassed a considerable fortune; and no doubt this is the case. After all, Queen Anne saw fit to knight him; and up till that time, this sort of thing had been the exclusive domain of the aristocracy and military types (and was certainly unheard of for a scientist). When he tired of academic life, he moved seamlessly into government affairs, serving in what one can only assume was among the most lucrative bureaucratic posts ever devised, the Master of the Royal Mint. By all accounts, he prospered for most of the nearly seven decades of his adult life. However, his record as an investor is, to be sure, somewhat mixed. Most notably, he is known to have lost a bundle in the infamous South Sea Bubble episode, a bizarre scheme under which the British government appears to have created a full boom/bust cycle in the single, fateful year of 1720, by issuing on no less than four occasions a form of convertible debt—without ever bothering to inform the investing public what the conversion ratio was.

The South Sea escapade was quite a hoot—even by today's somewhat jaded post-dot-com bubble standards. The whole country knew it would end badly; but this didn't stop everyone who was in a position to do so (including many members of parliament, Chancellor of the Exchequer John Aislabie and his staff, such literary luminaries as Daniel Defoe and Alexander Pope, and King George I himself) from grabbing every share they could get their hands on. During the tumultuous period between spring and autumn of 1720, some shares in South Sea and related enterprises increased 10-fold, attracting investors from such remote locales (particularly from an eighteenth-century perspective) as America and the Far East, before collapsing entirely and in

---

[1]Purists will be quick to point out that the German mathematician Gottfried Leibniz has at least as plausible a claim as the father of calculus as does our friend Newton. I am told that he published his theories a couple of decades before the appearance of the latter's landmark *Principia Mathematica*. To be perfectly honest, I have no informed opinion whatsoever as to who got there first. Here, as elsewhere, I'll claim author's privilege, as Newton is clearly the more appealing hero for this particular digression. However, let me do what I can to correct this by giving Leibniz his props as a righteously clever dude and someone who also would probably make a great trader.

the process ruining many a fortune and poisoning the continental investment climate for many years after.

In terms of Newton's involvement, he apparently used his considerable connections to grab a sweet slice of Round 1; but recognizing the unsound basis of the enterprise, he sold his early shares at a sizable profit, famously uttering, "I can calculate the motions of heavenly bodies, but not the madness of people." However, for reasons indeterminate, he dove back on in during the summer months and got slaughtered with the rest of the masses as the leaves began to turn on his country estates, losing his entire original investment and perhaps a lot more.

If it were possible to discuss the incident with Newton, he would no doubt agree that even perfect mathematical and statistical insight cannot save you from the caprices of the marketplace. That said, it is my belief that Newton's most famous efforts are even better oriented to the markets than they are to the physical sciences. For generations after he created his laws of motion, people believed that they perfectly described the dynamics of the universe. Then, early in the twentieth century, Einstein came along and pointed out that these laws don't apply at high speeds and in other nooks and crannies of the cosmos. This was part of the process of equating matter to energy, which, though arguably as important as Newton's key revelations, was known by even Einstein to fall short of explaining in a comprehensive fashion how the universe came into being and why it does what it does.

Over time, a Newton replaces a Galileo, an Einstein replaces a Newton; and bit by bit, we learn more, but not everything, about the inner workings of the cosmos. So it goes in the markets as well, which I would argue ebb and flow in a manner much more consistent with Newtonian theories than with those of any of his forerunners or successors. As traders, we live in a world where the natural state of prices are either at rest or in motion, where it takes an external stimulus to change this balance and where actions are typically met with equal and opposite reactions. For example, one very useful way of viewing the market downturn in the first decade of the twenty-first century is as a Newtonian response to the well-documented excesses of the last decade of the twentieth century. Yes, there are patterns of market behavior that more directly reflect Einstein's view of the universe—where instantaneous changes in core conditions, particularly as they approach zero or infinity, generate market events that are the financial equivalent of atom splitting. However, if one is careful, commits to clean living, and only involves oneself in markets where one understands pricing patterns, then one stands every chance of trading for an entire lifetime without ever encountering conditions that even remotely resemble nuclear fusion/fission. If Einstein and his cohorts like Fermi ever got into the business of trading, they would probably prefer complex instruments, such as derivatives. No doubt they would do well; but even here, they'd be the first to acknowledge their heavy debt to Newton.

It is therefore to the memory of that learned second holder of the Lucasian chair at Cambridge University (a spot currently occupied by that miracle of modern science, Stephen Hawking) that I dedicate my statistical tool kit. If we can look at the market universe with a measure of Newton's intellectual efficiency, we may live to avoid if not the big crunch, then at least at least the apples that seem to be forever falling on the heads of unwitting market participants.

Before we turn to the numbers, one additional word of caution is perhaps required. Please note that the statistical section and, indeed, much of the rest of the book contains numerous examples. Some of these use very large numbers; others apply more modest figures. Please do not be overly impressed by the former or depressed by the latter. The point here is that the same concepts pretty well apply whether you are managing $50 thousand worth of capital or $50 million.

Average P/L

This is a basic calculation of the mathematical mean of your daily returns, as derived by dividing your cumulative performance by the number of periods (e.g., days) the performance covers. You may find it useful to perform this calculation in terms of both dollars and percent of capital, the latter of which will help you to evaluate your performance across various levels of capital committed to the markets. For instance, if your account balance is, say, $50,000 at the start of a given period and your average daily return is $500, this would represent a 1% daily return. However, if over time your account balance grew to, say, $100,000, the $500 would represent only half this amount when expressed in percentage terms.

I heartily recommend that you calculate and compare these averages across different segments of your portfolio, over different time horizons, and so on. For example, you may want to calculate your average return on longs versus shorts in order to determine whether there is a discernible bias in your market orientation. Similarly, you can compare your averages across market sectors (for equities), underlying markets (for futures), segments of the yield curve (for fixed income trading), and so on. Look carefully here for differences in your unit performance. Are they tied to external factors such as market conditions or perhaps to areas of expertise or trading comfort? By calculating averages across these factors, you can begin to form an idea of what is working in your portfolio and what isn't.

Once you have mastered this relatively simple concept, you may wish to manipulate the calculation in such a way as to provide additional insights akin to those just described. One such adjustment is to separate your profitable and unprofitable days (or winning and losing trades) into separate data pools and to calculate the associated averages of these P/L pools. This will enable you to begin to compare your performance in winning situations to those in losing ones. In turn, this will be a critical theme that we revisit throughout the book, as I will argue throughout that no element of your trading success is more important than making sure you have extracted more from the market during profitable intervals than you have given back when events are working against you.

Standard Deviation

This second core element of statistical analysis is a bit elusive to define, but it is one of the most important components of our tool kit. As such, it bears spending some time and effort on standard deviation to obtain a fairly precise understanding so it can be efficiently applied. In order to do so, we must first introduce the concept of a *normal distribution*, which, stated simply, is a characteristic of most random data sets, ranging from people's heights, to their bowling scores, to their performance in the markets over time. There are very statistically complex definitions and associated tests respecting the normality of distributions; but, of course, the simplest and safest way to think of them is as those data sets under which, by grouping the range of outcomes by their magnitude, one observes a large concentration of data points around the mean, with the number of observations decreasing sequentially in either direction from the mean data point. If you plot this number of outcomes (y) against their absolute magnitude (x), you end up with a graph whose shape looks something like a bell, as depicted in Figure 3.4.

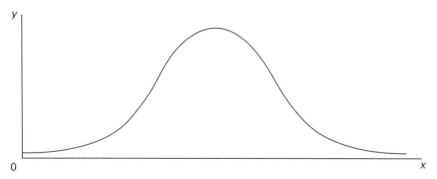

FIGURE 3.4 Graph of a standard normal distribution.

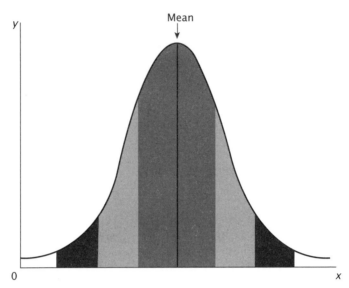

FIGURE 3.5 Normal distribution with standard deviation bands.

If we assume that a distribution is in fact normal (and this is an assumption, as we will reveal later, that you undertake with some degree of hazard), then it is entirely defined by its mean (defined earlier), which provides information regarding the magnitude of specific observations, and standard deviation, which is a measure of dispersion around this mean observation.

The standard deviation of a normal distribution is indicated by the width of the shaded bands illustrated in Figure 3.5.

The standard deviation will thus be measured in units of the x-axis, which, for our purposes, may be thought of as dollars or percent of daily return. The magnitude of this figure will become our main unit for measuring the riskiness in the portfolio.

Figures 3.6(a) and 3.6(b) illustrate normal distributions that are narrow (carrying minimal risk) and wide (indicating higher levels of exposure), respectively.

Figure 3.6(a) offers an example of a normally distributed data set with a small standard deviation (as measured by the width of the bands that are closest to the mean along the x-axis). A low standard deviation is one where most of the observations in a given distribution are close to the mean data point. If we think in terms of daily P/L performance, a low standard deviation would imply that the daily returns to a given portfolio resided largely within a narrow band of dollar-based or percentage-based gains and losses. In turn, this would be indicative of a low risk profile. By contrast, the large

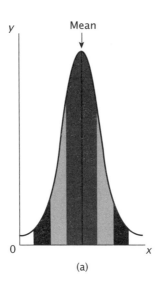

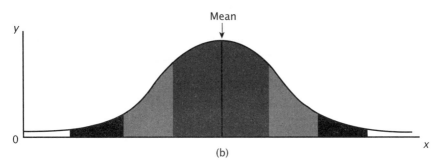

FIGURE 3.6 Examples of (a) small and (b) large standard deviations.

amount of *x*-axis space occupied by the distribution in Figure 3.6(b) suggests a much wider range of P/L outcomes, as would be consistent with a higher risk profile. Over the course of the next few chapters, you will begin, I hope, to understand just how powerful the standard deviation concept is in measuring the volatility of portfolio returns, which is exactly the notion we are trying to capture in measuring risk, or portfolio exposure.

Standard Deviations and Confidence Intervals. As I have suggested earlier, the standard deviation statistic, while not lending itself to simple definitions, tells us what level of distributional dispersion is

TABLE 3.1	Percentage of Returns Associated with Standard Deviation Intervals
Percentage of Normal Curve Area	**Mean ± Number of Standard Deviations**
50.0%	.674σ
68.3	1.000
90.0	1.645
95.0	1.960
95.4	2.000
98.0	2.326
99.0	2.576
99.7	3.000

consistent with a specified percentage of total observations being contained within the associated range, with one standard deviation on either side of the mean (indicated in Figures 3.5 and 3.6 by the innermost portions of the graphs) accounting for approximately 68.3% of all the data in the sample. By using multiples of the statistic, we can identify the magnitudes that would be associated with greater percentages of the distribution curve: with two standard deviations (indicated by the sum of the two innermost areas together in Figures 3.5 and 3.6) representing more than 95% of all observations, three standard deviations (covering the three innermost areas) representing more than 99%, and so on—again assuming that the data set in question is indeed distributed normally.

Table 3.1, which may come in handy for you in the future, maps specific multiples of standard deviations into corresponding percentages of the area underneath the bell curve in a normal distribution.

It is important to note that the tools of mean and standard deviation are typically viewed in financial markets, as elsewhere, as measures of estimation and prediction. In this sense, the left-hand column of Table 3.1 represents a *confidence interval* associated with a given number of standard deviations. For example, we would be 68.3% confident that a given observation will fall within plus-or-minus one standard deviation of the mean, 95.4% confident that an observation will fall within plus-or-minus two standard deviations of the mean, and so on.

The concept of a confidence interval in this sense is only as valid as is the tendency of historical distribution patterns to continue to replicate themselves (i.e., the past is a good predictor of future behavior). However, because (typically due to the introduction of new factors or information sets) the future will always deviate somewhat from the past, your confidence interval statistic will never be entirely accurate. For example, you are likely to experience a P/L fluctuation that you have identified as representing a 95%, more frequently or less frequently than the precise one day each month, which is implied in the calculation. Despite these shortcomings, the confidence interval concept is very important to risk managers and other control entities as a general indicator of the size of their current exposure. Be that as it may, for our purposes (and for reasons I will explain later), we will often be more inclined to maintain our focus on standard deviations as the purest measure of volatility.

How to Calculate the Standard Deviation Statistic. As this book is a practical guide to trading and not a treatise in statistical analysis, I will try to avoid the posting of mathematical formulas. The standard deviation statistic is as ubiquitous to the world of statistics as body temperature or blood pressure is to the field of medical science and can be calculated using embedded formulas in spreadsheet products such as Microsoft Excel or in any calculator with even basic statistical functions.

For the mathematically rigorous among you, and in the interest of public service, I offer the formula in its arithmetic form:

$$s = \sqrt{\text{var}} = \sqrt{\frac{\Sigma(X - \overline{X})^2}{N - 1}}$$

where s = standard deviation
var = portfolio variance
X = individual observation
$\overline{X}$ = sample mean
N = number of observations

Also in the interest of public service and full disclosure, I should tell you that some of the world's finest statisticians (certainly some of the finest I know) couldn't regurgitate this formula if their lives depended on it. So don't feel bad when you end up doing this the easy way and plugging it into Excel.

Sample Standard Deviation Calculation. In order to maintain some consistency in the use of examples, I ask you to return to the sample portfolio depicted in Figure 3.1. If you were to go to the trouble of calculating a standard deviation for this portfolio for the year 2002, you would derive a result of $25,349. Applying the logic we are using throughout this discussion, such a statistic implies that 68.3% of all daily P/L observations will fall somewhere between −$25,349 and +$25,349. Further, using the data from Table 3.1, we can establish a 95% confidence interval for future observations by simply multiplying the standard deviation statistic by the appropriate scale-up figure, in this case 1.96. Thus, the 95% confidence interval for this particular portfolio is ±$49,684, and we would expect no more than 1 out of 20 observations (about one trading day per month) to fall outside of these bands.

In addition to expressing this statistic in dollar terms, it is also useful to apply it against a percentage of capital. For simplicity's sake, assume that the account in question was trading with an introductory capital amount of $3 million. Under these circumstances, a one standard deviation figure would be approximately 0.75%, and the 95% confidence interval would be located between −1.47% and +1.47%. In turn, this means that only once a month would we expect a daily P/L observation, positive or negative, to exceed approximately 1.47% of capital, and this is one meaningful way of expressing portfolio risk.

Note, however, that we do not arrive at these numbers by simply dividing the dollar volatility ($25,349) by the introductory capital figure ($3 million) and scaling up to make the confidence interval calculation—a process that would return a higher result of 0.85% for one standard deviation and ±1.66% for a 95th percentile confidence interval. This is true because as profits and losses accumulate (in the case of this sample portfolio, I am happy to say they are profits), the capital base of $3 million changes accordingly. In order to calculate the most accurate version of the standard deviation (which, as we should bear in mind, is merely an *estimate* of portfolio exposure and, as such, will never be entirely accurate under any methodology), it is necessary to adjust the capital figure on a daily basis to reflect this P/L impact. However, for most purposes, you are probably just as well off keeping the capital figure constant.

Applications of the Standard Deviation Statistic. It should be clear to the careful reader by now that I really like this statistic. For one thing, it's typically represented in mathematical shorthand by the Greek letter sigma, as applied in the lowercase: σ. I find its curves to be very sensual and much easier on the eyes than its boxy, overmasculine uppercase counterpart: Σ.

More important, I believe that it is the most concise measurement of exposure to the markets. I use it as the primary unit of risk measurement in my own personal tool kit (yes, I have one), and I encourage readers to do the same. As is the case with many such measurements, its absolute magnitude is of less importance than the manner in which it changes across time, market conditions, financial environment, and so on.

Note that the standard deviation statistic is highly sensitive to the number of observations used to calculate it and that you are almost certain to derive different answers across different time spans. For example, the figure that you derive by using an entire year's worth of history may differ significantly from the result obtained by reviewing data over, say, the past

20 days. (Due to the principal of statistical significance discussed elsewhere, I recommend against performing the calculation on any data set consisting of less than 20 observations.) Do not be surprised by these disparities, which in fact can offer useful insight into the risk patterns that your portfolio is displaying. Indeed, I believe that you should remain at all times mindful of your standard deviation data, across various time spans, perhaps relying on rolling monthly (20-day), quarterly (60-day), and annual (250-day) windows as your primary guide. Compare and contrast these numbers. Try to tie back the highest and the lowest to specific incidents in your market experience. If there is significant disparity between the periods, you may want to investigate the sources of the higher number. Was it the result of extreme volatility in the markets? Did it correspond to a period when you (for whatever reason) decided to increase your overall market participation levels? Perhaps some combination of the two?

A continuous review of this information will help you in the critical task of determining your maximum threshold for performance volatility. How big a standard deviation is too big? Of course, this will vary from portfolio to portfolio and from situation to situation. As a general rule, I believe that the figure should not exceed 10% of the amount of capital you can afford to lose from the point of the calculation. For example, if your maximum tolerance for losses is, say, $100,000, I would recommend against trading in such a manner that the daily standard deviation of your P/L exceeds $10,000. I believe (and here purists will argue with me that the number is too small to generate a reliable result) that the best interval over which to calculate this is probably the rolling 20-day time span, as this is the one most sensitive to daily fluctuations. Moreover, if you don't exceed this 10% threshold in any given 20-day span, you place yourself in the best possible position for preservation of capital over longer time spans.

While the 10% threshold may, at first glance, appear to be somewhat arbitrary, let me assure you that I have developed this guideline very carefully, over a number of years and over wide ranges of market performance and conditions. While we will discuss the details of this at greater length in a couple of chapters, I have based it on the indisputable fact that markets often move by factors significantly greater than one standard deviation and that these large market movements often take place in direct succession. Therefore, the once-a-year conditions that cause prices to change by three standard deviations or more are events that would put a 10% portfolio, under the methodology set forth earlier, in considerable jeopardy of hitting associated maximum loss thresholds as the result of unforeseen volatility that operates as a perpetual threat to each and every risk-bearing portfolio. By operating below the 10% threshold, you place yourself in the best position to minimize the probability of avoiding the maximum loss level, around which any well-thought-out risk management program operates.

There are many other potential applications of the standard deviation statistic, some of which are best discovered through experimentation with this and other related statistics, many of the most important of which are described in the coming paragraphs. If you are willing to play with these numbers and apply them creatively to different elements of your performance data, you stand to benefit.

At this early stage of the discussion, I will introduce only one more concept for your consideration: the use of standard deviation in the calculation of risk-adjusted return. Specifically, it is common practice for portfolio managers and allocators of capital to express returns as units of volatility, with volatility being measured by the standard deviation of portfolio returns. For example, reverting back to our sample portfolio from Figure 3.1, the mean daily P/L for this account is $2,456, or 0.07%; and its standard deviation over the period is about $25,349, or 0.75%. By expressing these two statistics as a ratio, we begin to derive some notion of risk-adjusted return. Specifically, we can state that for the period in question, 75 basis points of daily risk generates 7 basis points of average daily return. While at this stage it is difficult to have an informed opinion as to whether this is good or bad performance, you should conceptually understand that this performance is better than that of a portfolio that yields the same return at a higher level of volatility. And you should understand that from this "risk-adjusted return perspective," we might be indifferent as an investor between this portfolio and one that was twice as profitable and twice as volatile.

Later on in this chapter, we will formalize the calculation of risk-adjusted return in a number of important ways, most notably by introducing such calculations as the Sharpe ratio and the Return over Maximum Drawdown (ROMAD) statistic.

Standard Deviation Statistic for Nonnormal Distributions. As indicated earlier, the standard deviation statistic is one that, in the strictest sense, can only apply to distributions that are characterized as *normal*, with most observations centering around an arithmetic mean and with a diminishing number of data points pushing away, in a bell-shaped pattern, from this center point. In market economics, this assumption of normality is often challenged, almost always on one of the two types of observable anomalies:

1. The distribution is materially *skewed* to one side of the mean.
2. Extreme observations tend to occur with more frequency than is consistent with the normality assumption (or *kurtosis*).

Purists will tell you that when a given distribution deviates from patterns of normality, the use of a standard deviation statistic to describe such concepts as volatility and dispersion becomes an increasingly questionable analytical methodology. Indeed, for distinctly nonnormal distributions, the standard deviation statistic may be entirely inapplicable.

Although very few markets or trading portfolios are skewed significantly to one side or another of their mean return profile (indeed, portfolios with high degrees of skewness on either side are difficult to sustain, due to financial constraints on the negative side and to the tendency for the market to quickly arbitrage away "superprofits" on the positive side), many tend to have more extreme observations than is perfectly consistent with the concept of normality. In these cases, the presence of outliers will cause the standard deviation to be higher than it would be if their magnitude or frequency adhered better to the normal distribution profile. However, the standard deviation is, simply stated, not a precise enough tool to identify these conditions, much less to quantify them.

I must tell you that the whole business of determining whether a distribution is actually normal or not gives me a headache, so I'm not going to spend any more time on the subject. What is more, I don't think you should trouble yourself much on this score either. In fact, my best advice to you (though it be blasphemy if uttered in the church of the pointy-headed) is to go ahead and calculate the standard deviations, without worrying about the validity of the normality assumption. When you do, try to write those lowercase sigmas with flourish and flair aplenty.

As Sly Stone said at Woodstock, it'll do you no harm.

Sharpe Ratio

Now that we have (more or less) thoroughly explored the concepts of both mean return and associated standard deviation, we can unite these concepts into what has become the industry standard for calculating risk-adjusted return: the *Sharpe Ratio*. This ratio is designed to normalize returns against their associated volatility, the idea being that a unit of return can be judged qualitatively in inverse proportion to the amount of volatility required to produce it. For example, consider two accounts: one that returned 25% in one year, with the first generating a standard deviation of 10%, and one that returned 20%. Under the Sharpe Ratio measurement, the first portfolio would be the better performer, because it ostensibly operated under a reduced risk profile while producing the same overall performance.

There are many variations to the Sharpe Ratio calculation, but all of them attempt to capture the following concept:

Sharp Ratio = (Return − Risk-Free Return)/Standard Deviation of Return

Note that the right side of the equation can be expressed in terms of dollars or percentages, as long as the same convention applies to each side. A few words about the individual terms, all of which are best expressed on an annual basis:

- *Return.* The amount you earn on assets.
- *Risk-Free Return.* This is the amount of money you can expect to earn on assets that are classified as "riskless" in the field of economic analysis, on amount of capital equivalent to the one that you are committing to the markets you trade. For all but a few specified situations, the appropriate rate of return is that of U.S. Treasury instruments. In the Sharpe Ratio calculation, the risk-free return is subtracted from the total return of the portfolio in order to isolate that portion of the performance that is tied to the assumption of market exposure. One rather elegant outcome of this is that an individual who takes capital and invests it in Treasuries earns exactly the risk-free rate and, therefore, generates a Sharpe Ratio of precisely 0, while portfolios that fail to earn even this modest level of return actually have negative Sharpes. Therefore, it is only for performance above the minimum benchmark of government coupons—and as such is deemed to be associated with risk-bearing market activities—that the Sharpe Ratio begins to recognize a positive, risk-adjusted return.
- *Standard Deviation of Return.* This is our old friend/nemesis, which we thought was beaten to death already, resurrected to apply as the risk component in a risk-adjusted return calculation. Note that here it is extremely important to express this statistic in the appropriate time spans—ideally, as indicated earlier, one year. Due to the specifics of the calculation (under which the figure varies directly with the square root of the number of data points), this requires either multiplication or division of the square root of the number of observations. For example, assume you have a year's worth of daily data that indicates a daily standard deviation of, say, $10,000, or 1.0% (assume $1 million of capital). In order to figure out the *annualized* standard deviation, we would have to multiply this figure by the square root of the number of trading days in a year. When weekends and holidays are removed from the calendar, this number converges to 250 (give or take a day or two), with the associated square root being about 15.9. Therefore, an account with a daily standard deviation of $10,000, or 1.0%, would have an annualized standard deviation of approximately $159,000, or 15.9%.

It is necessary to achieve this normalization of time spans across the Sharpe Ratio equation in order to derive results that do not fall into the category of nonsensical. Note that the equation allows for adjustments that account for such factors as partial data sets (e.g., half a year's worth of data) and for time periods other than daily. However, I will defer to my professional statistician friends for explanations of these mystic phenomena.

By now, you have probably rushed out to calculate your Sharpe and are wondering if you should be proud or ashamed. As a rule of thumb, I believe that individuals should almost always strive for Sharpe Ratios, calculated under the methodology just described, equal to or in excess of 1.0. For example, if we assume a 5% risk-free rate and a 15% annualized standard deviation of returns, the portfolio in question would have to return at least 20% in order to achieve this threshold—(20% Return − 5% Risk-Free Return)/15% Standard Deviation = 1.0. It is certainly possible to achieve significant financial objectives over extended time spans with Sharpe Ratios below this benchmark; however, the attractiveness of the returns from a risk-adjusted perspective quite naturally diminishes accordingly. In these cases, the providers of capital (whether it be you or some other economic entity) may very well decide there are better places to risk their money. At the other end of the spectrum, I have seen cases where portfolios can achieve Sharpes of 5.0, 10.0, or better for sustained periods of time. These are rather unique extremes and can only be reflective of either an uncommon market edge or some risks not well-identified by the standard deviation calculation; and I urge you to evaluate these situations with extreme care.

This brings us to the final element of our discussion on the Sharpe Ratio, namely, its limitations, which are largely tied to the accuracy of the standard deviation calculation as a proxy for exposure and to the applicability of historical returns and volatility distributions as a predictor of future performance. As indicated, the limitations of the standard deviation calculation derive from its assumption that portfolio returns are normally distributed; and, as we have demonstrated, this is not always the case. Moreover, past volatility patterns may not repeat themselves—particularly wherever and whenever volatility is calculated over shorter time spans.

To illustrate the kind of problems that these limitations can present, consider a portfolio that does nothing but sell deep out-of-the-money options, close to expiration. Because these options pay off in all but the most remote (in a probabilistic sense) outcomes, portfolio managers who employ these strategies can enjoy stable returns with low volatility for extended periods of time—often ranging into years. The associated high Sharpe Ratio, however, disguises the fact that every now and again, an abrupt market move will cause a substantial loss in these portfolios. When this occurs, we see both the limitations of σ in calculating exposures and the hazards associated with using historical returns as a proxy for future exposures. For these reasons, and a number of others, although the Sharpe Ratio remains an important benchmark for risk-adjusted return, it is best used in conjunction with analytics that don't rely on standard deviations as their exclusive measure for risk, such as Return over Maximum Drawdown (which we'll get to in a moment).

Median P/L

The statistical median is defined as the observation within the data set for which half of the data points are of a higher magnitude and half are lower. In perfectly symmetrical distributions, the mean and the median are identical (or nearly identical). However, in my experience, few performance-related data sets are perfectly symmetrical. Therefore, I suggest that you compare the mean and the median P/L observations in your portfolio across varying time horizons. Wherever the mean significantly exceeds the median, it is more than likely due to the fact that a handful of your most profitable days are bringing up your average. Similarly, where the median is significantly higher than the mean, it is probably due to the impact of a number of extreme negative outcomes on the average across the data set.

In either case, if the median and the mean diverge significantly from one another, it represents yet another opportunity to further explore the dynamics and the associated impact of activity at the tails of your P/L distribution. I highly recommend that you take this opportunity, by further exploring the associated causes, and so on.

Percentage of Winning Days

This is simply a straightforward percentage representation of the number of days where your trading ended profitably. While, at first glance, it would seem somewhat intuitive that a percentage target of 50% represents the minimum for profitable trading over the long term, I have found this not necessarily to be the case. As long as your unit returns on profitable days are sufficiently higher than they are on losing days, I have observed that an actual percentage of winning days as low as 40% can be conducive to profitable trading. The important thing here is to recognize, as I will elaborate on next, that this diagnostic combined with the "performance ratio" discussed in the next section represents a critical first-order P/L evaluation tool, as success in at least one of these two ratios is a necessary component of a profitable portfolio.

As with virtually every other element of our tool kit, the review of the *% winning days* statistic is most useful as a metric, which is tracked across multiple time periods and against such factors as external market conditions, level of capital deployed in the market, and seasonality. I invite you to drill as deeply as possible into your P/L data set in order to derive the best possible understanding of the conditions that are the greatest contributors to the probability of your ending the day ahead of the game, rather than a few steps back.

Performance Ratio, Average P/L, Winning Days versus Losing Days

My first law of trading dynamics: The key to risk-adjusted profitability is to extract more from the market when you are right than you give back when you are wrong. There are many ways to measure your performance in this regard, perhaps the most important of which, as we will address in subsequent chapters, is *transactions-level analysis*. However, as transactions-level data can be inaccurate, too voluminous to process, or simply unavailable, it is important to review this from a daily P/L perspective as well, which, in the overwhelming majority of cases, will be a close reflection of what happens on a trade-by-trade basis. As previously indicated, this "performance ratio" goes hand in hand with the % winning days statistic as a critical, first-order benchmark of trading performance. Look at it this way: In order to be successful as a trader, you either have to be right more than 50% of the time or make more on winners than you give back on losers—or (ideally) some combination of the two. Therefore, when an account is having difficulties, one of the first things I consider is whether the problem lies within the % winning days (indicating, perhaps, suboptimal selection) or in the performance ratio (indicating potential problems in the actual trading habits). In turn, this provides insights into potential inefficiencies and is helpful in prescribing the appropriate countermeasures.

The % winning days statistic and the performance ratio are interrelated. But make no mistake: The performance ratio is the more important of the two. This difference in their levels of criticality is dependent on a number of identifiable factors but most notably is governed by where the portfolio lies on the trading/investment spectrum. For long-term holders of positions, intuition suggests that accurate selection looms larger in importance then does any factor tied to the unit profitability on given days. By contrast, those who trade very actively will have the luxury of living with quite a lot of losers, so long as they are monetizing their winners at a sufficient premium. However, for virtually any successful account, it will be necessary to make more on your up days than you give back on your down days. Unless you operate in ways consistent with this objective, you will find your portfolio paddling up the performance stream.

What is an appropriate benchmark objective for the performance ratio? My experience tells me that somewhere in the range of 125% is entirely achievable, and I have worked with guys who have done much better, some of them exceeding that, some consistently achieving 200%+ in this regard. Play around with these statistics, and find the conditions under which you can maximize your performance ratio results. If these conditions happen to be scalable, you're on your way.

Drawdown

If you stick with this business of trading and investment, know this: You are going to spend most of your time in an unhappy state known as *drawdown*. This statistical concept, which is pervasive to the evaluation of all types of portfolio managers, has a very specific but often misunderstood definition. Specifically, *drawdown* refers to the difference between a portfolio's highest valuation over a given period and its lowest subsequent valuation. This means that your portfolio either is at a new record high for the period or, by definition, is in drawdown. Moreover, your status doesn't change until you have again reached a new high. Therefore, if you are managing, say, $10 million, earn $1 million over the next month, lose $50,000 on the first day of the following month, another $25,000 on the next day, and then make back the $50,000 on the third, you are experiencing a drawdown of $75,000, which won't be officially over until you make back another $25,000 and your account balance reaches at least $11,000,001. Because traders very seldom operate at new high account balances, they are almost always in at least a nominal condition of drawdown.

A thorough analysis of your drawdown patterns will offer you perhaps the most objective and comprehensive window into the risks inherent in your portfolio of any element of our tool kit. This is true for a couple of reasons. First, by using actual data as opposed to such statistical estimation tools as standard deviation, you eliminate the need for assumptions such as the implied normality of your returns. Your drawdown history is your drawdown history; and it doesn't matter whether it is based on a data set that is skewed, has excessive presence of observations in the tails of the distribution, or (alternatively) results in a portfolio histogram that takes on such a bell-like shape that you can hear it chime on Sunday mornings. Second, while other statistics we describe are typically single-point descriptions of complex, multifactored phenomena, the drawdown concept encompasses the depth, temporal interval, and associated recovery patterns of your actual exposure.

Because by my estimate and according to the definition specified you will spend at least 80% of your trading career in a condition of at least nominal drawdown, the concept lends itself to continual, broad-ranging analysis. Among the different drawdown-related factors of which you should track for each individual drawdown are:

- *Magnitude.* Of course, you will want to keep track of the value of your drawdowns, in terms of both dollars and percentage of capital allocated or deployed. Note that these figures lend themselves extensively to additional analysis. How are these drawdowns changing over time? Are they increasing or decreasing on an absolute ($) and relative (%) basis? Are they tied to specific market conditions? How do they correlate with your profitability over specified longer time periods (e.g., a year)? All of these questions can and should be addressed dynamically, always providing the potential for revealing new insights into your trading behavior.

- *Recovery Period.* It is also naturally very important to have a good sense of the timing dynamics of your drawdowns, which can best be expressed in terms of associated recovery periods. Here it is important to once again bear in mind the definition of *drawdown*, which is any negative P/L that takes an account down from its historical "high-water" performance mark. The Recovery Period statistic is thus a simple measure of the time it takes to reestablish a new high. Like the drawdown statistic, it lends itself to considerable additional analysis over multiple time periods.

- *Magnitude of Subsequent Incremental Gains.* As just indicated, a drawdown is not over until the account in question has achieved a new high-water mark. It is useful to then measure the amount by which the new high-water mark exceeds the old. This figure can be expressed as a ratio, with the drawdown statistic residing in the denominator, and will give you some idea of the trade-offs in your markets between risk and return. In particular, for some longer-term strategies (e.g., private equity investments), trade execution considerations and liquidity constraints may be such that you may have to suffer significant drawdown in order to achieve the desired returns. In such a case, it is instructive to understand the associated magnitudes. By contrast, short-term trading of liquid securities in relatively frictionless markets should not demand that enormous pain be endured in order to achieve your targeted objectives.

- *Return over Maximum Drawdown (ROMAD).* This statistic, in which annual returns are expressed as a percentage of the worst drawdown experienced over a specified period of analysis, actually represents what many people believe to be the most accurate available measure of risk-adjusted return. This is true primarily because drawdown is arguably the most accurate measure of portfolio risk. By tracking your drawdowns over, say, a number of years and particularly across a wide range of market conditions, you begin to get an idea of the full range of negative outcomes that can occur in your trading, along with the associated impacts. By comparing the worst of these to your annual returns, you provide yourself with a uniquely effective manner in which to express the risks and rewards in your portfolio, one that does not rely in any way, shape, or form on assumptions about the distribution of your returns.

For many professional trading accounts, including those tied to fee-based structures typically associated with the hedge funds and managed futures, portfolio managers are only paid for incremental performance. One very meaningful implication of this is that between periods where returns are calculated, if you are operating under this framework, you will not be paid for the revenues you have earned in recovering from a drawdown. This, in turn, has important implications for portfolio management. First, and perhaps needless to say, it means that you want to do everything in your power to minimize the magnitude of drawdowns as they take shape in their formative stages. However, once they have reached certain levels, the associated recovery process will require an investment in time on your part that may be accompanied with financial constraints that transcend your professional activities and impact your personal life. This may tempt you toward portfolio management options that are not entirely consistent with the decision path you would take if personal considerations weren't a factor, and the manner in which you conduct yourself at these junctures will have implications for your long-term well-being as a portfolio manager. If you become impatient and try to make back your losses too quickly, you may very well find yourself in a deeper hole, in the process threatening the viability of your entire trading program. However, in almost every case, it will not be practical to put off the paydays you seek forever.

For these reasons, I feel that using the drawdown thresholds as the basis for risk reduction is an essential component of any risk management program. Do yourself a favor and identify these thresholds at the beginning of a trading cycle. Then stick to this commitment. For example, you may decide to reduce your exposure by, say, 50% if you experience a drawdown of 10%. If you are able to do so, this will achieve two important results. First, it will go a long way toward reducing the magnitude of any further drawdowns in your account. Second, it may, over the long term, give you the confidence to take larger risks in aggregate, as you have established a framework that transforms the concept of drawdown from a mysterious and evil phenomenon that is lurking to do you no good at any moment into a controllable dynamic that is actually part of a sound risk-control program.

The major benefit of such an approach is that you avoid placing yourself in a position where your drawdown is too deep to allow you to revive your trading fortunes. The trade-off is that for any level of unit success you have subsequent to your drawdown, you can expect the associated recovery period to be significantly longer than it might have been had you not tried to make up your losses in the quickest possible fashion. However, I strongly believe that the extra investment of time is one that will pay off in myriad ways.

In general, by examining your drawdown patterns as part of a comprehensive statistical review process, you gain unique insights into your specific portfolio dynamics. You will better understand what went wrong, why it went wrong, and what it will take to correct the situation. Moreover, if you use drawdown as an "inverse barometer" of the amount of exposure acceptable for your account—reducing risk when significant drawdowns occur and increasing your exposure only when they are substantially erased—you stand to retain much more explicit control over your trading fortunes than you would if you operated in a vacuum with respect to this critical information metric.

Correlations

The final core element of our introductory statistical tool kit is *correlation analysis*. You ought to be at least nominally familiar with this concept, which involves identifying the extent to which two or more data series dynamically exhibit similar characteristics, most notably, for our purposes, across time. Correlation coefficients can range from +100% to −100% but (unless data series are simply disguised representations of a single concept, for example, the yield on a given bond and its price) typically fall somewhere in between.

By performing correlation analysis on the time series of portfolio returns, traders stand to gain unique and specific insights into underlying portfolio economics. For example, you may find yourself highly correlated to some benchmark stock index such as the Standard & Poor's (S&P) 500, the Dow Jones Industrial Average (the Dow, DJIA), or the Nasdaq Composite. More likely than not, this will be indicative of a long bias in your portfolio, which predisposes your account to perform more effectively when markets are rallying. However, this is merely one type of correlation analysis that can be applied to great effect to your P/L time series.

Following is a summary of some of the standard categories of correlation analysis that you may find useful in identifying the drivers of relative performance for your portfolio.

Correlation against Market Benchmarks.   This is the general case associated with the example provided prior, under which you might calculate "correlation coefficients" between your returns and the performance of various market indexes. Here, I recommend that you begin the process by simply identifying, in an anecdotal sense, the market indexes that might best capture the essence of your trading and then running some introductory correlations there. For example, if you are trading U.S. equities, you might begin with the S&P, the Dow, or the Nasdaq Composite. (This concept is largely analogous to that of a "beta" for an individual security. Therefore, when you calculate your correlation to the standard equity benchmark for the markets you are trading, it is not incorrect to think of this as your portfolio beta. If you wish to be creative, it might be interesting to compare your correlation to the equity markets to the average beta of the securities held in your portfolio.)

Similarly, if you are trading U.S. Fixed Income, the Treasury bond (long term), or the Eurodollar (short term), futures contracts might be the best place to start. With these basics in place, I encourage you to be creative, running correlations between your P/L and as many market time series as you can think of—whether they make intuitive sense or not. While you may not find any surprising interdependencies, you may gain one or two insights into the external market patterns that are likely to have the most dramatic impact on your performance. This is particularly true if you perform the analysis over multiple time periods, which I highly recommend. Doing so will give you a sense of how stable your correlations are, how they are changing over time and across market conditions, and so on—which in turn can be analyzed for insight into where your greatest opportunities and associated exposures reside.

As you review the dynamics across the different time periods, you should think qualitatively about external conditions at that time. For example, you may wish to determine whether your correlations tend to increase or to decrease during market rallies, breaks, and so on. Moreover, particularly during periods of market turmoil (e.g., third quarter of 1998), the markets themselves tend to correlate strongly to one another; and I believe it is extremely instructive to determine whether and by how much your own performance tends to converge or to diverge from market trends under these conditions. If you can avoid falling into volatility vortexes during these periods of disruption, you can take great comfort from a risk management perspective. Conversely, if, as is typically the case, your correlation to the markets increases along with their correlations to one another, you should be mindful of this and look to reduce your exposure when these types of extreme conditions begin to present themselves.

When calculating your correlation against market benchmarks, it is important to ensure that you are applying your P/L against the precisely appropriate data set, and this can be a tricky process. First, in order to determine whether your performance is correlated to the markets, it is critical to recognize the need to run your performance series against the *daily net change* in the market, not its *absolute level*. This is true because what we care about in this regard is whether you make money when the market is *going up or going down*, not whether it is at a high or a low price level. In addition, if you are trading international markets, you may very well find that the most relevant correlation data involves lagging one time series by a day to account for time differential (e.g., correlate your P/L against the previous day's price change in the appropriate market). Also, if the appropriate benchmark happens to be a futures contract, it is important to correct for the differential associated from the rollover from one delivery month to another, which, on the day it occurs, will generate a price change that may not be consistent with pricing patterns in the under-lying markets.

In general, the number of ways in which it is possible to derive inter-esting information from this type of correlation analysis is virtually limit-less, and I encourage you to approach this task with a sense of creativity, adventure, and discovery.

Cross Correlation Analysis. This type of correlation analysis involves the calculation of the statistic across different trading accounts. Needless to say, it is most relevant when the trading environment features multiple portfolios, either separate books managed by an individual deci-sion maker or some group of independent portfolio managers operating in cooperation (or at minimum proximity) to one another. In these cases, it is instructive to learn how the different accounts correlate with one another, again across different time intervals, market conditions, and so on. These types of analyses can serve to either corroborate or refute any notions that may exist regarding the extent to which multiple accounts are truly inde-pendent or are simply nominally different manifestations of a single trad-ing strategy. In turn, this can only assist the process of understanding the drivers of trading results and the identification of the frameworks that are most maximally organized for market success.

From a capital allocation perspective, correlation analysis is a critical tool in managing risk-adjusted return, as portfolio theory has long recog-nized the benefits of diversification in generating stable returns. In order to achieve such diversification, those in the business of funding portfolio strategies are naturally predisposed to minimize the correlations across the accounts to which they are allocating capital. Therefore, unless you are funding your own book, even if you don't care a whit about the manner in which your returns correlate with those of your peers, it's a pretty fair bet that your supervisor does. Accordingly, I urge you to be mindful of these factors even if you have neither the ability nor the inclination to calculate the actual correlations themselves.

If you do find yourself highly correlated to those around you—particularly if these correlations persist over time—it is unlikely that it is the result of coincidence. Take a careful look at your trading patterns as well as at those of your colleagues. More likely than not, there is an element of shared decision making. Try to determine in these instances whether all of the good ideas are emanating from a single source. Be as objective as possible in this process. If you conclude that there is a true, multilateral sharing of ideas, it can often represent the best of all possible trading environments. Conversely, if the idea generation process centers around one individual—whether it is you or one of your colleagues—be aware that this condition is highly unstable, lending itself to resentment and other negative dynamics. I recommend that you seek ways to remedy the situation, either by being more proactive in your contribution to the idea generation process or (if you are the Alpha of the group) by insisting that others step up their contributions. If the value proposition between you and your partners cannot be normalized, then it behooves you to ensure that the economic split of the profits accurately reflects the associated value contribution of the participants. Unless you can make this type of partnership effective and equitable for all concerned, it is likely to end badly, both in professional and perhaps in personal terms.

Serial Correlation. This final correlation concept is one that is slightly more complex; and unless you're one of us who find this sort of thing aesthetically pleasing, you can probably survive without going anywhere near this murky subject. However, the topic can have important implications for risk-adjusted profitability, so I'll say a quick word about it.

Serial correlation is a concept that measures the extent to which observations in a time series are influenced by earlier observations in that same series. To use a non-market-based example, one might apply this methodology to determine whether your golf score today is somehow impacted by your performance on the course yesterday. This is certainly true in my case, but I've played exactly one hole of golf in the past two decades, and this only at my dad's insistence. My attention span is painfully short, and my mind wanders if forced to focus on any effort for more than a very small number of minutes. Golfers, on the other hand, appear to need nothing so much as the patience and the presence of mind to endure a ritual that seems to me to go on for much too long and to proceed at much too slow a pace.

I am happy to report, though, that I did manage to avoid utter embarrassment on the one hole I did play, scoring a 5 on a par 3 and in the process amazing my dad, who has never been the biggest admirer of my athletic prowess and who has long been incredulous that I am able to get through such trivial tasks as shaving and riding the subway without doing myself bodily harm.

Hopefully, this anecdote will have convinced you that the calculation of serial correlations is a dangerous business. However, if you insist on proceeding, you should know that these statistics fall into the following two categories:

1. *Autocorrelation.* This concept measures the levels at which today's absolute performance is tied to absolute performance in the recent past. For example, in a stock portfolio using a momentum strategy, we might expect that yesterday's performance could greatly impact our result for today, as successful themes build on themselves, and (conversely) breakdowns in momentum create multiday losses until new pricing patterns present themselves. By contrast, in an arbitrage strategy, one might expect yesterday's losses to be a reasonably accurate indicator of likely strong performance today, and vice versa.

2. *Autoregression.* Autoregressive time series are those for which the main predictor is the amount that previous observations deviate from the mean of the data set. For instance, suppose you are trading an account that has an average daily P/L of, say, $10,000. The account would be considered autoregressive if it tended to perform excessively well or badly on a routine basis on days after it deviated from this mean significantly (say, making more than $20,000 or losing more than $5,000). Portfolios that are deemed to be autoregressive are ones that are based on either breakout strategies (futures system trading) or some type of arbitrage.

Note that serial correlation can be positive or negative and that it often has a dynamic "lag" element, meaning that the appropriate relationship may not be to the previous day's time series but rather to series that are several days old.

The science of determining the relative presence of serial correlation is applied heavily in the evaluation of individual financial instruments under the conceptual heading of *technical analysis*. The associated mathematical methodologies are rather complex and are certainly beyond the scope of this discussion. For more information on this topic, refer to discussions of ARIMA (Autoregressive Integrated Moving Average) and Box-Jenkins analysis, available in most standard statistical textbooks.

Suffice it to say that if you notice repeating patterns in your P/L time series, it may be indicative of serial correlation; and based on simple readings of the charts, you should be in a good position to take the appropriate corrective risk control measures.

"Kitchen Sink" Correlations.   Okay, so I lied. I have one more type of correlation analysis I need to cover. As "kitchen sink" implies, it involves correlating any two things that move against one another. Once you gather up a healthy head of steam in this regard, the process can be quite addictive. If you've followed the script, you may by now be gathering up untold numbers of time series, covering specific aspects of portfolio dynamics. You may, for instance, have accumulated data on such factors as capital usage, net market value, long/short P/L, number of daily transactions, average transaction size, average holding period, et cetera, et cetera, et cetera. While it's easy to get carried away, it is also not much of a stretch to say that there is potential benefit from calculating a correlation between any two such time series and, more specifically, by giving some thought to the implication of any significant result. For example, you may find that your net market value might be negatively correlated to your holding periods, which might reinforce the notion that it is easier to hold for extended periods of time positions with small directional overhang and more difficult to retain position profiles that have large net market exposures. Similarly, correlation patterns between transaction size and capital usage might reveal interesting insights into factors such as liquidity, transaction costs, and other dynamics that will be pertinent to portfolio performance.

Be creative. No matter what two factors you try to correlate against each other, I promise you that there have been sillier ones based on less intelligent premises.

BABY'S ON FIRE

It is very easy to take correlation analysis to extremes. I once worked with a guy who was obsessed with this and who would seek to find correlations in the strangest of places. At various points, he was pretty sure his performance was correlated to factors ranging from the Consumer Price Index to the ratio of investment on put options to call options.

While many of his colleagues found his methodologies difficult to understand, no one disputed the fact that he had traded profitably over broader and more diverse market conditions than virtually anyone in the firm. This individual and I shared a number of interests, and we bonded on such diverse topics as history, literature, and (naturally) rock and roll. Moreover, I was fascinated by his focus on correlation analysis and volunteered to try to help him unearth useful patterns from the data available to us.

We were soon correlating his performance to everything we could think of; and, like most fishing expeditions, we came up empty more often than not. However, we did hit on a couple of important themes over the course of this collaboration, most notably that he had an extreme positive correlation with two key external market factors: (1) the level of *volume* in the markets and (2) the level of *volatility*. Intuitively, this made sense: He had long been aware (albeit in somewhat of a subconscious manner) that he did his best trading when the markets were moving and when there was generally a good deal of trading action taking place therein.

Was this a revelation in his trading? Hardly. However, I like to think that it placed him in a position to size his market participation to the opportunities at hand. I saw some anecdotal evidence that he did indeed save his risk capital for active, fast-moving markets and that when things were slow, he responded by trading less. Correlation analysis thus helped him make better use of his resources.

I was less successful in convincing him that the Beach Boy's "Pet Sounds" is the most overrated album in the history of popular music and that Brian Eno's "Here Come the Warm Jets" is the most underrated.

"Baby's on fire, better throw her in the water."

I can't close this discussion without referencing an old platitude that cautions against confusing "correlation with causation." While correlation analysis can be extremely useful in understanding patterns, providing insights, and offering clues as to what is driving performance, it is crucial to resist the temptation of reading too much into associated outcomes. Ideally, like all other statistics discussed in this chapter, the calculation of correlations will evoke as many questions as answers. It will then be up to you to derive the applicable inferences and to make the appropriate adjustments with respect to your trading.

PUTTING IT ALL TOGETHER

Figure 3.7. is a consolidated report of many of the statistics discussed in this chapter. As can be seen, the report summarizes in graphical/tabular form a wide range of information pertaining to the performance of the account, in terms of daily P/L time series, capital usage, and so on. In later chapters, we will incorporate some individual transactions-level analysis. The data is presented, wherever possible and/or appropriate, in terms of both dollars and percentages. Such an overall snapshot, synthesizing the statistical concepts that I have found are most important, creates a useful framework for further critical analysis of portfolio performance— whether undertaken by the individual, by current or prospective

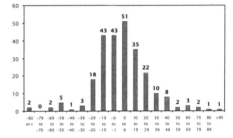

	7/1/02–9/30/02	10/1/02–12/31/02	1/1/02–12/31/02
Buying Power ($)	3,000,000	3,000,000	3,000,000
Return Stats			
Total P/L $	361,394	19,000	619,000
Total Return(% Buy. Pwr.)	12.05%	0.63%	20.63%
Avg P/L (Daily $)	5,647	297	2,456
Avg P/L (Daily %)	0.16%	0.00%	0.07%
Sharpe Ratio (Daily)	0.20	0.00	0.10
Volatility Stats			
Std. Dev. (Daily P/L $)	28,090	32,550	25,349
Std. Dev. (Daily % of Buy. Pwr.)	0.82%	0.91%	0.75%
Maximum (Daily $)	90,962	82,000	90,962
Minimum (Daily $)	(60,587)	(122,000)	(122,000)
Maximum / 1 Std. Dev. P/L	3.24	2.52	3.59
Minimum / 1 Std. Dev. P/L	(2.16)	(3.75)	(4.81)
Downside Deviation ($)	14,130	25,452	17,498
Daily P/L Stats			
Number of Days	64	64	252
Percentage of Up Days	50%	50%	54%
Percentage of Down Days	50%	50%	46%
Average Up Day	27,122	24,063	19,439
Average Down Day	(15,828)	(23,469)	(17,139)
Win / Loss Ratio	1.71	1.03	1.13

FIGURE 3.7 Sample consolidated statistical profile.

providers of capital, or by other entities on a need-to-know basis. It also illustrates the point with which I'd like to leave you concerning this topic: Avoid the practice of viewing each individual statistic in isolation; given their interdependencies, they are instead best interpreted "holistically," with an eye toward identifying the factors that reside on the periphery of your trading approach and (more important) that are true drivers of relative performance.

CHAPTER 4

The Risk Components of an Individual Portfolio

A man with a watch knows what time it is. A man with two watches is never sure.

—Segal's Law

O ur focus thus far has been on reviewing and understanding overall portfolio performance from a statistical/risk management perspective. Specifically, we have introduced methodologies that seek to characterize the risk components of trading accounts, as though these accounts were the most granular units of risk assumption that we could analyze. Of course, as I've already mentioned, this is not strictly true. In fact, as we will discuss at length in this chapter, it is within the power of the portfolio manager to engineer not only the overall level of exposure in the portfolio but also the characteristics of its subcomponents, such as distribution across markets and specific levels of exposure to such risk factors as position concentration, implied leverage, and correlation to underlying markets. This chapter describes the analytical tools that provide the basis for such control. Understanding and applying these tools effectively in the portfolio management process may very well represent the next step in your risk management evolution.

It is important to point out that when we speak here about risk *control*, we are not in all cases implying risk *reduction*. The techniques on which I will focus are designed to allow you to modify your exposures as you see fit: increasing them, reducing them, or redistributing them, as circumstances demand. As may have already occurred to you, sound risk management often demands adjustments that either leave overall exposure levels flat or actually increase them at times. If you can master these concepts and combine them with knowledge you may already have gained as a trader, particularly as to the optimal timing for "exposure adjusting transactions," you will have gained a significant competitive advantage over many other market participants who, for the most part in my estimation, tend to be very passive agents in the risk control process.

In order to move from an enlightened understanding of the magnitude and the distribution of the risks we are taking to a program that actually allows us to modify these exposures, we must aim our statistical tool kit at a specificity level deeper than that of overall portfolios. Specifically, we must focus now on the portfolio *building blocks*: the universe of financial instruments that we trade.

The same analytics that apply to entire portfolios can be used to evaluate individual financial instruments for their applicability to a specific set of risk management objectives based on factors such as current portfolio composition and market conditions. Therefore, in the pages that follow, you will notice some repetition of concepts introduced earlier. However, the manner in which we will apply these concepts differs from their earlier treatment in subtle yet important ways; and I encourage you to take the trouble to evaluate these distinctions, as well as the associated commonalities, as carefully as possible. By performing the analysis at both levels (i.e., that of the portfolio as well as of its subcomponents), I believe you can gain perspectives that are analogous to the insights one might achieve from, say, looking at a statue up close (i.e., in three dimensions) versus looking at a photograph of one (i.e., in two dimensions). Another advantage of performing these types of analyses at the individual position level is that the practice is actually geared toward figuring out how best to adjust your risk levels once you have decided such a change makes sense. For example, while the correlation analysis covered in Chapter 3 might argue for reducing, say, long market exposure, the individual position analysis would not only help select the best securities for doing so (given the specific characteristics of your portfolio) but also could assist in setting the size and then measuring the likely impact on portfolio performance.

Because this is such an important concept, we will cover it over three chapters. In the first installment, we will apply the tools we covered in Chapter 3 (in addition to some new ones of a similar nature) to individual securities so that you can make individual transaction decisions in a way that is mindful of their associated impact on your overall risk profile. Once you have learned how to include this type of thinking into your investment decision-making process, we will have completed our description of the portions of the tool kit explicitly designed to measure exposure. This puts us in a position to introduce and incorporate mechanisms designed to determine the levels of exposure that are most appropriate for portfolio managers, specifically sizing them at levels high enough to achieve target return objectives while, at the same time, ensuring that they minimize the probability of exceeding critical, predefined thresholds of profit/loss (P/L) stop-out. It is interesting that the process of setting appropriate exposure parameters, which is the essence of Chapter 5, is one that applies many now-recognizable elements of the statistical tool kit, including volatility, Sharpe Ratio, and a number of others.

With the statistical tools firmly in place, aimed at both the overall portfolio (Chapter 3) and its various subcomponents (Chapter 4) and applied as a means of setting risk levels in a manner consistent with both objectives and constraints (Chapter 5), we will turn our attention to the critical topic of identifying and evaluating the trading tools available to actually control and adjust volatility (Chapter 6). Here, we will focus on the specific alternatives available to you should you want to either adjust your risk profile (upward or downward) or redistribute your exposures for other strategic purposes. Again, the mastery of these concepts may be all you ever need (and may perhaps be all you ever get) in terms of a risk management edge.

In the meantime, we return to a critical question: Which statistical tools are most applicable to the task of risk management at the individual position level? *Volatility* and *correlation* (both old friends by now) come to mind, as you can not only calculate them for individual securities but also, as we will demonstrate, use them as a sizing technique for individual positions. For instance, if you are holding a $50,000 position in an instrument for which the volatility is 50%, all things being equal, this is roughly equivalent to maintaining a trade of $100,000 in a security for which the volatility is 25%. In a very meaningful (though imperfect) way, these positions have similar risk characteristics; and it becomes a relatively simple mathematical exercise to view your positions not just in terms of number of shares or contracts (bad), but in terms of dollar value invested (better) or units of expected volatility (better still). As we will discuss later in the book, the primary sets of circumstances under which these relationships break down are those involving large position sizes, where transaction costs begin to increase due to liquidity concerns. These concerns certainly arise with greater frequency in large institutional portfolios but should not deter anyone from understanding the volatility-adjusted exposures tied to the individual positions in their accounts.

You can generate similar incremental benefits by introducing the concept of *correlation* into the mix, which will give you some insight as to how much diversification positions on the same side of the market are generating for your portfolio and how much direct exposure offset you are achieving with positions on opposite sides of the market. With volatility and correlation firmly established as measures of individual position exposure, it is also useful to measure the interplay between the two—a concept captured perhaps most rigorously through Value at Risk (VaR) methodologies, developed by the money management industry over the past couple of decades to add precision to their own risk-estimation efforts. In this chapter, we will cover not only the benefits of VaR, but also its limitations—the latter of which, in part, has caused the money management industry to augment these methodologies with more-targeted tools, mostly captured under the heading of *scenario analysis*.

For those wishing to delve still deeper into these methodologies, there is an entire field of market evaluation, referred to commonly (if somewhat cryptically) as *technical analysis*, which is devoted to the science of studying the ramp-up/drawdown characteristics of individual securities over time.

Following is a brief description of the potential application of statistical tools in the measurement of the risk characteristics of individual market positions.

HISTORICAL VOLATILITY

I hope you have been practicing your σs because you're going to need them again here as we reintroduce the concept of standard deviation, this time as it applies to individual securities. These statistics are widely available for virtually every security on systems such as Bloomberg and Reuters (in fact, unless you are an expert in the securities in question, it might be a good rule of thumb to avoid trading any market where the historical daily price change time series is not readily available). You can also calculate these volatilities on your own by simple entering the daily pricing history for the instrument in question, computing a daily price change, and performing a standard deviation calculation using a program such as Microsoft Excel. If you choose the manual method, remember to annualize this statistic, typically by multiplying the daily figure by the square root of the number of trading days (250 or so) in a year.

In my view, you're best off expressing this statistic in percentage terms so as to render it fully comparable to statistics for other securities. For example, if you simply calculate the standard deviation from the price itself, the underlying unit of account will be share price points. You may find that you have calculated an annualized standard deviation for a given security of, say, 10 points. However, this figure has significantly different implications for a security that is trading at 20 than for one whose price is 100. By using percentage terms, we would find a 50% volatility for the first case and a 10% volatility for the second and should by now understand that the former security is probably dramatically more risky than the latter. In order to calculate volatility in percentage terms, simply express the price change in percentages by dividing this figure by the current price level. For example, a daily price change from 50.0 to 49.0 can be viewed as a change of either 1.0 points or 2.0%. Then, perform the standard deviation calculation on the percentage series.

Once you have calculated the percentage-based volatility for a given security, you can convert this to dollars of risk by multiplying the percentage term by the dollar size of your investment. The effect of this process is to express risk in volatility-adjusted terms. The good news here is that this concept lends itself entirely to comparison across securities. Thus, one can think of a $50,000 trade in a security with a 10% volatility as having roughly the same risk characteristics as a $25,000 investment in a 20% volatility security.

Because different financial instruments may have vastly divergent volatility characteristics, the implications of this concept on portfolio risk management are hard to overestimate. Indeed, it is hardly a stretch to say that they provide the backdrop for the development of risk management theory and practice in the institutional segment of the market (where it all began). Indeed, it was the realization that one could not measure risk without taking into account the single-variable and multivariate volatility characteristics of a securities portfolios that led to the development of the VaR models that drive much of the risk management focus of the professional trading universe and that we will discuss shortly.

In the meantime, however, you can apply the concept in a much more simplistic form by sizing your individual transactions in terms of the associated volatility you are willing to accept for each trade. For example, you may wish to establish as a guideline that no individual transaction should have an annualized volatility associated with it of more than, say, $1,000. Using this simple formula, you would know how much you would be willing to spend on a security that had a 10% annual volatility ($10,000), 25% volatility ($4,000), or even 100% volatility ($1,000) by simply carrying forward with the algebra. If you have a shorter-term trading orientation, you may wish to express volatility in terms of one-day standard deviation—a feat that you can accomplish by dividing the annualized volatility statistic by the square root of the number of observations in a year. Specifically, if we assume 250 trading days in a year, the factor, which converts daily statistics into annual ones, is the square root of 250, or 15.81.

As a final point regarding historical volatility, it is important to note that the results you get will vary with the length of the data set you use. To elaborate, it is entirely possible to calculate an annualized or daily standard deviation of returns for a given security, using, say, 20, 50, 100, 1,000, or indeed any number of daily points of observation (due to issues of statistical significance, I do not recommend calculating a standard deviation statistic for any data set containing fewer than 20 independent observations). However, the results you get for each individual series are likely to differ materially. While this reality introduces an additional layer of complexity to your analytical efforts, it also offers an opportunity to better understand your exposures. For example, if the standard deviation statistic for a security calculated over the past 20 days is significantly higher than the associated 250-day (i.e., one-year) figure, it indicates a condition of accelerating volatility in this financial instrument, which should be investigated further. In these cases, it bears asking why volatility has picked up and whether this condition is likely to persist indefinitely. For example, if the volatility spike can be traced to increased price action leading up to a scheduled event, such as an earnings announcement, one might choose to view the added exposure as a temporary phenomenon. Conversely, if the security in question is more volatile over the past month or so because of some more embedded change, such as deregulation, then perhaps it makes sense to err on the side of caution and use the higher number to calibrate your exposure on individual transactions. In any event, it should come as no surprise that I think that you should look at volatility across different time increments, at minimum focusing on the 20-day (one-month), 60-day (one-quarter), and 250-day (one-year) series as a means of obtaining a multidimensional view of the security's price dynamics.

OPTIONS IMPLIED VOLATILITY

The critical drawback of using historical data to measure the volatility of a given security is that history is not always the best predictor of future pricing behavior. For example, a security with relatively benign historical volatility characteristics may become extremely active in advance of a product launch; and, all other things being equal, there would be nothing in the historical time series data, per se, to anticipate and account for this. Thus, while the historical time series volatility analysis has been a mainstay of our statistical tool kit, we must now recognize that its ability to model future pricing dispersion is only as effective as past volatility patterns are in predicting associated dynamics in the future. However, there are relatively simple methodologies available to overcome these limitations that offer insights into future volatility patterns that transcend what can be inferred directly by historical volatility analysis.

One such methodology derives from the concept of *implied volatility* embedded in the price of every option. Implied volatility is a measure of the amount of price dispersion expected in a given security on a prospective basis that is implied in the price of a given option. If you are already familiar with the rudiments of options pricing theory, you will understand this concept; if not, it merits a quick review of its components and associated applications.

An option is typically defined in terms of its underlying instrument, strike price, expiration date, and buy/sell orientation (i.e., call options are those with a buy orientation; put options bestow selling prerogatives on their holders). These are the instrument's *static parameters;* and once they are established, its value is driven by two dynamic factors: (1) the price of the underlying instrument and (2) the expected volatility of this instrument. Strictly speaking, there is a third dynamic factor that impacts options pricing: the *applicable interest rate,* which establishes the opportunity cost of holding the amount of your premium in option value, as opposed to investing it in interest-bearing instruments. However, unless the option in question is (1) deep-in-the-money, (2) has a long time to go before expiration, or (3) some combination of the two, interest rate will not be a driving force in valuation; and we can ignore it for the purposes of this discussion.

To illustrate the interaction between underlying price and volatility in options pricing, consider the following extreme case: No rational economic entity would purchase a call option at a strike above the current underlying price, or a put option below this price, if the price for the underlying instrument was fixed and, thus, the expected volatility in the instrument was zero. This is true, of course, because it implies a 0% chance of the option finishing with some value at the time of expiration. Conversely, options for a security with an infinite volatility over a given period would theoretically be worth an infinite amount, as there is a theoretical opportunity to liquidate them at infinite intrinsic value.

The implied volatility pricing for all options with economic meaning resides somewhere in between these extremes, and it is not an exaggeration to say that a preferred method of expressing the price of an option—particularly for sophisticated users of options products—is in terms of its volatility. Options traders will often speak in terms of purchasing/selling this or that option at, say, 10%, meaning that this is the implied volatility at which they were able to execute an options transaction. To elaborate further on the associated pricing implications, the execution of an options trade at a 10% volatility implies that the parties in question expect the underlying security to exhibit an annualized standard deviation of 10% over the life of the option.

How does all of this pertain to the applicability of options implied volatility to our efforts to estimate portfolio risk? As it turns out, because implied volatility is quoted in the exact manner that historical volatility is expressed (i.e., in annualized terms), for the purposes of estimating price dispersion, the terms can be used interchangeably. In fact, implied volatility can be viewed very explicitly as the options market's attempt to predict what historical volatility will be in the future. We can therefore substitute options volatilities for historicals in order to size our associated exposure. *Perhaps surprisingly, we can do so without ever trading a single option.* For example, just as is the case with historical volatility, if we take a $50,000 bet in a given security with a 10% implied volatility, we would expect the position in question to fluctuate at an annualized, one-standard-deviation rate of $5,000. Again, we don't have to trade options to arrive at this estimate but can simply derive data from the options markets and apply it against our position in cash securities.

Options implied volatility thus has the advantage over historical volatility of encompassing not only historical time series information but also "qualitative" data and prospective economic inputs into its estimates of price dispersion. The measure gains further credibility through the fact that options traders are actually risking financial capital on the basis of implied volatility valuations. Take my word for it—this type of reality dose does wonders for the accuracy of financial models. From these perspectives, implied volatility arguably is the superior measure. However, like everything else in our statistical tool kit, it has shortcomings. First, because the implied volatility statistic is derived entirely from the manner in which options are priced, it is subject to the same idiosyncrasies that characterize the options markets themselves. Particularly during volatile intervals and periods of diminished liquidity, options pricing may deviate from what would be expected from the core economic characteristics of the security in question. Moreover, because volatility can be viewed as one form of expression of an options price, these anomalies will have a direct impact on the accuracy of the statistic.

For example, during periods of extreme market duress, prices and volatilities for all types of options are often bid up to levels beyond what would be justified by the underlying economic data; and the use of implied volatility as an exposure input might lead to inaccuracies in these instances. In addition, there is a well-known concept within the universe of option trading, referred to as the *volatility skew*, or *smile*, that describes the tendency for out-of-the-money options to trade at higher implied volatilities than those that are at, near, or in the money. It is therefore necessary to understand the relationship between the strike price and the underlying market price (i.e., the "moneyness") for the option on whose implied volatility you are relying. As a practical matter, I recommend the volatility for the at-the-money strike as the best approximation of future price dispersion, as this is the part of the options market that is least impacted by market inefficiencies.

Second, options pricing is also significantly impacted by the widely ranging liquidity characteristics of the market, and this too can interfere with the applicability of implieds as an indicator of exposure for underlying instruments. The "liquidity factor" is particularly acute either for small transaction sizes, which do not generate enough competitive bidding among market makers to fully reflect current market conditions, or for very large orders, where the current volume cannot efficiently accommodate the transaction size. In these cases, options pricing patterns can diverge materially from those that would prevail under ideal liquidity conditions (i.e., those resulting from transaction sizes large enough to capture the attention of the market, while small enough to operate within its liquidity constraints). Wherever and whenever this occurs, it will lead to implied volatility outcomes that differ, to varying degrees, from what can be best described as the rational equilibrium. In addition, options for the same underlier may have different volatility magnitudes for different expiration dates, particularly if, for instance, one option expires before a key information event (e.g., corporate earnings), and the other expires after this occasion.

For these reasons, while implied volatility offers a unique and critical insight into the likely price dispersion characteristics of a given financial instrument, it must be viewed, as with other elements of our tool kit, with a critical eye and a healthy degree of skepticism (which, like Chastity, to paraphrase that righteous man of letters George Santayana, should not be relinquished too readily). I believe that it makes sense to utilize both the implied volatility statistic and historical volatility figures, with both statistics calculated over multiple time spans. Line these up side by side, and examine the extent to which they deviate from one another. See if you can theorize why one figure might be significantly higher than the others. Is there pending news (which might push the implieds to levels well above the associated historicals)? Or are we in a period of anticipated calm after a particularly volatile interval (which might have precisely the opposite effect)? Once you have determined what is driving the disparity across volatility estimates, you can use these inputs to compliment one another in your evaluation of position exposures (they may also help you sharpen any hypothesis you may be forming about what's happening in the markets).

One final note: You can find extensive implied volatility data sets through news services such as Reuters and Bloomberg or in periodicals such as *Barron's*. You can also calculate them (if you have the option's price and static characteristics) either with simple options pricing packages available on the Internet or with financial calculators with basic levels of options functionality.

CORRELATION

Once again extrapolating from our P/L analysis tool kit, the concept of correlation can be applied to individual positions as easily as it can to entire portfolios. For example, every equity security has a beta statistic, which is the functional equivalent of a correlation coefficient between the instrument and its associated benchmark index. In addition, you can always calculate the correlations between any two instruments (whether they are equity securities or not) in your portfolio using spreadsheet tools such as Excel.

By being constantly mindful of the correlations across the individual positions in your account, you stand to learn a great deal about the diversification characteristics of your portfolio. You can determine whether, for example, long/short combinations are providing the appropriate exposure offsets. For positions on the same side of the market, correlation analysis will help you identify whether the positions are redundant or offer true diversification. Beyond this, if you are able to capture this data not only for positions that you may be holding at any given time but also for the other instruments you are evaluating and may hold at some future time in the investment cycle, you will place yourself in a better position to select the most appropriate securities to add to your portfolio in order to achieve whatever modification to your overall risk profile you desire.

For example, if you are holding a given stock position that you want to retain but feel it is vulnerable to a decline in the overall market, rather than sell it outright, you might choose to sell short a security that has a high correlation to the one you are holding, thus reducing your exposure while retaining your core position. The same general effect can also be achieved by purchasing a security that has a low or even a negative correlation to the stock whose risk you are trying to hedge. This isn't likely to be a revelation to you if you already engage in this type of activity routinely. I simply add that the use of sound correlation data in the management of these activities can only add to the efficiency of the process.

As with everything else, correlation data is time specific; and in calculating this statistic across different time spans, you are likely to achieve different results. Moreover, historical correlation data only describes past pricing patterns, which cannot necessarily be extrapolated forward with full confidence. Indeed, particularly in times of market stress, historical correlation data is likely to be of minimal use, as markets have a tendency to move in lockstep with one another under these circumstances (i.e., correlations converge to $\pm 100\%$). As is the case elsewhere, this limitation contains a hidden opportunity: I believe it is useful to compare correlations between securities across different time spans so as to gain a better understanding of interactive pricing dynamics across the fullest range of available market conditions.

VALUE AT RISK (VaR)

Through the efforts of modern-day financial engineers, a new paradigm has emerged: It is now possible, nay, even fashionable, to combine the concepts of volatility and correlation into a single, portfolio-based exposure estimate. This work, most of which has been conducted over the past 15 or so years, is most broadly synthesized under the heading of Value at Risk, which is now thought of as the standard methodology for risk management in the financial services industry. The underlying objective is to aggregate all risks in a given portfolio in such a way as to produce a volatility statistic at the portfolio level boiled down to a single number that will characterize overall portfolio exposure. This number is intended to predict P/L volatility, such that it identifies the size of P/L swings that are tied back to a specified confidence interval. For example, if the confidence interval used in the VaR calculation is 95% (as is often the case), then the risk number produced is designed to identify the P/L threshold such that a portfolio experienced a fluctuation in excess of this only about 5% of the time, or once in 20 days. Similarly, if the confidence interval is set at the 99% level, it implies that the portfolio in question should only experience a P/L observation in excess of this figure approximately once in every 100 days.

While VaR has inspired some well-deserved cynicism over the years, it's hard to argue against its conceptual merits. Think of it as a form of alchemy that transforms portfolios with multifaceted exposure elements into a single exposure-bearing unit. If you have little faith in the existence of alchemists (and let's face it, who doesn't these days?), it may be useful to think of your portfolio as being the equivalent of one giant security, the General Electric Corporation (GE), for example. Like your portfolio, GE has multiple business lines across virtually every important market sector, each of which must deal with unique and diverse risks on a daily basis. But also like your portfolio, there's not necessarily a great deal that ties these businesses together. While I'm sure that all of the unit managers enjoy the periodic schmooze fests up at the corporate headquarters in Stamford, Connecticut, it's hard to see, other than common ownership, what bonds exist among say, the presidents of the medical devices unit, the aircraft engine division, and the National Broadcasting Company.

Ah, but they do have that common ownership thing working, and those owners have the additional advantage of being able to own these businesses through the simplicity of a single security with a single price. And though it may not have occurred to you, dear reader, consider this: What is your investment account if not a mini-me version of a GE–type structure? Look at your next monthly statement and take pride in the diverse businesses you own: the world's leading software manufacturer here, an entertainment conglomerate built around an anthropomorphic rodent there, perhaps a virtual bookstore (and who among us hasn't hunkered to own one of those?), or an Internet search engine—maybe you even own GE stock itself. Why, you're a veritable Jack Welch! And why not have what he has (no, not the company-subsidized Manhattan duplex or the steamy romance with a former *Harvard Business Review* editor, but something even better): an ability to aggregate exposures into a single volatility unit that can be tracked holistically with an eye toward making appropriate adjustments. This is what we risk managers had in mind when we created VaR for you all those years ago.

Much has been written and said about VaR over the years, and I will resist the temptation to attempt to add significantly to this august body of erudition. However, as I think that VaR is a useful and effective portfolio diagnostic (and because most professional traders are likely to be governed by some sort of VaR calculation), it is important to have a general idea of the basic purpose and underlying justification of the approach, as well as some knowledge as to how the statistic is calculated.

Justification for VaR Calculations

The purpose of VaR is to provide an estimate of future P/L volatility, which, as I have argued earlier, is the essence of financial risk. Therefore, while the statistical tool kit described in the preceding chapter offers means of *evaluating* financial risk (i.e., after the fact), VaR methodologies are designed to *predict* this exposure. The evolution of VaR, which took place contemporaneously across the most sophisticated segments of the financial markets over the past couple of decades, can be traced to the desire of the financial community to improve risk control through the use of limits (for direct market exposure), collateralization (for counterparty exposure), and other remedies that would either help minimize loss or at least mitigate its associated impacts.

In seeking to better apply these concepts, the providers of capital and credit recognized and presided over what I believe to be a rational evolution (yes, occasionally even these knuckleheads deserve mad props)—from methodologies that dealt with individual instruments separately to an approach that was based on the level of actual performance volatility for the overall portfolios in question. However, because performance volatility (much like performance itself) is not known until after the fact, the focus turned toward approaches that would predict this variable; and the result is the development and institutionalization of Value at Risk. Although VaR can be both mystifying and maddening to those whose actions are governed by it, the methodology represents a significant upgrade over its predecessor approaches under which actual dollars of investment were used to set trading parameters. Under this less-sophisticated approach, many limit and collateralization regimes provided counterintuitive incentives that penalized investors for certain risk-reducing trades they might make and rewarded them (often inappropriately) for the assumption of additional exposure. For example, a trader whose activities were governed by the amount of dollars deployed in the market might actually be charged a higher amount against his or her limit or might face a higher collateral requirement for a spread position involving longs and shorts in highly correlated securities than he or she would for holding only one leg of this spread. This is in spite of the fact that overwhelming empirical evidence indicates that the full spread position will be far less risky than a directional bet of the same size. Of course, it would be a stretch to suggest that spread trading in every situation carries less exposure than outright speculation. The case of Long-Term Capital Management (LTCM) reinforces the notion that at certain levels of investment there is virtually no limit to the amount of risk inherent in a spread portfolio. The key distinctions here involve liquidity constraints and the use of leverage. Although no one would seriously argue that $1 invested in a long/short strategy involving highly correlated securities is much riskier than a $2 or even a $1 investment in either leg, spread strategies achieve the higher exposure through the use of leverage, often employing strategies whose dollar values are 50 or 100 (in the case of LTCM) times greater than the associated capital invested. Moreover, these situations are certainly exacerbated (again as occurred in the LTCM crisis) when position sizes exceed the ability of the market to provide sufficient liquidity to allow for orderly liquidation.

Indeed, despite the routine inconsistency with formulas that equate exposure to gross dollars invested, gross dollar investment collateralization/limit regimes are alive and well even in today's environment. Case in point: your securities portfolio, which allows you to purchase $2 worth of a single stock for every $1 of capital but would not allow you to hold more than $1 long versus $1 short for the same level of capital—even though the latter profile is likely, under most circumstances, to be far less risky. VaR programs (unless they're written by madmen) recognize this disparity. For reasons such as this, most everyone I have encountered whose trading activities are governed by limits will attest to the fact that a rational VaR system is far more conducive to the production of risk-adjusted return than many other methodologies available in the market.

Also, if you'll allow a moment's sympathy to us poor, beleaguered, and, yes, misunderstood risk managers, perhaps you'll not judge us too harshly for at least trying to create an effective exposure-measurement machine. I have had to deal with very complex portfolios, involving long and short positions in stocks, bonds, convertibles, options, and other types of derivatives all at the same time. In addition, these positions were typically denominated in as many as a dozen different currencies. How the heck was I supposed to make any judgment about exposure levels unless I did something to translate this rubric into (reasonably) homogeneous risk units? VaR may be silly and stupid and is certainly applied in ridiculous ways by people who have no business occupying the same galaxy as that inhabited by rational risk takers. But the only thing that I can think of that might be sillier or more stupid is to try to perform risk management on complex portfolios without something that was if not VaR then at least its functional equivalent.

Types of VaR Calculations

Over the years, three basic methodologies for calculating VaR have emerged:

1. *Variance/Covariance.* This is perhaps the most widely used VaR methodology, under which the program gathers volatility (variance) and correlation (covariance) statistics across all individual positions in the portfolio and combines them, using matrix algebra, into a single calculation of portfolio volatility.

   The basic equation under which the variance/covariance approach to VaR is derived is a calculation of the standard deviation of the portfolio under the assumption that its distribution can be described as *multivariate normal;* that is, the individual variable components (i.e., trading positions) in the portfolio will behave in such a way as to produce a normal distribution when viewed in aggregate. Under these circumstances, the portfolio's standard deviation (σ), can be calculated using the following formula:

$$\sigma = \sqrt{\sum_i \sigma_i^2 + 2 \sum_{i<j} \sum \sigma_i \sigma_j \rho_{i,j}}$$

where σ_i, σ_j = standard deviation of individual portfolio instruments
$\rho_{i,j}$ = covariance between instruments i and j

Do not be overly troubled by any failure on your part to fully comprehend the finer points of this nasty equation. For one thing, you have to be a bit skeptical about any mathematical expression that includes both capital sigma (which I have to admit is cooler when it has those little *i*'s and *j*'s underneath it, and even better if you can throw in—as often happens—a ∞ symbol on top) and small sigma. I'll make a little confession here: I've been at this risk management game for nearly two decades, and I can only recall one instance where I actually had to yank out this dubious formula to mollify some very fastidious Japanese guys. On the whole, I think you can pretty safely remove the formula from your memory bank—that is, if you'll promise me to take into consideration the following:

Using a combination of volatility and correlation statistics and (you'll have to trust me a bit here) a simple matrix-based expansion of the basic standard deviation calculation, we can derive a standard deviation estimate for complex portfolios, which should be more or less as accurate and applicable as those that we have calculated for individual securities.

Due in part to its relative simplicity, the variance/covariance approach to VaR has become the most frequently used of the VaR methodologies. It is widely available in risk management software packages and can actually be calculated, with relative ease, using spreadsheet programs—provided you have the proper volatility and correlation data. In turn, you can either obtain this data directly from a number of providers (such as RiskMetrics) or calculate it on your own, using historical pricing information for each position associated with the portfolios in question and converting these to a variance/covariance matrix. However, I must caution do-it-yourselfers away from underestimating the task of creating this matrix, the scope and complexity of which will vary exponentially with the number of individual positions in the portfolio.

For instance, a matrix for a portfolio of, say, 10 securities will contain 100 observations (10 × 10). However, if you double the number of positions in the portfolio, the matrix size increases fourfold to 400 (20 × 20). Indeed, by the time you reach 100 names, the matrix will have 10,000 individual data points; and if you ever were so ambitious as to model, say, the Standard & Poor's (S&P) 500 variance/covariance matrix, the number would rise to 250,000! For these reasons, I strongly recommend the use of external VaR programs for all but the most data-intensive traders; and if you must calculate your own VaR, you should at least purchase the variance/covariance matrix from an external data provider.

The variance/covariance approach to VaR is widely used because among VaR alternatives it offers the least calculation-intensive means of identifying a portfolio's exposure. However, for these reasons it is also the methodology that bears the greatest set of limitations.

First and foremost, it suffers from all of the potential inaccuracies associated with the key inputs to the calculation: volatility and correlation data, which may not be accurate predictors of future pricing patterns for the portfolios in question. Second, the methodology has no truly effective means for dealing with complex derivatives, such as options, which cannot be plugged neatly into a variance/covariance matrix. Indeed, most VaR programs use a simple adjustment, such as a delta-mapping for options, to convert these positions into fungible units of the underlying instrument. For example, a long call option for $1 million on stock XYZ that had a delta of .5 would receive identical treatment as a position of $500,000 in the cash market. For these reasons, the results must be interpreted with extreme caution. However, in spite of these limitations, the variance/covariance approach probably offers the best combination of simplicity and accuracy available to most investors (i.e., the benefits of its simplicity more than offset the costs associated with reduced accuracy) and is on this basis arguably the most applicable of VaR approaches.

2. *Historical Volatility.* Under the historical volatility approach, the VaR program actually recalculates a P/L for the existing portfolio, each day going back into the past in order to determine what the account would have made or lost over each day in the sequence. The program then ranks these P/L observations in ascending order and assigns the VaR number that corresponds to the loss associated with the confidence interval specified by the user. For example, if the historical VaR program you were using had the ability to look back one year, it would take your current portfolio, calculate a P/L for each day going back the full 12 months, and then rank these statistics. If you set your VaR confidence interval to be 95%, the program would then throw out the worst 5% of your losses (over a 250-day trading year, this would mean eliminating the worst 12 or 13 observations) and set your risk at the loss level corresponding to the next highest observation. The implied assumption is that you ought to be 95% sure, on a going-forward basis, that the daily losses should not exceed this figure.

Historical volatility is a significantly process-intensive VaR methodology because it requires the repricing of every single instrument over every single day covering the historical time interval selected. However, I believe that if it is possible to execute such a calculation, it may well be worth doing so, as historical volatility is generally viewed to be the most accurate of the VaR methodologies, at least for the vast majority of portfolios. A careful review of the underlying methodologies helps reinforce its basic advantages.

First, rather than relying on correlation data to impute the manner in which multiple securities will price themselves in relation to one another, historical VaR actually utilizes historical pricing to estimate the magnitude of associated exposure. This can be particularly important during times of market stress, when even static correlation patterns tend to break down. Second, unlike variance/covariance, historical VaR extends seamlessly (provided that the user meticulously incorporates the full set of inputs) to cover such derivative products as options—often with results that elegantly illustrate precisely why it is the preferred methodology among many risk managers who are in a position to choose their optimal VaR approach. Finally, historical VaR offers all sorts of opportunities for qualitative analysis against identifiable market episodes derived from real-world experience. If you see something in the results that interests you, it is very useful to look at the specific dates that generate these outcomes. This is an analytical tool that the other forms of VaR do not offer. Try to avail yourself of its benefits by evaluating both the likelihood for recurrence and perhaps even by formulating an associated contingency plan.

The binding limitations associated with historical VaR are those that pervade the entire business of statistically evaluating portfolio exposure. As we've discussed, these derive from the inability of past history to reliably predict future outcomes. In addition, as we've also covered, it is calculation intensive; and, as such, beyond the practical difficulties of executing the routine, it is probably more prone to error than other models. Individual bad data points can throw off results materially even when every other element of the calculation (involving perhaps hundreds or thousands of individual steps) is entirely accurate. However, if you are in a position to overcome these problems, I highly recommend its application wherever the data and systems are in place to render it feasible.

3. *Monte Carlo Simulation.* The Monte Carlo approach to VaR is similar in methodology to that of Monte Carlo pricing in the world of options trading. Under this method, the program regenerates large numbers of random, feasible price-change outcomes for individual securities (based on user-specified ranges of scenarios) and ranks them statistically according to their probability. It then assigns the VaR number tied to the "probability outcome" that corresponds to the selected confidence interval. For example, a Monte Carlo VaR program designed to capture risk at the 95th percentile confidence interval might reprice entire portfolios up to several million times in order to identify the full range of potential P/L outcomes and then set the VaR number such that 95% of the observations were below the figure and the remaining 5% were above it.

The advantage of Monte Carlo simulation is that by rigorously extrapolating market history across a huge number of results, it is possible to obtain a better picture of the full, prospective price distribution for the portfolio in question and thus have more information as to the probabilities associated with a wide range of outcomes. Moreover, Monte Carlo can be a useful methodology for portfolios bearing a high degree of optionality because it allows for the evaluation of virtually unlimited combinations of underlying prices and volatilities that combine to determine the value of the options in a given portfolio, including those associated with acute market conditions that can generate dramatic portfolio swings. However, for most simple portfolios, Monte Carlo simulation probably represents a bit of overkill, with any incremental accuracy to be gained in the process offset by the level of complexity and calculation intensity needed to execute the methodology.

It is worth noting that for all but the most complex of portfolios with extremely nuanced pricing characteristics, VaR results should be pretty consistent across the three approaches just defined. I think it's more important to use your time incorporating VaR than squandering resources selecting which method to use. Pick one that makes sense to you, given your portfolio characteristics and resource constraints, and incorporate it into your decision making. The rest, as they say, is irrelevant.

Testing VaR Accuracy

VaR models, as we will discuss shortly, vary in terms of their actual mathematical construction; but they are all designed, as we've covered, to predict performance volatility associated with a specified confidence interval. Specifically, all models will yield results that have a probabilistic component, *each producing a number that serves as a threshold that the portfolio volatility should violate with a specified level of probability.* As such, the accuracy of the model can be back-tested by checking how many P/L observations actually exceed the VaR figure over a given period of time and then tying the resulting percentage back to the confidence interval. If the two figures are consistent, the model can be said to be in good order; if not, then the model's assumptions and inputs must be examined in order to determine the source of the inconsistency (more about this later). This type of backtest is one of the simplest mathematical exercises we will cover in this book, and I urge you to periodically check to see if your actual P/L volatility is consistent with the model and parameters you are using. Some purists will argue that comparing actual portfolio volatility to VaR results is not an effective backtest because while the VaR calculation is based on the current portfolio as measured against historical price action, the test measures the accuracy of this calculation against *future* price fluctuation.

However, I would ignore this distinction for the simple reason that if your actual P/L volatility differs substantially from the results implied in the VaR calculation, it is failing to tell you anything—irrespective of the fact that it may be faithfully adhering to its core assumption base.

Setting VaR Parameters

At this very moment, you may be asking yourself which confidence interval is most appropriate for your VaR analysis. The bad news is there's no easy answer; the good news is that as long as you're consistent in its application, you pretty much can't go wrong.

First of all, if you use the variance/covariance approach to VaR, it doesn't matter what confidence interval you use because the numbers will simply increase linearly, according to the scale-up factors set forth in Table 4.1, which I have resurrected Lazarus-like, for the purposes of this discussion, from Chapter 3. Thus, under the variance/covariance approach, a 95th percentile confidence interval will equate, forever and anon, to 1.960 times a 1.000σ projection; a 99th percentile confidence interval to a 2.576σ; and so on.

Matters get a bit more interesting under both historical VaR and Monte Carlo simulation, both of which contemplate universes—remote though they may be—where portfolio returns distribute in ways other than normally. For example, historical volatility analysis will capture the fact that equity market distributions tend to have fatter tails than other financial assets; and if you are using historical volatility, you may find that the 99th percentile observation is of a significantly greater magnitude than 2.576σ. By the same token, the more complex your portfolio is (e.g., the higher the incidence of options and other derivatives), the greater is

TABLE 4.1	Percentage of Returns Associated with Standard Deviation Intervals
Percentage of Normal Curve Area	**Mean ± Number of Standard Deviations**
50.0%	$.674\sigma$
68.3	1.000
90.0	1.645
95.0	1.960
95.4	2.000
98.0	2.326
99.0	2.576
99.7	3.000

the likelihood that extreme observations will quantify themselves at surprising multiples of σ.

It is therefore a valuable rule of thumb that the more mathematically complicated the portfolio and the better the VaR measurement tools, the more useful it will be to apply higher confidence intervals. However, because most portfolios are simple and because most VaR systems lack the sophistication to identify the nuanced exposures at the tails of a distribution, there is generally only marginal benefit to be gained by using these more conservative estimates. As for me, I prefer measuring volatility in terms of a single standard deviation because it allows for the most direct comparison to the volatility of individual financial instruments and because, as we will see in the next several chapters, it can be used, through a modification of the Sharpe Ratio, as a means of sizing investment levels and volatilities to specific, risk-adjusted return targets.

Setting of VaR confidence intervals becomes most relevant when the VaR estimates are used as something other than a general indication of exposure levels. The most prominent example of this is the use of VaR as a benchmark against which limits or credit lines are set, as happens with perhaps most professional traders operating in the setting of large and small financial institutions. Typically, these institutions will impose restrictions on traders based on what they view to be acceptable levels of exposure as estimated by their in-house VaR programs.

When a capital provider sets trading/risk limits on the basis of a VaR analysis, the specific VaR methodology used in conjunction with the calculation looms much larger in importance. In my experience, fortunate indeed is the market investment professional whose VaR limits exist in harmony with her most rational view of the exposures she encounters in the marketplace. Unfortunately, everyone else will have to improvise, compounding the already considerable difficulties of maximizing profits by being forced to rationalize limits with an unclouded view of the true exposures in the portfolio. The only way I have found to accomplish these conflicting objectives consistently (as I will touch on shortly) is to reduce your risk taking to levels that fit comfortably within both the risk systems imposed on you and the amount of "true" exposure you are willing to accept in the markets. This will probably cost you money, as it will impede you from the assumption of maximum exposure profiles—particularly at high-conviction points when you feel that the exposures are justified.

STARLESS AND BIBLE BLACK

I want you to consider, for a moment, the hypothetical example of a bank—a large international bank—with big, far-flung trading operations and (of course) an unshakeable commitment to risk management. How committed was this bank to risk management? Very committed to risk management. It said so right in the brochure.

The risk departments of this bank, for obvious reasons, were sequestered in the deepest recesses of the organization's glittering corporate headquarters, located in the center of the financial district of a major Western city. It is in these highfalutin' environs that the keepers of the sacred risk management flame set about the task of creating their masterwork—the infamous *Black Box* (*Boitte Noire*). This goes to show that, among other things, black boxes, Rube Walker machines, and other dubious risk management devices exist on both sides of the Atlantic Ocean. Perhaps it was the thinness of the air on the upper floors; perhaps it was a desire to outshine their inferiors at competing organizations. But one way or another, they decided that any prudent risk management system must take into account not some of the risk but, gosh almighty, "all the risk there ever was."

On the wings of this lark, they flew right past the one, two, and three standard deviation thresholds, beyond the 95th, 99th, and even 99.99th percentile confidence intervals, all the way to the honest-to-goodness-no-turning-back 100th percentile observation. Off some glib tongue came the suggestion to use the 200th percentile; but another in the room had enough presence of mind to point out the oxymoronic nature of the concept, rendering at least one faction crimson with anger and embarrassment. In a face-saving gesture, rather than looking back at the worst outcome over, say, the past year, they took the (extraordinarily patriotic, in my view) step of going back to the very largest price change that had taken place in each market over the past decade. So enthusiastically was this proposal received that a particularly ambitious fellow in the group suggested that even 10 years was not a sufficient interval of analysis and that the only truly inspired answer lay in comparing today's positions to the worst price movements over the century just prior to the 21st ("Schizoid, man!!!" said the one trader present; but no one knew what he was talking about). I'm quite sure this suggestion would have carried the day had not one of the dour realists in the crowd pointed out the difficulties of obtaining 100 years of daily data for markets that in many cases hadn't existed even a generation earlier.

So they went forward with the 10-year plan. This meant that every position in equity markets had risk measured as though it lost as much as it might have on October 19, 1987; every interest rate position was mapped against the funding crisis in France in early 1994; and so on. Everyone congratulated everyone else on having created the most thorough risk system on the planet. And, in a spirit of true generosity (spurred in part by a threat of a mass walkout from traders on the desk), knowing that the Black Box was throwing off risk estimates that were five times as high as was the case for VaR programs operating with a 95th confidence interval parameter, the powers that be promptly quintupled everyone's risk limit.

The net result was a system where the risk estimates and associated limits were five times higher than those inherent in the previous structure. The bank was happy because it had demonstrated to *tout le monde* its single-minded commitment to prudent risk management. Traders were happy because for every dollar of risk they could take under the previous regime, they were now permitted to take *five* dollars. If some suspected that they had done nothing but effect some "limit inflation"—increasing both sides of the limit equation by equal amounts and leaving portfolio managers in exactly the same spot at which they had started—they did so quietly. The Crimson Kings of Risk Control had their Black Box, and it was their Epitaph.

Then, one day in the fall of 1997, something very interesting happened. On October 20, the 1987 crash data point (being exactly 10 years and 1 day old) rolled right out of the equity data series. The 10-year, worst-case loss in equity markets was reduced by more than 60 percent, in the process more than doubling the risk capacity for the bank's equity traders. Celebrations took various forms, including a couple of industrious fellows who decided to double down on stocks they were holding. Exactly one week later, October 27, 1997, the Dow experienced a drop even steeper than the one that had occurred 10 years (and 1 week) earlier. Those guys weren't seen much around the bank after that episode, but no one noticed. Meanwhile, the Black Box remains.

Use of VaR Calculation in Portfolio Management

Most professionals who trade the capital of financial institutions will be subject to some sort of VaR regime for the setting of their limits. However, even those who trade for themselves are subject to VaR governance, often in hidden ways. For example, futures and options exchanges use a modified version of VaR to calculate margin requirements for their products and insist that the brokerage firms that clear their contracts do the same. Therefore, unless you are doing nothing but trading equity securities for your own account, you are likely to be subject to some sort of VaR calculation on at least a subset of your portfolio.

However, whether you find your portfolio subject to an externally imposed VaR calculation, I submit that there is significant benefit to executing and analyzing a VaR methodology for your trading because it offers the best means of isolating the exposure characteristics of your combined position profile at any given time. In addition, VaR serves as one of the best indicators of actual level of *market participation* available to the typical investor—a subtle point, but one that bears pausing over in order to ensure a full understanding. Consider two portfolios that each have $1,000,000 invested in the markets. One portfolio is full of high-flying stocks; the other has boring dividend-paying assets. Although the same dollars are committed to the market from each portfolio, I would argue that the high-flying portfolio is *more fully invested* and has a higher degree of *market participation*, largely due to the fact that it will experience more acute financial impacts to any level of price action in the markets than will the dividend portfolio. VaR has no purpose other than to measure these concepts, and I particularly endorse your taking the steps necessary to understand the time series dynamics of the VaR calculation, starting with a routine periodic measurement of its predictive accuracy (i.e., the back-test). Study its ability to adhere to the confidence interval assumptions you have specified (as described in the previous *Testing VaR Accuracy* section).

Once you have achieved a sufficient level of accuracy in this regard, you can then use the VaR statistic as yet another means of ensuring the efficient use of your capital. If your VaR numbers are increasing, it means that your exposure is on the rise; and (rationally speaking) this should only take place when (1) there is sufficient risk capital available to increase the bet and (2) profit opportunities are rising in a manner that justifies the increased exposure. For this reason your VaR should be positively correlated to your overall performance. If it isn't, it may be due to a failure on your part to manage your risk capital efficiently and to identify your best opportunities on a "look-ahead" basis.

Wherever and whenever it is feasible to do so, I also recommend that you review the "intermediate" calculations associated with your VaR program in order to identify the elements of your portfolio that are contributing most strongly to your overall exposure. This can be done in most programs by comparing the risks projected for a single position across all names held in your portfolio. As is the case across time, the greatest contributors to your overall exposure should be those that are tied to your best opportunities, and these ideas should generate your greatest profits over the longer haul.

If there is significant mismatch between the positions that are producing your greatest overall exposure according to the VaR calculation and those that are most directly responsible for your P/L, take it as an indication that you could be managing your overall position more effectively and that greater profitability can be achieved by reallocating your risk capital in such a way that the lion's share of your revenue derives from the trades for which you feel the highest level of conviction.

Once your VaR program is up, running, and in stable production, think of it as a barometer of your risk. Set ranges of acceptable VaR outcomes and stick to them. Make sure that when you do find yourself operating in the upper portions of the range, you have done so because you believe that such additional risk assumption is justified by the quality of associated market opportunities and does not derive from "investment creep," boredom, or any of the other factors that can cause investors to initiate and maintain positions in their portfolios for reasons that even they cannot explain.

To summarize, VaR, with all its limitations and prone though it is to cartoonish overemphasis, gets a bad rap. For one thing, when portfolios are truly complex—in particular involving multiple-asset and -instrument classes, such as stocks, bonds, and options—it's difficult to contemplate a method for aggregating exposures that doesn't operate under the basic VaR framework. The same can be said, to a lesser but still considerable extent, for portfolios with long/short orientations or even for one-sided, single-instrument-class portfolios that make an effort at diversification. In each case, a well-framed VaR calculation ought to be a valuable tool for the sizing of exposures at both the individual and the portfolio levels. I can't think of a single situation (polytechnicians included) where a trading operation isn't better off with some sort of VaR–based model than without one. As a risk manager, I shudder at the thought of operating without VaR, or at least something that closely resembles it. And in the more complex environments I've had to manage, proceeding without a risk aggregation tool such as VaR would be laughable. As an investor, if you take the trouble to understand the strengths and weaknesses of the VaR model that applies to your account, the methodology can provide all kinds of additional useful insights into both the internal and the market-related dynamics of your account.

SCENARIO ANALYSIS

I have spoken of VaR as a form of alchemy, through which those wishing to predict future P/L dispersion for portfolios with multiple and complex financial instruments seek to express that dispersion in a single numerical estimate. Hopefully, I have convinced you that imprecise though the methodology might be, there is considerable merit in the effort. In order to address the imperfections associated with the aggregation process, as well as those tied to the methodology's inability to elegantly express certain specific types of exposures, the risk-obsessed among us have created the concept of *scenario analysis.*

As implied in the name, scenario analysis is designed to measure the exposure associated with specific, user-defined contingencies in the markets that are not well captured by other methodologies. Most typically and perhaps most effectively, scenario analysis is applied to various arbitrage portfolios where the interplay between individual instruments is less easily captured by VaR's more brute force mapping of positions in an account into easy-to-comprehend risk factors.

For purposes of illustration, I offer some examples of the application of scenario analysis to three specific types of arbitrage portfolios:

1. *Relative Value Fixed Income.* This strategy, rendered somewhat infamous by the Long-Term Capital Management episode of a few years back, involves the simultaneous purchase and sale of fixed-income instruments with similar but nonidentical economic characteristics that exhibit pricing divergence, in the hopes that this divergence disappears over the life of the transaction. Often, this may feature the purchase and sale of bonds with similar credit qualities across differing maturities or of bonds with differing credit qualities across the same maturity. In the case of the former, a prudent risk manager might want to know what happens to this portfolio if interest rates continue to move in nonintuitive ways that are adverse to the portfolio, and he or she might design a set of scenarios to cover the following such contingencies:

   - Interest rates change by the same magnitude across the yield curve (called a parallel shift).
   - Rates at earlier maturities increase at a faster rate than those at further out maturities (flattening twist), or vice versa (steepening twist).
   - Rates at both ends of the yield curve remain relatively constant, while those in between these endpoints either increase or decrease.

   By using scenario analysis, one can determine the exposures associated with these types of subtle price movements with a great deal more precision than by using other methods of exposure estimation.

   In the case of relative value plays involving instruments of differing credit quality, the designers of scenario analysis routines will typically try to estimate the impact of changes in *credit spreads*, defined as the premium that lenders will demand of borrowers of lesser credit quality. Like the yield curve manipulations mentioned immediately earlier, these exercises are likely to capture risks that are assumed away by the aggregations embedded in the VaR calculation.

2. *Convertible Bond Arbitrage.* The typical configuration of a convertible bond arbitrage portfolio is one under which the portfolio contains inventories of bonds that are convertible into stock, as hedged by short positions in the cash equity securities of the same corporations. Because these bonds are typically highly correlated to their associated stocks, most VaR programs would fail to register much exposure. However, there are scenarios under which these portfolios (perhaps due to the demands of the firms that provide leverage to convertible

arbitrage portfolio managers) might suffer from the worst of all possible combinations: The bonds drop in value while the equities experience a contemporaneous rise. It behooves those who either manage or fund convertible arbitrage portfolios to have a clear understanding of the risks associated with these worst-case scenarios.

3. *Options Volatility Arbitrage.*   For those intrepid few wishing to capitalize on subtle and theoretically unsustainable discrepancies in the volatility pricing of options with the same or highly similar underliers, it is prudent to create a scenario analysis that specifically targets conditions under which these mispricings extend themselves. Due to the nonlinear and (often) leveraged nature of options portfolios, this process can often identify exposures that a VaR program or other risk-estimation methodology might otherwise miss.

It is also not unusual for risk managers with oversight responsibility of large portfolios involving multiple asset classes (e.g., global macro portfolios) to contrive scenarios under which all financial instruments either decouple from each other or begin to move in lockstep—in dramatic adverse fashion. These so-called event-risk scenarios are very prevalent in the risk modeling of large financial institutions and provide the considerable benefit of informing all involved parties (including high-level decision makers who are perhaps somewhat removed from the day-to-day portfolio management process) as to the institutions' best estimates of worst-case loss. However, as a day-to-day risk management tool, I find them to be of limited use.

The main point here regarding scenario analysis is that particularly for certain complex portfolio types, it will often behoove the portfolio manager to move beyond widely used instruments of portfolio risk estimation into something much more targeted to their specific exposures. If this applies to you, you probably already know it and are aware that you are probably the best engineer of the appropriate scenario analysis. However, if your portfolio involves nothing more than directional speculations in specific markets, scenario analysis is probably overkill.

TECHNICAL ANALYSIS

Most traders are familiar with the time series evaluation of the historical pricing patterns of individual financial instruments, commonly referred to as *technical analysis.* Over the past few decades, an entire science of technical analysis has emerged that involves myriad methodologies that are mind-boggling in their number, range, scope, and complexity. It is not my intention here to delve too deeply into these mysteries (we've enough ground to cover as it is); however, I do believe that the rudiments of technical analysis can be effectively applied as a risk management tool.

Specifically, it is important to remain mindful of the "technical" characteristics of the financial instruments you are trading. This is true both prospectively for positions you are adding and in terms of the management of the positions you are maintaining on your sheets at any given time. In order to accomplish this in even a basic way, it is necessary to introduce the concepts of *support* and *resistance*. You probably deal with these concepts every minute of every day, and I don't mean to insult your intelligence by providing basic definitions. However, on the odd chance that you are either unacquainted with or confused by them, the following general descriptions may be of use:

- *Support Level.* The price for a given security that represents a repeated lower bound of a trading range. Financial instruments that do violate support levels are often considered to have more risk for downside price movement, as the violation indicates that the market may have revised downward its perception about the core valuation level that exists.
- *Resistance Level.* The price for a given security that represents the upper bound of a trading range. Financial instruments that violate resistance levels are often considered to have more opportunity for upside price movement, as the move above resistance may suggest that the market may have revised upward its perception as to the maximum level of valuation that exists.

There are a number of methodologies for determining the support and the resistance levels for the securities you are trading, many of which involve the use of moving averages and other simple statistical techniques. In addition, a careful review of time series charts will provide you with a general idea as to where the support and resistance levels are for the securities you are trading. Once you have estimated these pricing points, they represent ideal levels of review for position initiation/liquidation.

For example, many traders use the violation of support/resistance thresholds as the catalyst for either position initiation or liquidation. However, even if you choose not to adopt this approach, it is still important to be mindful of these technical thresholds because there is a heightened probability that once violated, the associated position is likely to experience an increase in its volatility. Also note that this volatility can go in either direction. Technicians make a living by buying financial instruments that have penetrated resistance and selling them when they break through support. Oftentimes they are right, but they are also often wrong. The main point is that once these levels, which represent perceived equilibrium of supply and demand for economic assets, are well known by markets and once they are breached, it is typically an indication of heightened differences of opinion as to the proper valuation. In my experience, these events are often signals that new intervals of volatility are indeed on the horizon.

If you wish to probe deeper into the concept of technical analysis, you will find a limitless array of tools at your disposal. For example, technical models that possess a higher level of sophistication than simple, support/resistance algorithms often feature in-depth analysis of the relationship between volume and pricing, taking such forms as momentum analysis and relative strength indicators. Again, in each instance, there are associated risk management implications that can be harnessed in a constructive manner. However, I caution you against overdoing it in this regard; it is easy to fall into deep analytical traps using technical analysis that are not at all guaranteed to enhance your portfolio management skills on any level. My best advice is to start slowly, understanding the areas of historical price stability for the securities you are trading, and to have some sort of game plan when pricing patterns violate these equilibrium levels.

Measures of volatility, correlation, VaR, technical analysis, and scenario analysis can all be useful in helping you determine and manage the specific levels of exposure in your account. Each can be distilled into intuitive, mathematically uncomplicated, quantitative descriptions of either portfolio risk characteristics or exposures in individual positions that an investor might hold. In my experience the use of these techniques has both direct and indirect benefits, with the latter taking the form of unearthing a deep well of potential knowledge about the markets in which investors operate that can be mined in a multitude of beneficial ways, some of which we will discuss in subsequent chapters.

CHAPTER 5

Setting Appropriate Exposure Levels (Rule 1)

Happy, who is happy?
Was there not a serpent in Paradise itself?
And if Eve had been perfectly happy beforehand,
would she have listened to him?

—William Makepeace Thackeray
The Virginians

At this point, it can be hoped that you have established your methodology for quantifying your portfolio exposure in terms of both its historical characteristics and its future consequences. Empowered with these tools, a couple of critical questions regarding portfolio management should come to mind.

1. How can I establish appropriate exposure ranges for my trading such that my risk is neither excessive nor too low to attain my objectives?
2. What should I do to adjust my risk profile if I feel it is either too high or too low?

In this chapter, we will focus on the first of these questions, while leaving the second question to be the central issue attacked in Chapter 6. Although there are certainly limitations as to how much control you can directly exert over your profit/loss (P/L) volatility, the methodologies that I describe are designed to increase such control considerably and in the process to place you in the best possible position to achieve your performance objectives while minimizing the damage if events play out that you did not anticipate.

DETERMINING THE APPROPRIATE RANGES OF EXPOSURE

Read this next statement very carefully, kids, because it's important: *It is up to the capital provider to determine the appropriate risk ranges for the trading portfolios that it is funding.* This means that if you are trading with anything but your own proprietary capital, the risk management call will ultimately belong to someone else. However, this does not imply that the exercise of determining appropriate exposure ranges is one that you can avoid, as I believe that it is an important one for virtually all portfolio managers—whether you are self-funded or otherwise.

This is true because the guidelines that your funding entity is likely to provide will offer little in the way of details beyond setting an upper bound of acceptable portfolio exposure; and these figures may or may not be entirely rational from a risk management perspective. Moreover, while your management will almost certainly be excessively vigilant (if not entirely sensible) in establishing and enforcing risk limits at the upper end of the range, they are likely to provide you with very little guidance as to what an acceptable lower bound for your risk ought to be. This concept is more important than most traders realize, as they are often conditioned to believe that less risk is always better than more risk. However, this is often far from the case. And I wish I had a dime for every trader I know who was profitable on a unit basis but simply did not take on enough risk to generate a revenue stream large enough to cover the fixed costs of his or her accounts or to meet minimally acceptable rates of return on invested capital. Sadly, even tragically, the talents of these traders go fallow, simply because they never feel comfortable enough to take the risks necessary to achieve the absolute revenues that are fully within their power to achieve. The same dynamic may also apply if you are self-funded; I have encountered many individual traders who make money consistently but at the end of the day aren't properly compensated for the time and effort they put into trading activities because they simply aren't taking enough risk.

For all these reasons, I strongly recommend that you take the trouble to establish and routinely review exposure ranges that fit your circumstances in terms of both minimally acceptable risk levels and the more intuitive upper bounds. This section will offer guideline on setting these ranges.

In order to arrive at the appropriate figures, let's draw from that relatively small but often untapped resource—common sense. Clearly, we want to set our exposure ranges such that when we operate on the lower end of the spectrum, they still provide us with a sportsman's chance to reach our profitability objectives, while, when operating at the other end of the range, they offer an acceptably low probability of hitting what we have defined as our largest tolerable economic loss (whether stipulated by an external funding entity or self-imposed). In other words, we always want to take enough risk to enable us to achieve our goals while not extending beyond a point where the likelihood of exhausting (or, heaven forbid, exceeding) our risk-taking resources becomes a dangerous possibility.

While there is no question that setting these parameters is a subjective process, limited in its accuracy by our universal inability to predict the future, our statistical tool kit provides us with the basis for setting these ranges in a manner that should positively impact our ability to achieve our dual objective of reaching our goals without assuming undue exposure. Specifically, the model features a dual methodology that draws on such concepts as Portfolio Volatility, Sharpe Ratio, Targeted Return, and Maximum Acceptable Loss in order to identify the exposure level sufficient to reach our targets while minimizing both the probability and the magnitude of loss-threshold violations.

Method 1: Inverted Sharpe Ratio

We'll start the process by focusing on the less intuitive task of developing a methodology for setting a sensible lower bound for portfolio exposure. If we accept the critical notion that risk and return are interrelated, then we ought to be able to express one in units of the other. Indeed, as we have already covered, some of the most important work done in the era of financial engineering is the expression of return in units of risk. Most famously, and most relevantly for our purposes, these concepts are embodied in the Sharpe Ratio calculation, which you may recall is a ratio of returns to their associated volatility.

If we can estimate our Sharpe Ratio with relative accuracy, we have a pretty good notion of the kind of return we can expect for a given level of performance volatility. But what if we are looking to ask the opposite question? What if instead of wondering what return we can expect, given the riskiness of our portfolio, we want to figure out how much exposure we need in order to generate the level of performance we desire? As it turns out, with a quick sleight of algebraic hand, we can manipulate the Sharpe Ratio equation to determine both what a given level of volatility will produce in terms of returns and (more important for our purposes here) what level of volatility is consistent with a given performance target. In order to understand this critical concept as thoroughly as its importance demands, let us take the steps involved one at a time. Begin by resurrecting the basic Sharpe Ratio equation:

Sharpe Ratio = (Return − Risk-Free Rate)/Portfolio Volatility

The Sharpe Ratio can be thought of as a scorecard of your performance as a portfolio manager from a risk-adjusted-return perspective. It also is a measure of the amount of return you are likely to generate for a given dollar of risk, which, as argued earlier, is a concept that is expressed most succinctly in the portfolio volatility statistic. Thus, once you have carefully analyzed your Sharpe Ratio and are comfortable that the number you have calculated is one that you can sustain, you can invert this equation to determine what level of return you are likely to generate for a given level of risk assumption. Note that for the purposes of this discussion, we will designate this figure to be the "Sustainable Sharpe." It differs from the "actual" Sharpe Ratio derived for selected time sequences by containing a qualitative overlay that bases the figure on a conservative assessment of what you are likely to achieve in the future, given the dynamic nature of market conditions. The "actual" Sharpe Ratio is based solely on your trading history. Our "Sustainable Sharpe" is one that uses the historical Sharpe (and perhaps other inputs) to derive a lower bound for what we can confidently achieve as a Sharpe Ratio on a going forward basis.

The results of this algebraic maneuvering are as follows:

1. (Return − Risk-Free Rate) = Sustainable Sharpe × Portfolio Volatility
2. Portfolio Volatility = (Return − Risk-Free Rate)/Sustainable Sharpe

These equations define a concept that I will refer to as the Inverted Sharpe Methodology for setting exposure levels. The first equation is designed to provide you with some idea of the amount of return you can expect given your Sustainable Sharpe and your current level of volatility. The second will tell you what kind of portfolio volatility you should target in order to yield a specific return (again given a Sustainable Sharpe).

Both equations can be extremely useful in the determination of appropriate target ranges of exposure. To illustrate, consider a portfolio with the following characteristics:

Target Return:	25%
Risk-Free Rate:	5%
Return − Risk-Free Rate:	20%
Sustainable Sharpe:	2.0

We take the target return, the risk-free rate, and the Sustainable Sharpe as constants in this analysis, meaning in the case of the Sustainable

Sharpe that the account in question believes it can generate more than $2 in return for $1 of exposure it takes. The variable in these equations is portfolio volatility, which, as you will recall, is our proxy for risk. Now let's plug various volatility scenarios into the inverted equations in order to determine what they say about performance. In order to do so, however, we must take a careful look at our options for characterizing volatility. In the Sharpe Ratio calculation, volatility is represented as the standard deviation of portfolio returns. So, whatever statistic you are currently employing as your benchmark exposure measurement, it must be mapped back into standard deviation units in order to produce meaningful outcomes. Perhaps the best alternative at your disposal in this regard is the results of a Value at Risk (VaR) calculation, which have the advantage of being based on current portfolio characteristics. If you have access to a VaR calculation, it is therefore possible to substitute this figure into the denominator of the Sharpe Ratio, as long as you take care to scale down the confidence interval statistic to the one standard deviation level (for example, if you are using a 95th percentile VaR, you can map it back into a one standard deviation figure by dividing by 1.96). If you choose not to use a VaR approach, the best alternative is simply to calculate a one standard deviation P/L volatility.

Returning to our example, let us first assume that by our best estimate the portfolio is managed such that its projected, annualized volatility is 7%. Inserting this figure, along with the Sustainable Sharpe and Risk-Free Rate parameters into equation 1, and solving for Return, we find that this portfolio is likely to produce returns of approximately 19%—respectable, but significantly below our target return of 25%.

This analysis begs the question of what portfolio volatility is consistent with a 25% return target, again assuming the portfolio in question is able to sustain a Sharpe Ratio of 2.0. We can arrive at this answer quite simply using the second equation by inputting Return, Risk-Free Rate, and Sustainable Sharpe, and solving for Portfolio Volatility. Carrying through these steps with respect to the sample portfolio profile generates a result of 10%, implying that a portfolio with a Sustainable Sharpe of 2.0 should generate about 10% annualized volatility in order to produce returns of 25%.

In considering these concepts, it is important to understand that the algebraic manipulations of the Sharpe Ratio that are embodied in the two equations are nothing more than rough approximations of the amount of volatility that is consistent with a given target return, based on historical risk-adjusted performance. The algebraic results will never be entirely accurate because, in the first place, the figure you select as your Sustainable Sharpe Ratio will almost certainly deviate from both your historical performance and from your best guess as to what actual Sharpe you can produce in the future.

Moreover, I must caution against too literal an interpretation of any results you produce in this type of analysis, which, among other things might indicate that those who have lower Sharpes should assume higher risk profiles in order to achieve specified return thresholds (instead, the responsible solution involves targeting a lower return profile). However, when viewed from the proper perspective, the Inverted Sharpe Equations offer useful insights into the appropriate sizing of your risk profile. This is particularly true in cases where (as often occurs in my experience) the volatility characteristics and target returns are entirely inconsistent with one another.

For example, on the one hand, the sample portfolio in our example may target 10% annualized volatility and still come nowhere near the 25% return target. On the other hand, we can state with a great deal of confidence that if this account produces volatility in the low single digits, say, 3%, it has very little chance of ever hitting the 25% objective (indeed, it can only do so if the actual Sharpe Ratio is more than triple the estimated Sustainable Sharpe). By the same token, if this account trades to an annualized volatility profile of, say, 30%, the projected returns would be 75%—a figure so far in excess of the targeted objective as to raise questions about either the appropriateness of the target or the level of risk assumption, or some combination of the two. The point here is that by combining information about your Sharpe Ratio with expectations of return, you begin to create a picture of what type of risk levels are appropriate to these objectives; volatility levels significantly below these ranges will almost guarantee a failure to achieve associated targets, whereas figures vastly above these thresholds give rise to potential inconsistencies between return targets and risk tolerances.

Method 2: Managing Volatility as a Percentage of Trading Capital

As you may have surmised, the Inverted Sharpe Ratio method is best adapted to determining the lower bound of exposure that is consistent with reaching your targeted objectives. The main insight that it will provide you in determining the appropriate associated upper bound is that if your volatility is too high, it will project out a return that far exceeds your objectives. While this information may be useful, it doesn't address the binding constraint to risk assumption, which, as we all know by now, is the limited availability of risk capital. Clearly, in determining an upper bound of acceptable exposure, we would want to be motivated by a methodology that both minimizes the probability of our reaching our largest allowable loss and ensures that if, in fact, we do experience hard times, we don't end up with a number that considerably exceeds this figure.

The challenge, therefore, is to identify a threshold of exposure that expends, without exhausting, the full measure of risk capital allocated to the account. Reviewing this concept intuitively, the brain (well, at least my brain) moves fluidly to the following premise: In a rational portfolio risk management program, maximum exposure threshold should be tied to P/L performance over routine and identifiable cycles (e.g., one year). As a matter of good business judgment, I'm sure that you'll agree that your risk-taking prerogatives are much broader when you have accumulated some bankable P/L to work with than they are when you're down money and struggling to trade on.

The logical extension of this argument is that your maximum risk tolerance is fungible against your P/L, and the process of establishing an upper bound for your exposure begins with quantifying this interplay. Our methodological approach begins by introducing the concept of *trading capital*, which is defined simply as the sum of your maximum loss tolerance and your period-to-date P/L:

$$\text{Trading Capital} = \text{Risk Capital} \pm \text{P/L}$$

where   Risk Capital = largest allowable loss for the period

This simple equation defines the current amount of "losable" dollars associated with a given account until it hits the previously defined maximum loss threshold. For example, if an institutional trader has been given the right to trade until he or she has lost $5 million, then the trading capital on the first day of the year is $5 million. If the account subsequently makes $2 million, trading capital increases to $7 million. Similarly, if this account loses $2 million, trading capital is diminished to $3 million.

With the concept of trading capital established, we can apply it as a measure of risk-taking *capacity*. As the figure rises, we have more room for exposure and can expand our risk taking accordingly: by taking on larger position sizes or by deploying larger amounts of capital into new ideas, or some combination thereof. By the same token, as trading capital is diminished, so too is our ability to bear the negative consequences of risk taking, and our upper bound for market risk assumption must contract accordingly.

The next step is to formalize this into an equation that expresses risk-taking capacity as a function of trading capital. While some may argue for complex formulas that may (or may not) bring some added precision, it is my experience that you can operate quite effectively by simply fixing upper exposure bands as a fixed percentage of trading capital. Once you have framed the issue in this manner, the exercise of establishing a maximum is reduced to one of selecting the appropriate percentage threshold. Here, again, there is room for divergent opinion; but based on years of experience in monitoring traders in drawdown, I think that this number should not exceed 10%. In other words, as a rule, maximum volatility (expressed in one-day, one-standard-deviation terms) should not exceed 1/10 of trading current capital. In mathematical terms:

$$\Sigma_{P/L} < \text{Trading Capital} \times 10\%$$

where $\Sigma_{P/L}$ = VaR calculation at one-standard-deviation confidence level, or 20 standard deviations of P/L.

Again, if you have access to a VaR program and can convert the output to a one-standard-deviation confidence interval, it represents probably the best proxy for $\Sigma_{P/L}$, as it is tied directly to the risks that currently characterize your portfolio. However, the 20-day average volatility is a very good proxy of the kinds of risk that you are currently taking. In either case, here's my rationale behind establishing 10% as an appropriate upper bound:

If $\Sigma_{P/L}$ reaches 10% of the amount of capital you have left to lose at any given time, then we can expect with relative frequency (one observation out of six, or better, if we've figured it right) a loss that meets or exceeds 10% of your remaining risk-taking capacity. While a loss of this size would clearly be acceptable from time to time, we must be mindful of the fact that according to our standard deviation theory, market moves of two, three, and even four standard deviations occur routinely throughout the trading cycle. Indeed, most market mavens agree that these types of outlying observations happen with more frequency than is indicated by the probabilities typically associated with a normal distribution. As we have discussed briefly, this phenomenon is commonly referred to as kurtosis, or "fat tails" for the more pedestrian among us. Like it or not, fat tails are a reality in the markets. And I for one am glad for their presence, for the world would certainly lose some if its charm without them.

When a fat-tailed event, say, to the tune of three or four standard deviations does occur in the markets, if our volatility assumptions hold, a portfolio that has volatility of 10% of its trading capital may be exposed to losses that are between one-quarter and one-half of its remaining risk capacity. Needless to say, this is a potentially very serious erosion of risk capital. Moreover, as you have no doubt experienced, these types of extreme market movements tend to happen on multiple days in succession (or at least in very close proximity to one another), meaning that markets that have three- or four-standard-deviation moves in a single day can often experience much larger fluctuations before the dust settles and the market stabilizes. Thus, at volatility levels much above 10% of trading capital, traders can literally find themselves one adverse market event away from having blown through the lion's share of their reserve. It is for this reason that I view 10% as an appropriate upper bound.

Of course, portfolio construction plays a major role in the percentage selection process. For portfolios operating in liquid instruments for which the P/L tends to be in proportion to moves in underlying markets, there is arguably some breathing room here. By contrast, liquidity-constrained portfolios, and/or those where the P/L impact may be orders of magnitude of the price movement in underlying markets (e.g., portfolios with a great deal of optionality), it may be necessary to be even more conservative. However, while we may quibble with the applicable percentages, I see no compelling arguments against the notion that trader volatility should be scaled to trading capital, and I encourage you to adopt this approach in as thorough and as timely a manner as you can.

There are a couple of very important practical implications to trading under a discipline that ties P/L volatility to trading capital. First, on the upside, it implies that as your profits build, so does your risk-taking capacity. Among other alternatives, you can use these additional resources in ways that may spur your development as a trader—by trading in larger sizes; by experimenting with new asset classes, sectors, or instrument types; by modifying your long/short profile; and so on. Ultimately, by making a long-term commitment to the continued expansion of your portfolio management horizons, you stand the best chance of maximizing your success over time. However, in order to do so, you will routinely be compelled to operate in ways that will deviate from your normal trading habits; and by far the best time to do this is when your trading capital has increased through profit accumulation. The extra cushion this provides offers you the opportunity to assume new kinds of portfolio profiles at magnitudes of exposure that will not eat significantly into your risk capital.

Let's say you start out the year with risk capital of $1 million. Under our trading capital approach, we would not recommend that your daily volatility, as expressed in units of standard deviation, extend much beyond $100,000. Now let's assume that you make an additional $1 million during the first quarter of the year. Your trading capital has now expanded to $2 million, and your maximum recommended exposure has similarly doubled, to $200,000. The additional risk capacity can then be deployed entirely or in part in the development of complementary trading disciplines that will enhance your arsenal. This is the ideal situation under which to either try new strategy variants or increase your risk by scaling up your trading sizes.

In either case, it is important to undertake these developmental efforts at limited levels of exposure. If you do try some new, different, or scaled-up activities, determine in advance the amount of risk capital you wish to allocate to this exercise. Perhaps, carrying forward with the preceding example, the appropriate figure is $500,000, or half of your accumulated profits for the period in question. It is very important to adhere to this discipline and to terminate the developmental activities if you subsequently lose an amount equal to your specified threshold. The very process of stretching your portfolio activities at a point when you have reached a benchmark level of profitability, investing a portion of these profits into the further development of your portfolio management skills, and then terminating this activity, if necessary, at specified levels of loss can be enormously empowering. Arguably, you'll have renewed opportunities for such experimentation in the future (such as when you have rebuilt your P/L to levels where the risk is justified); and in the meantime, you have demonstrated the ability to manage the associated outcomes of broadening your trading horizons to acceptable levels of loss.

Now let's examine what happens when your trading capital contracts. At volatility levels below the introductory threshold of 10% of your trading capital, the risk of a single event or series of events pushing you toward the precipice is minimal. However, as we have said, this is not the case when you have generated a significant negative P/L for the period in question. Under these circumstances, the percentage-based impact of material negative P/L observations on your loss reserve increases exponentially, and it becomes imperative for you to scale down your risks accordingly.

To illustrate, let's return to our earlier example of a portfolio that has been allocated $1 million of risk capital/potential losses. Let's assume that after the first quarter, this portfolio suffers losses of $500,000, in the process reducing trading capital by 50% to $500,000. If you continue to generate $\Sigma_{P/L}$ of $100,000 (as would be consistent with our model for full investment at a cumulative P/L of $0 for the period), you have increased the probability of meeting or exceeding your stop-out level by an order of magnitude as (due once again to the fat-tailed nature of the markets) a single 5σ market event; or consecutive price movements on the order of half this size are much more commonplace than most investors are aware. Moreover, because these types of market swings can happen abruptly and without warning, a failure of this portfolio to scale back its exposure to reflect its reduced ability to absorb losses creates a material positive probability that the account not only reaches its $1 million loss threshold but exceeds this level by a significant amount.

Note that this is particularly true for portfolios that operate in markets characterized by liquidity constraints because in these cases the very efforts undertaken to reduce exposure may exacerbate volatility—in the process causing negative price action that can push valuations to levels not justified by the underlying economics of the situation—simply because the market is aware of the portfolio manager's acute need (as well as those of perhaps others in a similar situation) to liquidate his or her position. Not that it's overly relevant to this discussion, but in these cases you may find that in addition to being compelled to confront the consequences of having hit your economic stop-out, you may be subject to the further indignity of watching positions you just liquidated under duress bounce back to neutral or even positive P/L levels once the market understands that it has squeezed out all those who are operating near their financial constraints.

IF A TREE FALLS IN THE FOREST . . .

The late 1990s offer a treasure trove of case studies of what to do and what not to do when managing liquidity-constrained portfolios under conditions of drawdown. Many of these lessons emanate from the hedge fund community (where morality tales are sometimes more plentiful than investor returns), and I ask you to consider the sad ending of a hypothetical hedge fund, once pre-eminent but now defunct, whose name I can't state specifically (even hypothetical hedge funds are notoriously publicity-shy) but I can tell you that it derives from one of the sturdiest and tallest trees in the forest, the sequoia dendron gigantum, or redwood tree. For nearly 2 decades, this mighty colossus towered over its competition, in terms of both returns and assets under management, inspiring the humble admiration of the saplings that comprised the majority of its neighbors.

Unfortunately, one of the laws of the forest is that even its mightiest denizens eventually yield to the forces of nature; and by the time the leaves began to turn in 1998, it was apparent to most observers that the salad days of our angular protagonist were very much behind it. However, like all great warriors of the untamed market wilderness, the fund was destined to experience its fall in the throes of battle—and not by its unilateral withdrawal from the arena in which it had so long reigned as champion.

Did it get bested in a single, defining incident? Hardly. These things seldom are as clear-cut in the markets as they are in nature. Looking back, however, there is one event that stands out above all others: a massive bet, gone awry, that one of the world's benchmark commodities would devalue significantly, relative to one of its peers. I don't know how big the exact position was and couldn't even verify with certainty that the trade actually took place; but according to widespread market scuttlebutt, it amounted to several billion dollars.

That there were sound fundamental justifications for this position there is little doubt. Some of the smartest commodity traders in the world had been predicting such a shift in sentiment for many a month. Speculative frenzy had pushed the commodity's price to well beyond where its natural sources of demand could continue to make use of it. The fact that they were starting to utilize less efficient substitutes was evident in the price action of these commodities. Many speculators who had ridden the upward trend to once (or perhaps twice) in a lifetime profit levels, were rumored to be getting out while they still could.

The problems here had to do with size and scale. Against the backdrop of the Russian default, the collapse of Long-Term Capital Management, and a rapidly deteriorating state of capital markets on a global scale, even the most intrepid investors were busy engaging in wholesale portfolio liquidation in a frenzied effort to accumulate cash and consolidate losses. Then, one afternoon, there was a multi-billion dollar bid for a clearly overvalued commodity. Quickly, quickly, the market surmised that a large hedge fund was liquidating its largest holding—and rumors flew about the relative level of duress that precipitated such liquidation. Our redwood was known to have been badly wounded in the Russian debacle; and as nature has ordered, nothing that moved wanted to risk being in the path of the giant, if by chance, it were to come crashing to the ground.

All of a sudden, there were no offers for the overvalued commodity, as afore-mentioned and newly endowed speculators decided that, gosh darn it, maybe the commodity wasn't so overvalued after all. Over a two-day period, it rallied another 20%. None of us who witnessed this activity could ever recall a single trade on the part of an individual investment entity ever causing such a major price disruption in a market generally thought of as being so liquid that even the world's leading central banks could only effect changes a fraction that size, and this only with a concerted, coordinated effort.

Though its formal demise didn't take place till a couple of years later, everyone could see that the mighty sequoia, which once, as the saying goes, looked like it would indeed grow to the sky, was losing all its sap. Join me if you will in bidding it a fond, if belated, adieu. We are not likely to encounter its like again in our lifetimes.

The concept of reducing risk in portfolios that have experienced a significant drawdown has critical implications for the entire trading/investment process, and I believe that it is perhaps the single most important discipline that exists in the field of risk management. To understand this concept as thoroughly as we ought, we must review the drawdown dynamic from the point of view of both the capital provider and the portfolio manager.

First, from the perspective of the entity that supplies the capital, be mindful that due to the everchanging nature of the financial incentives under which portfolio managers may operate, their interests may diverge materially from yours at certain thresholds of drawdown. This occurs because portfolio managers, in a rational compensation system, draw the lion's share of their financial incentives in the form of a percentage of their profits. In this way, under even modest levels of positive return, everyone's interests are properly aligned; and portfolio managers have every positive incentive to manage their ongoing trading/investment activities in such a way as to produce the maximum risk-adjusted return that is available, given their trading style, market conditions, and other factors.

However, the same cannot be said for these interests when the portfolio in question is substantially in the red. In that case, the financial relationship between capital provider and portfolio manager undergoes a dramatic shift—primarily as the result of two factors. The first is tied to a concept called *high-water*, which serves as the basis for remuneration for the majority of fund management enterprises. Under the high-water approach, investment managers are paid their percentage cut only of the revenues associated with net, incremental additions to the value of the assets. For example, a trader who is entitled to 20% of the profits in a high-water payout regime and who loses, say, $1 million does not get his or her 20% of the revenues associated with recovering these losses. The trader receives the 20% only when he or she produces positive P/L above the $1 million. Traders who operate in deep deficit face the prospect of not getting paid for the revenues they generate until they have made back the full measure of the losses they have suffered. Under these circumstances, the portfolio manager has a great incentive to minimize the amount of time it takes to effect this recovery and has a tendency to believe (incorrectly, as it turns out) that the best means by which to accomplish this is by assuming a higher risk profile.

Second, capital providers tend to be very impatient with portfolio managers in drawdown and are quick to withdraw their funding in favor of investment alternatives that offer better prospects. The associated risk of funding loss further incentivizes traders in drawdown to increase their risk to remove, with the greatest possible expediency, the condition that threatens their livelihood.

The confluence of these factors presents a potentially disastrous divergence of interest between the capital provider and the portfolio manager, as the former's payout function is still "linear" (i.e., she derives essentially the same benefit from an incremental dollar of revenue as she does when the portfolio manager in question is flat or up money), while the latter's economics are "binary" (i.e., he only gets paid on an upswing in his P/L large enough to eradicate his deficit, otherwise he earns nothing and perhaps loses his funding to boot). Under these circumstances, the portfolio manager has a very substantial incentive to seek out unacceptable levels of market exposure that will put him back in the black if he is correct about the markets but render him no worse off—economically or from a career perspective—if he is wrong.

For capital providers whose objective is to maximize risk-adjusted return, there are few responsibilities more important than taking the steps needed to ensure that their portfolio managers in drawdown do not ramp up their exposures. They must manage these responsibilities through the imposition of limits, the reduction of working capital, or any other means available. Failure to take this step can lead to situations where, for obvious reasons, the losses associated with individual portfolios vastly exceed the maximum amount specified in the funding arrangement.

While the provider of capital has every incentive to ensure that portfolio managers in deficit don't assume more risk than is dictated by their trading capital, he or she should not, as a rule, be averse to these traders using their full risk capacity as defined by the Trading Capital Equation. Once the account is deeply in the red, so long as the portfolio manager is adhering to the disciplines associated with the 10% Rule (or appropriate derivation thereof), the downside for the capital provider is capped with a reasonable degree of certainty at the economic stop-out; and the risk/rewards associated with the portfolio (so long as it exhibits the appropriate exposure characteristics) are actually no worse than those associated with positively performing portfolios. In fact, they are arguably much better—due to the high-water concept, under which any positive P/L generated by portfolio managers in drawdown falls directly to the bottom line—unfiltered by trader compensation percentages that won't accrue again for the trader until he or she has made back the loss. Therefore, unless the capital provider has given up entirely on the trader in question (at which point the relationship should be severed, irrespective of current P/L considerations), he or she should feel very good about funding drawdown portfolios—provided, again, that the portfolio manager is living within his or her risk limits and otherwise practicing sound risk management

However, the landscape looks vastly different to portfolio managers operating from a deficit position. As we've shown, these individuals will face significant temptations to trade their way out of their losses over shorter time periods by assuming higher levels of exposure. I will argue strongly that they should resist this temptation for the following reasons. First, professional portfolio managers who take pride in their work and who seek to earn their compensation by maximizing risk-adjusted return understand intuitively that increasing their exposure from a deficit position runs against the interest of their investors. Specifically, they recognize that while they are, from a compensation perspective, no worse off if they lose an amount equal to their economic stop-out, or an amount much greater than this, their investors will feel this difference on a dollar-for-dollar basis. It can be hoped that at least a subset of professional money managers will, on the basis of pure professional pride, resist the temptation to rapidly trade out of any hole that they have dug for themselves by increasing the amount of market exposure they are assuming to levels that exceed or even approach the levels associated with the time period of the drawdown.

Second, the notion that it is in your interest to accelerate your recovery through higher risk assumption is entirely false. While such action may appear to work to your benefit in the short term, it is, on the whole, an approach with potentially disastrous career consequences. By failing to adhere to the disciplines of the 10% Trading Capital Equation, you show an inability (or, at minimum, a negative predisposition) to act in a manner that is consistent with the critical principals of capital preservation and sound risk control. True, the market may bail you out; and if it does, you may live to fight another day. But even if this happy outcome becomes the reality, it contains a much larger element of luck than may be apparent at the time of your recovery. Further, there is probably a much greater chance that your additional risk assumption comes at a time when, viewed from an objective perspective, market conditions don't justify the additional exposure. After all, the only time when you are confronted with such an alternative is after a serious episode of negative P/L, which in almost all cases is symptomatic of unfavorable market conditions or less-than-optimal decision making on your part, or some combination of the two.

Ask yourself now, without the answer being clouded by conditions of trading duress: Is this the time that you want to place the ultimate faith in your ability to have identified sufficient market opportunities to justify an increase in exposure? When viewed objectively, I believe that the answer, in almost all cases, would have to be no.

Even if, in retrospect, the forces of nature combine in such a way as to have justified additional risk taking, my experience is that 99.99% of the traders out there will face multiple incidences of large-scale drawdowns over the course of a career. If your response to each situation is to increase your risk as a percentage of trading capital, it is only a matter of time before you experience not just a blowout, but perhaps a blowout of epic proportions. If you are managing other people's money, it pays to be mindful that the universe of potential constituents is a limited one and that they are becoming increasingly sophisticated in evaluating portfolio-manager reaction to conditions of performance duress. An incident in which you blew through a large portion of your risk capital and then lost more money through a failure to adjust your risk profile downward will be extremely easy to identify and equally difficult to explain away. Any capital allocator who values his or her job and/or wealth will avoid these types of portfolios like the plague. For self-directed traders funding their own portfolios, the consequences of having luck run out at undue levels of risk, at a time when these traders are in the midst of a deep drawdown, should be only too obvious.

It is abundantly clear to me that from all rational perspectives, the only reasonable alternative for traders in drawdown/deficit is to reduce exposure down to levels reflecting a fixed percentage of their trading capital. In addition to minimizing the probability of hitting down-and-out thresholds, such an approach virtually ensures that in instances where accounts do approach these thresholds, they can be liquidated before the actual loss number exceeds the stop-out level by a meaningful amount. For the worst-performing portfolios that adhere to this discipline, the P/L path approaches the stop-out level in an asymptotic manner, with exposure decreasing at each downward leg of the P/L spiral.

The contrast associated with the approach of adhering to a fixed level of volatility tied to trading capital, as opposed to one that does not adhere to this discipline, is depicted in Figure 5.1. Believe it or not, I drew this

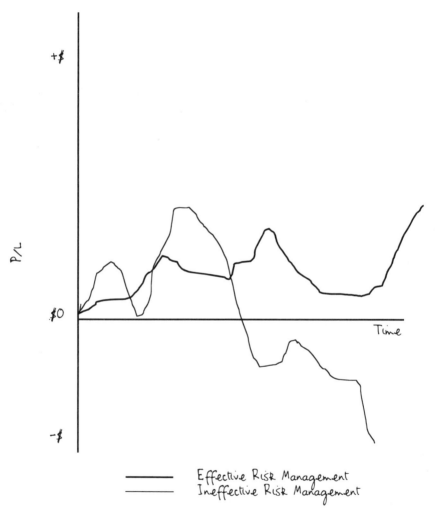

FIGURE 5.1 Time performance graph of effective and ineffective risk management performance.

diagram myself, and I am immensely proud of my handiwork. If you ever want me to draw you a diagram, I'd be glad to try. Just don't expect miracles like Figure 5.1, which only can be wrought from the artist through a process involving divine intervention.

In addition to its indisputable aesthetic merit, Figure 5.1 is instructive from a risk management perspective as well. As can be seen, the thin-line portfolio is one where the trader sets an upper bound of exposure as a reasonable percent of trading capital. When this account experiences a deep drawdown, it removes risk in an orderly fashion and, in the process, ensures that the loss does not violate the stop-out threshold. The thick-line portfolio, by contrast, is one where risk does not adjust downward with negative P/L but instead stays constant or increases over the course of the drawdown. Here, as can be seen, there is virtually no limit to the amount of loss the portfolio can ultimately experience; and in many cases the actual figure will exceed the associated down-and-out by material amounts. If you buy into notions regarding the sanctity of the economic stop-out threshold, then I am sure you'll agree that the best means of controlling your exposure is to stick to the disciplines that derive from operating within the framework specified in the 10% Equation.

Adherents to these principals must be mindful that maintaining maximum risk capacity as a fixed percentage of available trading capital—particularly during periods immediately after intervals of deep drawdown—is one of the most difficult tasks I know of in the field of portfolio management. In more cases than not, and particularly for those whose drawdowns take them deeply into a negative P/L position (i.e., as opposed to ones that merely reduce accumulated profitability for the period), such a commitment means a willingness to invest meaningfully long time periods to the recapture of P/L for which, due to the high-water concept described earlier, there is no attendant compensation. And if this prospect weren't unpalatable enough on its own, it is my observation that a commitment to operate at reduced risk levels in the wake of a drawdown will often coincide with periods of large perceived opportunity in the markets that comprise a trader's core focus. Indeed, even if this isn't the case, from the perspective of the trader, it almost always seems as though it is.

Finally, as you begin to recover your losses, there will be a significant temptation to view the problems that caused the drawdown as an anomaly that is not likely to repeat itself and to accelerate your assumption of exposure at a rate faster than is specified by the 10% Trading Capital Equation. *I urge you to resist these forces,* as the manner in which you deal with them may, in my estimation, have a substantial bearing on your future career prospects as a trader/portfolio manager.

Inevitably, the voices inside your head will begin to tell you the following stories:

- The episode of your recent (albeit partial) recovery offers incontrovertible evidence that your problems are behind you.
- Great trading/investment opportunities exist right now; but they may disappear—perhaps for good—by the time you've accumulated enough risk capital to take full advantage of them.
- At current risk levels, your trading compensation prospects are unacceptable and are likely to remain so for an unacceptably long period into the future.

When you combine all of these arguments, they make for a compelling case to increase your exposure as quickly as possible now that happy days are indisputably here again. However, you increase at great peril to your long-term prospects for the simple reason that if your fortunes take a turn for the worse at this critical juncture, the results can be devastating. Depending on how much incremental risk you have taken on, you stand every chance of taking your portfolio values to new lows. If this happens, it may wreak considerable havoc on your confidence as well as on the confidence of those who own the capital you are managing. Often this phenomenon can cloud your ability to make sound market decisions (after all, you are now wrong twice: first, on the original drawdown, and second, on your ramp-up), which can severely hinder your ability to make money even under favorable market conditions. By contrast, if you have maintained your exposure as a fixed percentage of your trading capital, you have both limited your risk on the downside and ensured that even if you miss a few good opportunities, you have nevertheless demonstrated the ability to manage your exposure effectively under times of duress. Under these circumstances, you stand to have a long, satisfying career as a trader, instilling yourself with confidence and increasing the trust in your judgment among those who are impacted by your trading fortunes. In the end, I believe this is well worth the investment you make by resisting the temptation to increase exposures beyond those that tie back logically to your capacity to absorb losses.

BORN TO RUN

Let's take a brief journey into the world of our imagination, where there exists a land, located in a deep hole somewhere in the middle of the wilderness, in which everything a trader looks on is higher than he or she is. I refer, of course, to the Kingdom of Drawdown. It is a very drab, tedious place, where visitors always appear to be in a great hurry to leave. In fact, some might go so far as to call the Kingdom downright depressing. Certainly no one who visits is ever very happy, and the permanent residents are often described as the walking dead. Indeed, I have often wondered what it is about Drawdown that makes it so popular, with traders of every level of skill visiting there routinely and its register of full-time residents increasing each day. In terms of its topography, the Kingdom of Drawdown looks much like New Jersey, with the same size and shape but without the Bruce Springsteen affiliation. In fact, its main transportation artery is a near-perfect replica of the New Jersey Turnpike, with a toll-based structure under which the deeper into Drawdown you travel, the higher the toll you are forced to pay at the end of your journey.

Although it is a Kingdom, Drawdown has no king. Instead it is ruled by two aristocratic fellows who wear plumed, festooned garments and who make sure, through their sheer nastiness, that no one ever has a good time on their watch. One is the Duke of Risk Reduxus, whose job it is to make sure that no one within the Kingdom walls goes too fast on the turnpike (he is rumored to have socialist leanings). His partner (said to be related to the Duke by blood or marriage) Count Compus Interuptus, runs the turnpike toll booths and spends his days making sure that he grabs every last available shekel that the good citizens could muster through their labors.

Our tale takes place in the infamous third quarter of 1998, which was a very important period in the Kingdom's history, as those who were there can verify. Drawdown was in fact very crowded that Indian Summer (by many accounts, this is the peak of their tourist season), playing host to many of the world's best traders—many of whom were unfamiliar with its terrain and each of whom was eager to make the visit to the Kingdom as short as possible. However, with so much traffic on the turnpike and with the Count's henchmen waiting to collect their fees, it was very difficult to get out; and the scene of untold numbers of traders and investment managers, each carrying the baggage of large portfolios and each desperately trying to return home, was one of the saddest that this reporter has ever had the responsibility to describe. Gradually, an idea arose from the multitudes, an inspiration of sorts: Each of them could individually increase their speed by traveling lighter. Though there was scant communication among them, they decided that the best way to proceed was to shed their portfolio baggage. So they hurried to the market village of Drawdown (which was way down around Exit 9), seeking to liquidate their holdings at the best price they could. Unfortunately, the merchants of the town had a keen eye for value, and all of the traders were pretty much selling the same wares. Naturally, prices plunged dramatically, and many traders had to travel out of the market village, ever deeper into the Kingdom, to find buyers for their wares. Moreover, at the rate at which their portfolios were being liquidated, it was becoming increasingly clear that many traders would not be able to raise the exit toll and might be stuck in the Kingdom of Drawdown forever.

One of the groups that participated in this sad pantomime was a company called Jai Lai investments, a very well-known and well-thought-of enterprise that hadn't, truth be told, spent much time in Drawdown, instead managing brief and infrequent stays over a long history. Jai Lai had two traders who were leading the expeditionary team at that time, known respectively as *Doofus* and *Rufus*. These two were boyhood pals and virtually inseparable from the time they first swapped football cards in the 1970s. As trading partners, they had made a great deal of money together, and they were very much taken by surprise when the world turned upside down in the fall of 1998. However, their responses to these episodes were very different. Doofus was Jai Lai's specialist in charge of trinket collection, and what a job he did! In the years before our story began, he had accumulated such an assortment of knickknacks and thingamabobs as to leave the average observer plainly speechless. There were enough Peruvian Pelts and Turkish Treasures to make your eyes water. There were baubles from Brazil, Danish pastries, Malaysian mish mosh, Venezuelan victuals, and even some stuff from places no one had ever heard of before. Oh, Doofus was very proud of his collection and, being a bit mercurial by nature, entered Drawdown with something of a haughty attitude. His pantaloons were flush with drachmas, pesetas, rupees, and even some dollars at the time; and he wasn't particularly concerned about hanging around the Kingdom for a bit. He figured he was driving a Ferrari on a road full of Chevys and could burn his way up to the exit booth pretty much any time he so chose. As the winds blew colder, he began to notice heavier traffic on the turnpike, but he wasn't overly troubled by this trend. Moreover, he had no inclination of any kind to reduce his collection of odds and ends (which had taken years to accumulate) at wholesale prices to facilitate his departure.

In fact, being a natural-born contrarian, he got the very clever idea of buying when his colleagues were selling; and the sight of him bidding with the locals against his trader buddies is one that few who witnessed it are likely to soon forget. Of course, the selling pressure turned out to be so intense that after a while, even Doofus couldn't stem the drop in prices. As this happened, Doofus sold everything, including his Ferrari, at bargain-basement rates; and in the late stages of this process, he could be found not near the exit gates or in the market, but rather sitting on a park bench, legs crossed, reading the *Daily Mail*. In the end, his entire stake was wiped out. And the really sad thing about this is that by all accounts had he been selling with everyone else in the Drawdown market square instead of buying, he likely could have raised the cash to bail himself out. Instead, he became a permanent (somewhat legendary) resident of Drawdownville. When I last checked, he'd built some lovely condos on the hillside, which are now fully occupied by traders with similar, if less dramatic, stories to tell.

Rufus's visit to the Kingdom took a very different course. He, too, was a world-renowned collector and held many of the same types of treasures contained in the satchel of his boyhood pal. However, most of us who knew them both suspected that he had made better bargains for himself and had purchased better-quality stuff, at better prices from the same merchants patronized by Doofus. Rufus was very upset at the notion of spending one minute more in that sorrowful space than he had to. When he sensed his markets were turning troubled, he began to sell everything. In fact, he was among the first sellers of the stuff that Doofus was buying. As such, in retrospect, Rufus got what were very handsome prices for his holdings. It took months; but by the time he was finished lightening his load, he had plenty of cash to pay the exit toll. Later that fall, the winds started to blow favorably for Rufus and those of his ilk, and he ended up making more money than he ever imagined possible.

Most of us have visited the Land of Drawdown and will do so again before much time passes. The message of this fable is clear: If you wish your stay there to be a brief one, it pays to travel light.

DRAWDOWNS AND NETTING RISK

Another extremely critical implication of deep drawdowns, which applies exclusively if you are working as part of a multistrategy trading team, is one referred to within the industry as *netting risk*. Specifically, netting risk is the contingent cost of having to pay out portfolio managers in a multistrategy portfolio who are compensated on the basis of a percentage of the revenues they produce from an overall revenue stream that has been diminished by the presence of unprofitable accounts. As any multistrategy fund manager will tell you, such netting expenses are pure poison to the profitability profile, and the management of netting risk thus becomes a core focus of any rational multistrategy risk management model.

To illustrate why this is the case, consider a trading team of two individuals funded by a third party under a scheme where each trader is paid 25% of his or her profits. Now envision a scenario where one of the traders makes $1 million in a year, while the other loses $1 million. The net revenues of the enterprise are precisely zero, but this does not obviate the funding entity's responsibility to pay the profitable trader the $250,000 he earned through his portfolio management efforts. Undeniably, the condition of expenses that cannot be offset by revenues is both bleak and unsustainable. From the point of view of the investors, the minimization of netting risk has to be a top priority.

If you are a member of a multistrategy trading team, you should recognize that any negative returns you generate become contributing factors to one of the most debilitating expenses that a trading firm can experience. The deeper you go into negative territory, the more acute is the problem your situation presents. Therefore, by cutting your exposures if your account becomes even marginally unprofitable, you align your action with the interest of your investors; and this, my friends, is a situation you should constantly strive to create and maintain.

ASYMMETRIC PAYOFF FUNCTION

I'll close my arguments regarding the need to reduce risk during drawdown by discussing a widely established but largely underapplied concept, which I will call (in part because this is the name that everyone uses) the *asymmetric payoff function*. Specifically, I refer to the reality that drawdown reduces not only investment returns but also the capital that is available to deploy in the markets to recover the associated losses. Therefore, at every incremental level of percentage-based drawdown, the percent return needed to recover these losses increases at a geometric rate.

Perhaps the best way to explain this is through the use of an example. Let's assume that I am a portfolio manager in charge of assets valued at $1 million. If I lose $100,000 in the first month of operation, or 10%, not only do I have to make up this $100,000, but I have to do so with only $900,000 of investment capital left to deploy in the markets to recover these losses. The $100,000 represents 11.1% of the $900,000 available to me, so I must make 11.1% in order to recover a 10% original loss in my account. Moreover, this relationship will apply to a 10% drawdown, no matter whether the account in question contains $500 or $5 million.

As drawdown increases, so too does this disparity because a deepening loss profile contemporaneously increases the size of the recovery needed to get back to even while reducing the capital available to do so. Thus, a $250,000, or 25%, loss must be made up against $750,000 worth of capital, implying a 33% recover hurdle; and the trend continues from there. Indeed, by the time my account lost $500,000, or 50%, my recovery task would involve making back $500,000 on the $500,000 of remaining capital, which translates into a 100% recovery hurdle.

The relationship between the percentage-based drawdown and associated recovery hurdle is specified below:

$$Y = X/(1 - X)$$

where X = drawdown rate (in percentage terms)
        Y = recovery hurdle (in percentage terms)

To further illustrate, look at Figure 5.2 and Table 5.1, which solve for Recovery Hurdle (Y) in the equation at various levels of Drawdown (X).

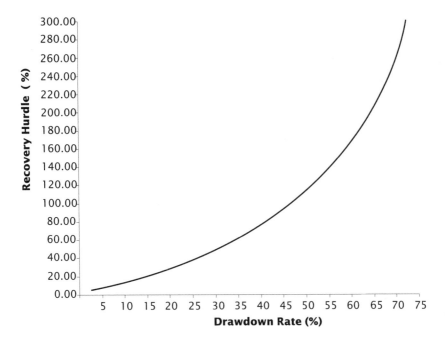

FIGURE 5.2 Drawdown rates and associated recovery hurdles.

TABLE 5.1	Drawdown Rates and Associated Recovery Hurdles
Drawdown Rate	**Recovery Hurdle**
5%	5.3%
10	11.1
15	17.6
20	25.0
25	33.3
30	42.9
35	53.8
40	66.7
45	81.8
50	100.0
55	122.2
60	150.0
65	185.7
70	233.3
75	300.0
100	∞

I am particularly struck by the last line of the table, which would also apply to the graph if we could create a vertical access that reached up to infinity. That's right—if you lose all your capital, then the implied, percentage-based return you will need to recover these losses is infinite.

And now, my dearly beloved brothers and sisters, my sermon is over, and I step down from the pulpit on this topic. If you haven't yet acquired religion regarding the need to cut capital as fortunes move against you, then I fear you never may.

CHAPTER 6

Adjusting Portfolio Exposure (Rule 2)

He's a worldwide traveler, he's not like me or you,
But he comes in mighty regular, for one who's
  passin' thru,
That one came in his work clothes, he's missed his
  last bus home,
He's missed a hell of a lot of busses, for a man
  who wants to roam,
And you'll never get to Rome, Son,
And son this is Rule 2.

　　　　　　　　　—Paul Heaton, Beautiful South,
　　　　　　　　　　"Liar's Bar"

I open this chapter by offering mad props hat to one of the best (and, sadly, unrecognized, at least in the States) bands since the Beatles. If you haven't already done so, please do me a solid and check out Beautiful South. Feel free to blame me if this turns out badly; but in so doing, remember to temper justice with mercy, as I always have done with you (well, almost always—that time when you doubled down on your 10-year-note position in front of the monthly payrolls report, you deserved everything you got from me, and then some).

Throughout the preceding discussions, I have highlighted the critical importance of adjusting your exposure to account for your performance relative to your objectives, for drawdown management, and for other realities of the profit/loss (P/L) cycle. Call this Rule 1. Rule 2, with a grateful nod to my favorite musicians from Hull (along with the late great Mick Ronson), is that effective portfolio management demands an explicit

understanding of the alternatives available in the marketplace to bring
about such adjustment whenever the situation so demands. Your specific
path for risk modification will, of course, depend greatly on the type of
portfolio you are managing, as well as on factors such as prevailing market conditions, your recent fortunes from a P/L perspective, and other
"situation-specific issues." For instance, the steps that you would take to
modify risk on, say, a portfolio of U.S. government securities are by definition different from those that would be appropriate for a portfolio of
global equities. Similarly, a portfolio of derivatives will often require
exposure adjustment measures that are different from those needed for a
portfolio comprised of cash securities. Also, as implied earlier, risk adjustment to stem acute and abrupt losses will assume forms highly different
from the occasional tweaks to your exposure that you might wish to
undertake under happier circumstances.

With all of these qualifiers in mind, there is a common thread to the
types of risk-adjustment steps that you can take—irrespective of the
composition of your portfolio—to meet the requirements of the current
situation you face. Some of these are described in this chapter.

SIZE OF INDIVIDUAL POSITIONS

I'll begin by stating the obvious: Size matters. *In almost all cases, the
volatility of your portfolio will vary directly with the size of your individual positions.* In fact, in most cases (involving not only cash securities
but also derivatives), the relationship between position size and portfolio
exposure will be linear. Absent compelling evidence to the contrary, it's a
pretty safe bet that for any given position you put into your portfolio, a
position twice that size will be twice as risky, whereas positions half this
size are likely to generate half the exposure.

There are a number of ways to make this concept work for you in the
markets. For example, you might either add or take away from your positions in existing names so as to meet your appropriate risk profile. Or you
might wish to adjust your position size only on incremental trades. In
either case, you can take it on faith that one surefire way to manage your
exposure is to assume that larger-size positions means greater volatility,
and vice versa. Also bear in mind that while the relationship between position size and volatility will in most cases be linear, this linearity will break
down at very large transactions sizes due to liquidity constraints. For portfolio managers with large pools of capital behind them, there are levels of
position size where the risk profile changes dramatically. In cases where
your trading size crosses these thresholds, you are likely to discover that a

given percentage change in the sizing of your position may have a much larger impact on your overall portfolio exposure. Note, however, that you will only manifest this additional portfolio volatility at the entry and exit points of the transaction. For the entire period in between, your P/L by definition will be a linear function of transaction size, where if position of size X generates $\$Y$ of volatility, those of $2X$ must generate $\$2Y$; and so on. It is therefore important to remain mindful of the liquidity characteristics of the markets in which you are trading and to map them carefully into your overall risk management architecture.

We will cover this topic in much greater detail in subsequent chapters.

DIRECTIONAL BIAS

While not applicable to all strategies in all markets, it is often a good idea to maintain a healthy mixture of long and short positions within a portfolio. This is particularly true in portfolios where the individual instruments contained therein tend to be highly correlated, such as those focused on equity securities or commodity futures. All other factors remaining equal (particularly those tied to the amount of leverage in the portfolio), a balanced mixture of longs and shorts is a less risky profile than one in which all speculations are pointed in the same market direction. For example, a portfolio that has a long position in corn and a short position in wheat is likely to be less risky, on a unit basis, than one that features dual longs or shorts in these same commodities. Similarly, an account that is long IBM and short Microsoft is likely to carry less exposure than one that contains the same securities held on the same side of the market.

As portfolios scale up in size, the need to operate on both sides of a given market becomes more pronounced, and I strongly urge this kind of two-sided market orientation as being one of the best means of maximizing risk-adjusted profitability.

However, I should tell you that this challenge is, in my experience, one of the most difficult in advanced portfolio management. This is because most traders and, indeed, most markets lend themselves more directly toward a single-sided market orientation. For example, it was plainly easier to trade the long side of the stock market in the last half of the 1990s, first, because the market enjoyed a sustained rally for the entire period; second, because the equity markets are structurally organized under all market conditions to favor long bets through such mechanisms as the "uptick rule" for short sales, the rather complicated "borrowing-based" mechanics of short selling, the rules that compel large institutional portfolios to operate exclusively on the long side of the market, and other factors. We must bear in mind that short-selling in the equities markets represents, when results are characterized in terms of their extremes, an asymmetric bet under which gains are limited by the fact that a stock cannot price itself at a value less than zero, while potential losses are, at least in theory, unlimited in nature, as there is no upper bound to the value at which a security can trade. By contrast, when I was in the futures markets, traders constantly told me how much easier it was to trade the short side of the market, but then again no one ever accused this crowd of seeing any glass as being half full.

Though it can be difficult both psychologically and practically, I believe it is important, wherever possible, to practice the discipline of trading on both sides of the markets, as the potential benefits from adopting such an approach far outweigh the associated annoyances. In the first place, most providers of capital are more comfortable funding portfolios with a dual market orientation than they are investing in portfolios where the risk is single-sided. I'm not sure that I agree with this philosophy on pure risk management grounds (one of my main tenets of risk control is that a dollar of risk expressed one way is no more hazardous than a dollar of risk expressed another way), but the dual approach certainly mitigates certain event risks—such as being long insurance stocks when planes crash through buildings.

Beyond this, to whatever extent that your portfolio faces external volatility constraints (and trust me, it does), a great way to manage your associated exposure is to achieve some balance from a long/short perspective. Long/short portfolio management is also a very useful tool for risk control in those cases when you are hoping to benefit from correctly identifying an information catalyst (e.g., a product announcement) but are unsure when the catalyst will take hold. In these situations, by utilizing a balanced portfolio approach, you will be much more able to maintain your positions during the adverse overall market conditions that may occur in the period before your catalyst works its way into the pricing of the instruments you are targeting (more about this in a moment).

One common misconception holds that in order to be a successful long/short player, it is necessary to operate profitably on both sides of the market. While, all other things being equal, this is certainly a desirable outcome, I would argue that there are important benefits to be gained by operating with a relatively balanced market-direction orientation even if you do no better than break even or lose modestly on the side where you are less comfortable operating. As indicated earlier, by doing so, you reduce your exposure to broad-based market events, such as crashes. A portfolio that is entirely on one side of the market is exposed to the full fury of these episodes, which, as we have already discussed, are likely to cause all securities to move in lockstep with one another. Perhaps as important, the presence of some well-adapted two-sided market exposure will greatly enhance your ability to stay with your best ideas—across all market cycles—and thus capitalize in those situations when you feel a high level of conviction that a certain scenario will play out but less sure as to the precise timing.

Let's take a moment to more closely examine my assertion that a long/short position orientation also reduces the need to be absolutely accurate in terms of market timing, shall we? In my opinion it is much easier to make money by trading well-researched ideas in individual securities—particularly those where you believe you have specific edge—than it is to predict whether the overall market is going up or down. If you make more narrowly defined positions such as individual equities and commodities your money-making focus, my experience is that many of your best trades will be ones that you have put on somewhat more in advance of the moment you would choose if you could trade through the "rearview mirror." In these cases, positions on the other side will protect you from adverse movements in the overall market that may take place in advance of the event on which you are seeking to capitalize. I believe that it is critical that you do so because otherwise you run the considerable risk of being blown out of your best ideas due to the idiosyncrasies of the macroeconomic environment; and if you routinely fall victim to this, my friends, you are doing nothing more than spinning your wheels.

At the end of the day, then, unless you have a particularly accurate crystal ball, you're likely to face a choice between the following outcomes with respect to your best ideas: You're going to be either early or late to the party. Most traders have the experience and the savvy to recognize that the latter alternative is unacceptable: Being late means missing the trade altogether. Ergo, for many of your key money-making transactions, it may be necessary to put your position on somewhat in advance of the point at which would have been ideal, from a risk/reward perspective, as viewed after the fact. The immediate attendant consequences are that you are going to have to manage the volatility of the position along with the associated uncertainties as to the correctness of your opinion. If you can master both of these (and if you have, indeed, assessed the situation correctly), then to paraphrase Rudyard Kipling, yours will be the world and all that's in it, and which is more, you'll get paid, my son.

In fact, if you can master both the risk control and the "conviction-based" aspects of being early with your best ideas, you stand not only to monetize them, but also to maximize them through the process of adding to your position at increasingly favorable price levels, an approach comfortingly referred to in the financial markets as *averaging*. Of course, this is a dangerous method, and one that is best practiced only by experienced traders who (1) are pretty damned certain that they are right about the idea in question, (2) have sufficient risk capital to stay the course, and (3) have the skill, experience, and discipline to manage the process effectively. I don't want to put too fine a point on this and will stop short of suggesting the averaging methodology to all but my most sophisticated and highly credentialed readers. However, I do believe that the concept is illustrative of the manner in which the tool kit can work to the advantage of effective risk takers with a true market edge. Also, and perhaps more to the point, a two-sided market orientation is, at minimum, extremely useful to anyone attempting if not to average into a high-conviction position for which the payoff timing is uncertain, then at least to maintain a core exposure.

Let's consider a rather crude example. I've heard (through the grapevine, of course) that you've fallen in love with a small-cap pharmaceutical company called XTC, which you strongly believe is about to receive approval from the Food and Drug Administration (FDA) for a drug that simultaneously cures depression and enhances sexual performance (I know this is far-fetched, but I'm told that such things are, at least in theory, possible). Because you are very thorough, you have carefully studied the clinical trials, have read everything the FDA has said on the topic, have spoken to doctors who say that this is a great breakthrough, and have analyzed the financial numbers thoroughly. Heck, there are even rumors around (though not started by me) that you were part of the clinical trials and had a wonderful experience in the process.

Unquestionably, you've done your homework here, and it appears you do indeed have an edge. But some smart money is betting that the FDA will send XTC back to the drawing board this very month. To make matters worse, as of late, the entire small-cap pharmaceutical market has been trading like some poorly fashioned version of Federico Fellini's *8½*. Finally, the market as a whole is very volatile, and some experts believe it may crash at any time. These things spook you, but you're pretty sure that XTC will get its approval and that when it does the stock should double. The only problem is that you don't know when the approval will be forthcoming.

So how do you stay with this position long enough for the drug to get approved and you to get paid? Well, a long/short approach will certainly help your cause. Perhaps you could pair this position off against a pharmaceutical stock that does not have such a catalyst. Walk a little ways further with me through this tortured example. Picture for yourself another small-cap pharma company, formed out of the merger of two separate pharma concerns, the Lucy Companies and the Skye Corporation, that then acquired a third enterprise, Diamond Pharmaceuticals, to form the Lucy, Skye, and Diamond Corporation. Its ticker symbol is LSD, and it is seeking regulatory approval for a drug that either enables people to fly or makes them think they can (I forget which). Further assume that your research—as thorough as it was on XTC and extending back several decades—indicates that the "federales" are a smidge less keen to approve this particular product. Wouldn't that make a swell pairs trade? If you sold short some LSD and resisted the temptation to liquidate it prematurely, it might enable you to hold your XTC through a full range of overall market and sector-specific conditions while still enabling you to make your big score when XTC did win its approval.

By contrast, if you were holding both XTC and LSD on the long side, the consequences might be much more severe, matters might soon start to get out of control, and there are circumstances when you might have to bail out of both prematurely, which would not be good at all. If there is no LSD (or functional equivalent) available, you might prefer to sell short the DRG index—a sort of smorgasbord (or cocktail, if you prefer) of pharmaceutical concerns that trades as a single security on the American Stock Exchange—to achieve the same ends. Failing this, there's always the opportunity to sell broad-based indexes, such as Standard & Poor's (S&P) 500 futures, which will protect your position in some, if not all, of the types of situations that might otherwise force you to sell XTC before its time.

If you are able to hold XTC through the approval process, you can call it a victory—irrespective of whether you liquidate your LSD, DRG, or S&Ps at a profit or at a loss. When viewed at a safely objective distance from the actual portfolio management process, it is easy to see how a two-sided market orientation, with one side serving largely as instruments of risk control, could offer better risk-adjusted returns than one that focused exclusively on either longs or shorts. Moreover, in these circumstances, it would be logical (and perhaps even in some cases desirable) that the aggregate P/L for the hedging side of the market would be negative. However, in my experience, these factors offer little direct solace to many portfolio managers who often feel the pain of losses on the hedging side much more acutely than they do when the ideas for which they have the highest level of conviction liquidate to negative P/L. So prevalent is this trend that many equity traders with a long orientation are convinced that they are getting killed on the short side of the market—even when their short trades are doing no worse than breaking even or generating modest profits!

I have spent a great deal of time thinking about this phenomenon, and I suspect that the pervasive reluctance of many portfolio managers to operate on the hedge side of the market, along with the associated tendency to experience heightened levels of stress over what they perceive to be losses from this activity, is entirely psychological in nature. In my experience, not only do traders perform much better statistically on the hedge side than they generally believe, but their overall profitability improves with the proper level of attention to hedge-oriented trades in ways that may be difficult to perceive.

My friend Mo, the movie producer, is a perfect example of this type of thinking. As is consistent with his artistic temperament, he had a tendency to fall in love with all of the stocks that he trades. "Fine," I told him over beers one night (I have found over the years that beer and even stronger waters are very useful tools of the risk management trade), "but you'd have a better chance of owning them at the right time if you could find some off-setting shorts, and hang on to them." From time to time, he'd take my advice; but I could always count on him to whine about just how much his daring forays into the short side of the market cost him. When we finally looked at his trading sheets, I'll be damned if the schmuck hadn't actually made money on his shorting! After I finished slapping him upside the head, I made him promise me that he would do two things: (1) Keep shorting, and (2) shut up about it. Of course, he did neither. Looking back at these events, I suspect that Mo's move to Hollywood was just about the best trade he ever made.

Operating a balanced portfolio is a very labor-intensive operation; and in order to do so effectively, it may be necessary to spend the lion's share of your time seeking out appropriate hedges for your portfolio. The process is more difficult than you might currently suspect because, among other things, you need to select a security that will protect you from adverse events without negating your upside when your catalyst plays itself out. What is more, factors that qualify a position as a good hedge are neither identical nor, unfortunately, the mirror opposite of those that characterize your best opportunities. Often the methodology involved in identifying opposite-side market positions designed to reduce your overall exposure is entirely different from that through which you would seek to identify your highest profit positions.

Specifically, the identification of a proper hedge involves the selection of a security not for its likely profitability prospects, but rather for its ability to offer protection against negative outcomes in the market that do not change your fundamental desire to hold the security on which you are focused from a profitability perspective. For example, if you are long GM because you expect an overall rise in auto sales but are fearful of an uptick in interest rates, you might consider an offsetting short in, say, Ford. However, in doing so, you run the risk that Ford benefits by an equal or greater amount than GM if auto sales do spike up. The hedging universe is rife with problems of this nature, and I don't believe it's inaccurate to state that there are almost no situations where even a perfect hedge on paper cannot go badly awry. For these reasons, you may spend more of your time, if you're smart, identifying and analyzing hedge alternatives than you do identifying profit opportunities. Such a time commitment may not be a particularly enjoyable prospect; but if you are able to successfully maintain a two-sided approach toward portfolio management, the prospects for risk-adjusted return across an increasingly high level of capital under management will ultimately justify the extra effort required.

Finally, the most relevant benefit of a balanced long/short market approach for those who practice this art effectively is that it is an effective tool for explicitly controlling portfolio volatilities in a manner that is more or less seamless to their core trading practices. For instance, a long/short equity player wishing to increase his volatility might allow his net exposures to fluctuate more broadly than is the norm, while a trader wishing to dampen her P/L swings would choose to operate within more narrow bands and with a higher degree of balance. In a dual-orientation portfolio, these adjustments occur naturally within the ebb and flow of the portfolio management process. By contrast, if you focus exclusively on one market side or the other, the process of controlling volatility through dynamic hedging is both disruptive and fraught with hazard.

POSITION LEVEL VOLATILITY

Another manner in which traders can directly control the magnitude of their P/L fluctuations is through the strategic inclusion of individual security volatility in their selection criteria. Though the relationship between the volatility of individual securities within a portfolio and that of the portfolio as a whole is a complex one, it is safe to assume that the selection of higher-volatility securities in your portfolio will increase your exposure, whereas the avoidance of these instruments will have a risk-dampening impact. Therefore, during times when you wish to increase market exposures, one alternative at your disposal is to substitute away from securities with low volatility in favor of those with higher volatility characteristics. Similarly, one way to dampen exposure is to effect the opposite type of substitution, replacing highly volatile securities in the portfolio with those that are more stable by standard statistical measures.

While I certainly endorse the concept of both understanding individual security volatility and using this as one factor in your portfolio selection process, it is important to caution against overreliance on this component of your selection methodology. As I have argued, the ideal selection criteria for any given investment opportunity is its incremental impact on prospective risk-adjusted return for the overall portfolio. Stated more simply, it is imperative that you make your decisions on the basis of which opportunities will provide the highest level of incremental return for the amount of incremental exposure assumption they entail. In order to use this selection process as effectively as possible, the decision maker must have a grasp of the volatility characteristics of his or her prospective trades, but he or she also must be aware of the upside opportunities that are implicit in the trade. Indeed, if the true criterion for investment inclusion is risk-adjusted return, then it is as incorrect to make decisions on the basis of volatility characteristics alone as it is solely on the basis of return opportunity. The ideal model incorporates both concepts, and I encourage you to bear this in mind when managing the volatility characteristics of your portfolio.

Also be mindful, as we will discuss in the next chapter, that one very effective means of "normalizing" the exposure in your account is to size your positions according to their volatility. For example, if you buy $1,000 worth of a stock that has a 50% annualized volatility, this, in risk units, is the rough equivalent of spending $2,000 on a stock whose volatility is 25%. Most professional traders use this type of analysis in determining the appropriate size of individual positions within their portfolio, and I encourage you to do the same.

TIME HORIZON

An additional if less intuitive way of managing your portfolio volatility is through the manipulation of your holding periods. Specifically, the longer that you hold positions in your account, the more volatility you are likely to experience. To fully understand this interplay, it is important to recall the relationship between volatility and time, as set forth in previous chapters. In particular, you can convert a daily standard deviation statistic into the appropriate figure for your particular holding period by simply multiplying the percentage-based figure by the square root of the number of days you intend to hold the position. For example, if you plan on holding an individual security with a daily volatility of 1% for 100 days, you would anticipate a standard deviation over this period of 10%.

While the plain implication of this interplay is that your volatility is a direct, positive function of your holding periods, the specifics of this relationship will vary from security to security, from one situation to the next. Herein lies both the opportunity and the hazard. As indicated previously, attempts to deconstruct the risks associated with individual positions into single volatility numbers require us to make certain simplifying assumptions about the manner in which volatility expresses itself in the marketplace that simply don't hold true in real-life situations. The most glaring of these oversimplifications is one that suggests that actual price fluctuations will distribute themselves evenly across time. This, of course, is seldom the case. For example, the previously referenced security with daily volatility of 1% that we intend to hold for 100 days might generate enough price fluctuation within a week or two to account for the entire 10% volatility we would expect over the period. This would be particularly true when information pertinent to the valuation of the security is concentrated within specific dates, such as earnings reports. In these cases (which, by the way, account for the vast majority of market activity), not only the holding period for individual securities will determine how much of the volatility you capture in your trading, but also the timing of your entry and the exit points.

Counterintuitive though it may seem, the idiosyncratic manner in which volatility distributes itself across time actually creates opportunities to control risk through the management of holding periods. As an example, consider the case of the day-trading methodology that has come into mainstream popularity over the past several years: Day traders, by definition, are usually in and out of their positions within a single trading session; and by operating with holding periods that are typically measured in terms of hours, if not minutes, they often miss even the core of single-day volatility that is implicit in our one-day, one-standard-deviation statistic. Thus, by extending their holding periods from intraday to overnight, day traders often stand to increase their exposures by much more than that implied by a simple, linear expansion of their holding periods. Of course, day traders wishing to modify the amount of time they are willing to hold positions for the purpose of *decreasing* their market exposures have much less latitude. Any move to shorten holding periods that already fail to extend beyond one trading session is not likely to reduce the risk of loss in individual securities and may in fact increase it—due to such unavoidable market factors as commissions, bid/offer spreads, and other types of transactions costs.

By contrast, those whose holding periods extend beyond one day have a better opportunity to use this variable as a means of targeting the appropriate exposure levels in their portfolios. Once again, a useful rule of thumb is that your exposure will increase and decrease as a function of the square root of the number of days you hold the position. Thus, the risk associated with holding a position for a week (five trading days) is slightly more than double (i.e., the square root of five) the risk that would be associated with a single day; a position carried for a month would be just over four times the daily amount (i.e., the square root of twenty); and so on. What is more, you can achieve additional refinements to this formula by being mindful of the information calendar, leading to opportunities for adjusting exposure upward and downward as appropriate, around the timing of the release of pertinent market information, such as earnings announcements and economic reports.

Finally, just as there is diminishing risk impact available in the adjustment of high-velocity day trading, so too do the impacts reduce themselves at the other end of the spectrum. Specifically, if your trading style typically involves retaining positions for intervals of several months or longer, the modification of your holding periods by even very large, percentage-based amounts is unlikely to have much of an impact on the management of your exposures. The reason for this is that over longer holding periods, volatility patterns tend to smooth themselves out, converging toward the equilibrium levels that in most cases can be ascertained through close observation of such factors as historical pricing patterns and options implied volatility levels. Under these circumstances, traders and investors are likely to capture the full measure of the volatility inherent in each of the securities they hold in their portfolio. However, it is still possible for long-term investors to use holding periods as a means of controlling exposures, specifically by increasing and decreasing their position sizes around the anticipated release of economic information that may be pertinent to their position profile, as suggested earlier.

DIVERSIFICATION

One proven way to control portfolio exposure is through the manipulation of diversification. While the mathematics of this concept are vague at best, the idea itself is intuitive: The more diverse the portfolio, the lower its risk profile. In turn, diversification itself can be diffused into two separate components: (1) the number of securities included in a given portfolio, and (2) the similarity of the pricing characteristics across these securities.

As is the case with the other methods to adjust portfolio exposure, diversification can be used as a tool for two-way risk control, allowing investors to adjust their risk profiles upward or downward as the specific situation requires. This means that investors wishing to increase their risk profile can accomplish this objective by reducing the number of positions in the portfolio or by selecting securities that have more common pricing characteristics, or some combination of the two. Conversely (and perhaps more typically), diversification can be used as a tool for exposure reduction by a program that features larger numbers of securities and ones with more diverse economic characteristics. To illustrate, an account with a single security obviously is as undiversified as a portfolio can get, whereas one that featured, say, a hundred names across various market sectors would likely display some characteristics of diversification, taking the form of smoother return streams on both the upside and the downside—particularly across longer time horizons, which are more likely to yield a full range of market conditions.

However, while it is easy to maintain a running count of the number of securities held in a given portfolio, establishing the level of pricing similarity between securities is a complex process, often more an art than a science. A good qualitative starting point is the rudimentary economics of the securities themselves. For example, if you are trading equities, you can assume that in order to achieve a meaningful level of diversification, it will be necessary to hold positions across a number of industries—ideally those that are subject to different business cycles. Similarly, if you are trading commodities, a portfolio of materially different asset classes (e.g., grains and energies) is likely to generate higher levels of diversification than one that is focused in a single set of "substitutable" product types (e.g., wheat and corn). These dynamics also carry forward to the remaining segments of global capital markets, most notably fixed income and foreign exchange.

In addition, it is important to be aware of the actual, statistically observable correlations among the securities you are trading, which will be inversely related to the level of diversification you are able to achieve in your portfolio. In other words, the higher the level of correlation among the individual securities in your portfolio, the lower the benefits of diversification you are likely to derive. Intuitively, this makes sense, and the use of correlation analysis is entirely compatible with the fundamental strategy of selecting securities with differing underlying economic characteristics. However, while the qualitative approach to constructing a diversified portfolio may in most cases appear to be sufficient, correlation analysis will add accuracy and precision to the process. Often enough, the apparent commonalities (or lack thereof) among positions in your portfolio will be deceiving, and you will inevitably run into situations where financial instruments that have little or no economic overlap are in fact highly correlated, as well as those where seemingly closely related securities offer widely divergent pricing characteristics. In these cases, quantitative correlation analysis can be of enormous assistance in the development and maintenance of a portfolio diversification profile that is consistent with your objectives for risk-adjusted return.

As a final point, it is important to be mindful of the diminishing benefits of diversification. In particular, as you spread your portfolio over an everwidening set of individual securities, the impact on risk adjustment of the addition or removal of an individual asset will decrease. At some point in the process, the portfolio will take on the characteristics of an index; and the addition (or, for that matter, removal) of individual transactions may actually have the opposite effect of the one that is intended. In addition (and at the risk of stating the obvious), the more positions you have in your portfolio, the more work you have to do with respect to both analysis and position management; and this implies a diminishing edge with every incremental position that you add in the name of diversification. Presumably, if diversification never enters your mind, you will only put on trades that you believe have met the full measure of your criteria for effective return generation. As you add positions in order to diversify, by definition, you begin to relax these criteria. At some point, this will begin to cut into your profit profile; and in extreme cases, you run the risk of obliterating any opportunities you might have otherwise had to make money from your original investment hypothesis.

For these reasons, I suggest that you establish a base level of positions that you are comfortable managing and increase/decrease your diversification levels by nominal amounts as a means of adjusting your exposure at the margin. The selection of this base number of positions is largely a qualitative process for which no formula is likely to generate the appropriate answer. The number should be sufficient to avoid an undue level of position concentration while at the same time allowing you to devote the appropriate level of attention to each individual position. Whether this happy medium can be achieved with 5 positions or 50 is a function of a number of variables, including the complexity of the markets in which you operate, the level of resources you have at your disposal to manage your book, and your own personal portfolio management style. The point is that your use of diversification as a tool of risk control should not cause you to stray from your base number of positions by more than, say, 50%. Thus, if you comfortably manage 5 positions under normal circumstances, your efforts to engineer your diversification should generate a range of as many as 7 or 8 or as few as 2 or 3. Similarly, if your base number is 50, the range might be 25 on the low end and 75 on the high.

LEVERAGE

A widely discussed but often misapplied concept of risk control is that of leverage. Indeed, there has been so much misinformation about leverage in the discussion of financial markets over the years that it is, in many ways, difficult to find the appropriate point for introducing it into our discussion. However, as leverage, when properly measured, is undoubtedly part of the risk management landscape, it is essential for portfolio managers to have at least enough understanding of the concept to enable them to grasp its impact on their portfolio exposures.

Therefore, I begin with a simple definition. For our purposes, *leverage* can be defined as the ratio of the economic value of a given portfolio to the amount of capital available to fund it. Because leverage, no matter how it is defined, is always expressed as a ratio, its level can be controlled through manipulation of both the numerator and the denominator. Specifically, individuals wishing to increase their leverage can do so by either increasing the value of the assets in their portfolio or decreasing the amount of associated capital allocated to fund it, or by some combination of the two. Similarly, a decrease in leverage can be brought about by any combination of reduced asset size and increased capitalization.

As a general rule, leverage and portfolio volatility are positively correlated. However, there is a virtually unlimited set of exceptions to this rule. For example, because the numerator of the leverage calculation is simply the total aggregate value of the positions in the portfolio (i.e., without regard to market direction), a given market-neutral, long/short portfolio with very minimal risk has a higher degree of leverage than one that simply contained the long positions in the same portfolio—*in spite of the fact that the latter is likely to be the more risky market profile.* Beyond this, leverage statistics have vastly different implications across asset classes and across instrument classes within a given asset class. For example, the use of a specified amount of leverage in a fixed-income portfolio will generally have less-acute impacts than will the same profile in equities, due to the fact that equity markets routinely have higher levels of volatility. For identical reasons, within the fixed-income group, leverage will be more impactful at the long end of the yield curve than it will for short-term trading instruments.

Beyond this, certain derivative instrument classes are designed to engineer precise leverage for investors because they offer trade-offs that involve both the cost of the investment and the probability of their bringing about a favorable outcome. Most notable among these is options, which we will discuss in the next section. However, speaking in terms of their implications for leverage, it is important to note that options provide wide ranges of methods for amplifying or reducing leverage, which cannot be characterized in any simple manner for the purposes of understanding their impacts on portfolio exposure.

For complex portfolios that cut across asset and instrument classes, the relationship between leverage and portfolio exposure is a complex one for which no specific formulas are applicable. However, most portfolios are less than complex and have a much narrower and more stable focus. Wherever this is the case, it is a fairly safe assumption that increased leverage translates fairly directly into increased portfolio exposure, and vice versa. From this perspective, leverage is clearly a very useful tool for risk control—provided that whatever steps you take to either lever up or delever your portfolio are undertaken in a balanced manner. Be aware that any actions you take to use leverage to control your risk will have disproportionate impacts if the associated increases or decreases in position sizes are not distributed in a fairly even manner across the entire portfolio. A good rule of thumb is that any leverage-based adjustments should not alter the core economic composition of the portfolio, only the overall size of the investment.

On the whole, it is safe to conclude that manipulation of leverage is one of the more powerful mechanisms at your disposal to manage your exposures: increasing it by some combination of larger position sizes and smaller capital basis, and decreasing it by reduced position sizes or capital injections. However, it is important to be mindful of the constraints that will apply to your leverage activities. If you are trading your personal account, you should really view your leverage exclusively as a function of the total pool of investment capital at your disposal. Any smaller number is really an artificial constraint, and any larger figure implies borrowing: a practice (I strongly discourage) that, while broadening your capital base, actually increases your leverage at any level of investment. If you are trading professionally, using the capital of other individuals and institutions to fund your activities, you should be acutely aware that the capital at your disposal is not a concept you can directly control.

In terms of the ranges of investment sizes available to traders, these are bounded from below by zero and from above (for most markets) by some combination of market regulation, credit considerations, and other external factors. For example, in the U.S. equity markets, it is well-known that Federal Reserve Regulation T limits the size of a given portfolio (calculated on a gross basis as the sum of long and short positions) to twice the amount of capital posted in the account in question. Futures traders are constrained from a leverage perspective by margin requirements, which are ostensibly tied to the amount of volatility inherent in the underlying instrument in question. Over-the-counter derivative leverage is determined contractually by the parties to the transaction and can often significantly exceed the leverage available in exchange-traded markets.

OPTIONALITY

As we just noted, one of the most powerful ways of managing the market exposure for a given portfolio is through the use of options. Indeed, because options can be constructed in so many different ways to address myriad exposures, it is possible to use these instruments to create virtually any type of risk profile that is desired—from those that are very sensitive to movements in underlying securities to those whose value is largely independent of underlying price and instead are tied to other market factors, such as the level of volatility that is perceived to exist within the instrument in question. Moreover, particularly for short sellers of options, there are infinite numbers of strategies for which the associated market exposure is virtually unlimited.

For these reasons, an entire branch of market science has evolved around the concept of options trading, featuring dozens of similar yet distinct pricing models, an extensive set of descriptive diagnostics covering the relationship between a given option and its various inputs (underlying price, volatility of instrument in question, time to expiration, etc.), and so on. Indeed, the options landscape is vast and complex and, for the most part, beyond the scope of this book. However, there are a number of basic options strategies that allow investors to adjust the risks in their portfolios in order to achieve an exposure profile that is better adapted to their investment objectives, and it is therefore important to address these in a simple, straightforward manner.

With this in mind, let's take a look at the specific elements of options trading and investing that render it such a useful tool for risk control and adjustment.

Nonlinear Pricing Dynamics

Options differ from cash securities (and, to a lesser extent, futures) primarily because of the fact that there is a wide range of contingencies that impact the payouts associated with them. The first and certainly among the most important of these are those associated with *time*. No options exist into perpetuity (otherwise their value would in many cases be infinite), and all have fixed expiration dates beyond which they are no longer valid (i.e., the options buyer no longer is entitled to the rights of the option under the terms of the contract). Because of this, options instruments will react differently to pertinent economic information at different points in their life cycle, with more abrupt/less continuous pricing impacts typically occurring at points close to expiration (particularly when the underlying instrument is trading at or near the option's strike price, as further discussed later) and more continuous patterns at earlier dates during the lifetime of the instrument.

Relationship between Strike Price and Underlying Price (Moneyness)

The second critical contributing factor to option nonlinearity is a concept called *moneyness*, or the extent to which the instrument is in or out of the money. To calculate an option's moneyness, you simply need to compare the value of the underlying price to its strike price (i.e., the price at which the underlying instrument will change hands in the event that the holder of the option chooses to exercise it). Options prices will react very differently depending on their associated moneyness—particularly as they approach expiration. Indeed, at expiration, an out-of-the-money option is worth zero, while an in-the-money option is worth the difference between the strike price and the underlying price (this is the option's so-called "intrinsic value"). This dichotomy causes exponential types of movements for options at or near the money as underlying markets change in value and display shifting price dispersion characteristics.

Implied Volatility

We already covered the topic of *implied volatility*, which, as you may recall from Chapter 3, is a useful means of characterizing future volatility, both for the options themselves and for their associated underlying instruments. Because implied volatility is as dynamic a concept as underlying price, it can shift abruptly, often causing discontinuous movements in the price of options that may or may not be consistent with the associated moves in underlying securities. For example, the holders of call options on a stock about to report earnings may find that a positive earnings announcement generates a less favorable price movement than is consistent with the release—due to the market's belief that the stock will be less volatile after this announcement.

Asymmetric Payoff Functions

With most financial instruments, a long position and a short position executed at the same price have pricing characteristics that are of identical magnitude and opposite direction. Not so with options, where the payoff characteristics between buyers and sellers, and thus the associated risk dynamics, diverge widely. In order to understand the underlying causes of this anomaly, it is simply necessary to review the basic dynamics of the transaction.

Under an option transaction, the seller grants the buyer the right, but not the obligation, to execute certain trades under specified conditions at some point in the future. In consideration for these rights, the seller receives a cash premium, which is his to keep and which binds him for the life of the contract to the terms and conditions implied in the option. Once the premium changes hands, external conditions determine the fortunes of the participants.

If, on the one hand the market moves in such a way that benefits the option holder, the benefits may far exceed the associated costs (expressed in the form of premium). These benefits can be monetized in one of two ways: (1) by the sale of the option itself or (2) by taking the position in the underlying markets, through the exercise process. Under these circumstances, the seller of the option is faced with exactly the opposite return dynamics, potentially losing multiples of the premium taken in by virtue of movement in the underlying market.

If, on the other hand, the market moves against the interests of the option holder, the value of the option converges to zero, causing the holder to lose up to the entire value of the premium, which typically translates into profits for the option seller.

The entire range of outcomes can be viewed as one where for the holder of the option, there is unlimited upside, with the downside being confined to the value of the premium. For the seller, the best that can be expected is to retain the premium, while this entity faces theoretically unlimited risk if the market moves against the short option position. This payoff matrix is largely identical to the one experienced between the buyer of insurance policies and the insurers that grant them, and this is why many types of long options strategies are often characterized in terms of the purchase of portfolio insurance.

While the market typically views the selling of options as a far more risky activity than their associated purchase, it is, in my view, hazardous to make broad generalizations in this regard. Indeed, depending on market dynamics, there are certain options strategies (e.g., the purchase of extremely expensive options immediately after a market event) where the risks are in fact much greater on the long side than on the short side, under wide ranges of likely market outcomes. Many of the more experienced short sellers of options employ sophisticated hedging strategies that can mitigate most, if not all, of the key risk factors we've discussed. For these reasons, the use of options is an extremely complex market strategy and one that can often lead to surprising results, even for seasoned market participants. I suggest that you proceed with the appropriate level of caution (some good software wouldn't hurt matters either).

Leverage Characteristics

In addition to the aforementioned characteristics, it should also be pointed out that there are material levels of leverage inherent in virtually all options trading, that the associated leverage characteristics are dynamic and complex, and that (like virtually every other aspect of options trading) the exercise of drawing broad conclusions regarding the relationship between options and leverage is one that is full of hazards. In order to understand this, we must again return to the rudiments of the options trade itself.

Purchasers of options pay premiums in exchange for contingent rights to hold specified amounts of target securities. The premium can be thought of in these cases as invested capital. Many investors like to think of the ratio of the underlying value to this premium as the leverage factor. For example, if an investor paid, say, $1 million for an option to buy $100 million worth of

U.S. Treasury securities, the implied leverage in this transaction is 100 times. However, this leverage, needless to say, has much different risk characteristics than a portfolio that simply takes $1 million and uses it as collateral to purchase $100 million of the same U.S. bonds, with the main difference being that while the holder of the option cannot lose more than the premium he or she invested, anyone invested in cash securities at 100-to-1 leverage can realize losses beyond the level of the investment.

By contrast, short sellers of options are receivers of premium and are often viewed as making no investment and, therefore, achieving infinite leverage on their portfolios. The seller of the U.S. Treasury security option described in the preceding paragraph would be the net recipient of the $1 million in premium and would have exposure to the same $100 million of underlying market risk. However, in most cases, it is entirely erroneous to characterize this as an infinitely levered position. In the first instance, the overwhelming majority of options short sellers (including, in my opinion, all of the smart ones) engage in some type of hedging, whether it involves an offsetting position in the underlying markets, long options positions with risk-mitigating market characteristics, or some combination of the two. As such, there are very few pure "short sellers" of options. Beyond this, every legitimate brokerage firm in the world requires options sellers to post margin ideally equal to the value of the premium plus an amount equal to the likely worst-case loss that the position could experience. Finally, even if the short options portfolio in question is unhedged and uncollateralized, any legitimate market participant would at least set aside sufficient risk capital in order to fund associated losses if the position moves against them.

From these perspectives, we can reasonably conclude that the calculation of a leverage factor for short options portfolios is a complex and ambiguous process that is probably viewed most rationally as a function of both the margin collateral required to fund them and the amount of risk capital rationally allocated to them.

Absent the necessary precautions, the naked short sale of options is in most cases irresponsible and almost always a losing strategy over the long term. However, if incorporated into a sound risk-control program that features some of the components we've mentioned, short selling of options can have more attractive risk-control features than long options programs, which often generate large losses while providing false comfort as to their actual levels of exposure.

To reiterate: Options are mathematically complex and extremely idiosyncratic. Options markets are notorious for packaging certain types of economic attributes on the surface while imposing subtle costs in hidden ways. Therefore, it is critical to proceed with extreme care when entering into an options strategy. First and foremost, this means taking the trouble to understand the full measure of the associated risks. However, risk evaluation is only the beginning. In order to guard perpetually against myriad unforeseen outcomes in options trading, it is also necessary to thoroughly evaluate all transactions costs implications as well, including commissions, bid/offer spreads, and tax considerations.

Because of these complexities, I highly recommend that you seek some sort of partnership with trustworthy and options-savvy individuals before including options in your portfolio mix (even if these are your brokers). Even then, it's best to start out small, carefully evaluating the range of outcomes you experience (both expected and surprising) at small levels of risk capital. Through this process and over time, you'll be in a better position to discern which conditions are most conducive to your success in these markets and which aren't likely to work to your advantage. In turn, this will place you in the best position to incorporate options into your investment activities efficiently and to separate yourself from the untold ranks of those whose use of these markets serves as little more than fodder for market professionals who make a living by simply understanding the inefficiencies with more precision than the masses do.

GREEK ALPHABET SOUP

I am currently working with an equity options trader who uses options to try to capture short-term trading flows in the equity markets—much in the same way a run-of-the-mill short-term U.S. equity trader would with stocks. Equities have been very volatile lately, and he's made a particular effort to keep his portfolio neutral in terms of directional market exposures. The standard way of doing this in options-land is to achieve something called *delta-neutrality*—a condition under which put and call positions (long and short) offset one another in terms of their reaction to moves in underlying markets. He has been quite the zealot about this, and, as such, we were both surprised at how badly he was getting nicked in a recent wicked market rally. On further inspection, we spotted the problem: The options he was holding that had a negative delta (meaning they would tend to move in the direction opposite that of the underlying market—something almost exclusively associated with long puts and short calls) had much higher betas than did his long delta positions (long calls and short puts). As a result, though his overall options position was neutral in terms of raw dollars, due to the beta mismatch, his portfolio had a very deeply embedded short bias. From now on (so I told him and he agreed), he'd have to monitor his beta-adjusted delta position.

Reminds me of that old bumper sticker that remains one of my faves: "My karma ran over my dogma."

SUMMARY

These are just a few of the methodologies available to portfolio managers wishing to seize more direct control of their portfolio exposures. There are others, of course, but those we've covered are the most basic ones available. Moreover, there's precious little, in my experience, in the way of risk control that can't be achieved through the use of these tools. While I caution yet again against overapplication of these tools as a portfolio strategy (while it's relatively easy to get caught up in investment methods that have a primary orientation toward risk control, such an approach is clearly suboptimal to one that features enlightened position selection and execution management), when applied strategically to situations that merit the specific adjustment of portfolio exposure, they can have a significant, positive impact on your experience as an investor.

In closing, while we are moving in a rather linear fashion from a passive, uninformed view of risk management to one that is active, based on the benefits conferred by the power of information, I caution against making changes to your risk profile simply for the purpose of change itself.

In the words of John Milton, "They also serve, who only stand and wait."

CHAPTER 7

The Risk Components of an Individual Trade

Trifles make perfection and perfection is no trifle.
—Michelangelo Buonarti to a friend

Having for the moment exhausted my inventory of anonymous British rockers to exploit, I now ask you to take a journey deeper through the past and to consider the experience of Michelangelo: the man who put the Renaissance in the term "Renaissance man." It is difficult to imagine another individual who so dramatically altered the landscape of human perception in so many diverse and beneficial ways and over such a long, difficult period of time. Forsaken by his benefactors (the Medicis), nearly skewered by the Savonarola, indentured for decades by popes, and disdained by more popular contemporaries (ranging from Leonardo to Raphael), Michelangelo, over his long lifetime, nevertheless succeeded in reinventing the related fields of painting, sculpture, and architecture. Don't expect to draw any direct, market-related wisdom from his example because guys like him don't make great traders. Their minds weren't made for such lowbrow nonsense.

But Michelangelo, toiling away for decades at his craft, focusing on the details of the task—an earthly figure here, a cherub there—until the entire history of creation is told on a ceiling, had given us the gift of some insights that we surely can use. Let's focus our attention now on that most basic component of an investment program: the individual trade. Here, we will attempt to determine whether by focusing on trifles we can add a little dose of perfection to the portfolio management canvas on which we paint.

At the risk of stating the obvious, your trading/investment success can be viewed as nothing more than a financial scorecard of the buy and sell decisions you make in your portfolio, as measured across all asset classes and as weighted by such factors as investment size and market volatility. It follows that whosoever achieves a systematic mastery of the science of trading stands a great chance of achieving even the most ambitious of investment objectives, while those who fail to do so will find themselves at a most bothersome disadvantage in this regard. In turn, if you wish to maximize your performance in the markets, it's important to develop a solid and consistent quantitative handle on your performance at the level of the individual transaction. In this chapter, we discuss ways you can accomplish this task with relative ease.

YOUR TRANSACTION PERFORMANCE

The basic methodology for portfolio review at the trade level involves collecting and analyzing components of your individual transactions, based on aggregation of such pertinent information as time, date, underlying instrument, price, quantity, and counterparty. If you are able to gather this data in a manner that is efficient to the subsequent analysis, as will be described later in this chapter, you can then evaluate it for insights as to the drivers of your success over any given period. It is my experience that this can have important implications for effective portfolio management, enabling those responsible for this process, among other things, to gear their resources toward those components and conditions that are most likely to produce the desired outcomes and away from those tied to their areas of greatest frustration.

The collection of transactions-level information is a more difficult undertaking than the data-gathering processes we've covered so far. Principally, this is due to the size of the task. Many portfolio managers trade very actively, and the practical difficulties associated with collecting multiple data elements for each transaction can be manifold. Also, the information-gathering process can be subjective, even down to the definition of what constitutes a trade. For example, if you buy 100 lots of a position, executing it across 10 trades over several hours, is this 1 trade or 10? Further, if this transaction is viewed as a single trade but has multiple counterparties and prices involved, how can you classify these attributes with consistency?

Transactions-level analysis is rife with bothersome details such as these, but the benefits you can derive from resolving these difficulties render the effort well worth the hassle. To further set your mind at ease on this score, I will begin this chapter by describing a methodology designed to rid you of many of the ambiguities inherent in the exercise. With the appropriate set of assumptions in hand and with an associated commitment to the process, I believe it is possible to analyze your trading decisions and modes of operation in ways that can spotlight correctable inefficiencies and facilitate the scaling-up of unusually effective components, often with significant positive implications for your bottom line.

As has been the case with the rest of our data gathering and analysis, we will begin by establishing the appropriate analytical framework, then attempt to create tools that characterize and measure performance efficiency, and finally point out alternatives for modifying trading/investment behavior when opportunities identified in your transactions-level analytics indicate the need to do so. The first step is one of identifying and maintaining the appropriate data from your trading records.

Key Components of a Transactions-Level Database

In order to perform effective analysis on the transactions that comprise your portfolio, it is plainly necessary to gather and to store all discernable and relevant aspects of the individual trade. The recommended attributes that should be included in the data set are:

- Instrument name.
- Date and time of transaction.
- Buy/sell indicator.
- Price.
- Quantity.
- Executing broker/counterparty.
- Commission.
- Order type (e.g., market, limit, stop, etc.).
- Native currency denomination.

In addition, depending on the type of instrument traded, it may be necessary to record:

- Maturity (for fixed income) or expiration (for futures and options) date.
- Coupon rate and frequency (fixed income).
- Put/call indicator (for options).
- Strike price (for options).

While these informational elements will more or less completely define a given transaction (at least for most types of trading), there are other indirect pieces of information that you need not record for each trade but that will be implicit in the information already gathered and that you should by all means include in your subsequent analysis. These include:

- Asset class.
- Sector designation.
- Security-specific data (volume, correlation, volatility, shares outstanding, etc.).

Again, while it is not necessary to gather and include this information in your database, it is important to be aware of its existence, to identify sources for these statistics, and to set up a framework for subsequent capture of this data. For example, let's assume that for reasons of simplicity or targeted-market advantage, a portfolio manager restricts her universe of securities traded to, say, the Standard & Poor's (S&P) 500. In order to analyze transactions-level performance for this portfolio, it would be useful to know something about the volume of these securities, not to mention their volatilities, betas, sectors, and other market characteristics. However, it would be neither necessary nor indeed efficient to record these statistics every time the portfolio manager executed a trade in one of these names. Rather, this information is best obtained from other sources, including electronic-pricing mechanisms such as Reuters and Bloomberg, as well as financial print publications, such as *Barron's*.

Defining a *Transaction*

As a final consideration in setting up your trade-level analysis tool kit, you must decide what among your transactions activity specifically constitutes a "trade." This is particularly important for active traders (including professionals) who very often maintain a core position in a given security while scaling up and down the exact quantities they are holding at any time on the basis of market conditions. For example, an experienced trader, anticipating a sustained market rally, might put on a core position of 100 S&P 500 futures with the expectation of holding it for several weeks.

However, within this time interval, he might reduce or expand this position as the relative prospects for such a rally become more or less apparent over time. For the purposes of subsequently analyzing this trade, it will be necessary to determine which elements of this sequence fully comprise the transaction. Is it each individual execution? Is it the position as a whole, with each execution folded into it? Perhaps some combination of the two?

Unfortunately, there is no universally correct answer to this question, and there are trade-offs no matter which method you adopt. As a rule, I lean toward an approach under which a *single transaction* is defined as the set of executions that establishes and liquidates a given position without crossing over either from long to short or from short to long. In the preceding example, the unit of the trade would include every execution that comprised the initial position size of 100 lots along with any trades that either increased or reduced the position down until it reached or transcended the zero threshold. If the portfolio manager actually reversed his position during this sequence, the execution that reversed the position would be split into two components: one that took the account down to zero (which would be included as part of the original, initiating trade), and the other that established a new short, with the latter being defined as the beginning of a new trade that would be in place until the account was then flat the position.

This approach has the advantage of grouping into a single transaction all individual executions that were tied to a common theme (in the example provided, a belief that a benchmark index will rally); however, this arguably comes at the expense of some precision. This is particularly true if the portfolio manager believes that the scaling up and down of a trade held for longer durations is strategic enough to merit separate analysis.

If you choose to group your executions in the manner just described, you will need to assign a single price to the transaction in order to perform the types of analyses contemplated in this chapter. You needn't bother being particularly creative here, and the best approach is probably one that is called "weighted average" in the nomenclature of statistics or "volume weighted average price" (VWAP) in the nomenclature of the markets. This number is derived by multiplying the number of shares or contracts by the price, across each execution, summing these figures, and dividing by the overall number of shares or contracts grouped into the transaction. For example, if you buy 30 shares of IBM at 120 and 70 shares at 121, you would multiply 30 by 120 and 70 by 121, add the two products, and divide the total by 100. The result of 120.7 is a good proxy for the average execution price of the transaction.

The alternative approach involves defining each individual execution as a distinct trade. This is the most granular level at which to conduct analysis and arguably offers the highest level of precision. However, this methodology also carries some hazard—particularly for traders putting on larger position sizes who, due to liquidity constraints and other factors, may require several executions in order to establish and liquidate their fully invested position sizes. For instance, in our S&P example, due to price sensitivity, a portfolio manager wishing to establish a long position of 100 contracts might choose to do so across several individual executions, across several hours. In the trader's mind, this may very well be a single transaction; however, when he subsequently attempts to determine its statistical characteristics, it will be impossible to reconstruct it into a unit that is conducive to analysis. Moreover, statistics (which we will describe in greater detail later) such as win/loss ratio, average trade size, and a number of others will be obscured by viewing each execution separately.

For these reasons, it is my view that the former method of grouping all executions tied to the initiation and liquidation of a position in a single name, on a single side of the market, is the preferred one. However, it may very well be worthwhile to engage in some experimentation with both approaches in order to obtain the broadest possible understanding of the statistical characteristics of your trading. Ultimately, you are by far the best judge of what constitutes a transaction within your trading universe. As always, the discovery process itself justifies the effort.

Position Snapshot Statistics

In addition to tracking what happens at the individual transaction level, it is important to apply statistical measures to snapshots of your portfolio as they exist over time. Think of your individual transactions as being brushstrokes on the dynamic canvas that represents your portfolio. From one perspective, its content is best described by the brushstrokes themselves; but from another, the best way to look at it is in terms of what is visible on the canvas at any time. The logical way to review the content of your portfolio is to capture and analyze the individual positions that comprise it on a periodic basis. The ideal frequency for subsequent statistical analysis is daily, as this offers the most precise set of meaningful datapoints; however, even if you do nothing more than analyze your month-end statements, you will find yourself gaining unique and useful insights into the drivers of your success.

The key statistics you will want to retain from routine snapshots of your portfolio are relatively few and entirely intuitive (comprising what you will recognize as a standard position blotter); yet from them, as you will see, emerge myriad interesting analytical opportunities. They include:

- Ticker or instrument name.
- Entry price.
- Current price.
- Entry cost (can be derived).
- Current market value (can be derived).
- Unrealized P/L.

The retention of this information in a database will allow you to create the following time series for subsequent analysis:

- *Dollar Investment in Individual Securities.* Most of us trade the same instruments on a recurring basis. Every day the dollar amount of these investments will change by virtue of price fluctuation alone. The process of trading, of course, adds to the fluctuations. It will be useful to maintain a running total of these position sizes in order to determine subsequently their impact on your return profile.

- *Total Long/Short Capital Utilized.* This figure is simply the amount of dollars invested on the long side of the market across all positions and the total dollars invested on the short side on the same basis. This will also be a useful statistic to maintain in time series form for subsequent analytical purposes.
- *Gross Market Value.* This is defined as the sum of the dollar values of your longs and shorts. Remember to reverse the sign of the short positions so that they are added to your longs, as opposed to subtracted.
- *Net Market Value.* While Gross Market Value is the sum of all positions, long and short, Net Market Value is derived as the difference between longs and shorts. In time series form, this will give you an idea of your tendency to trade with a directional bias as well as of the extent to which this bias shifts over time and across market conditions. In addition to being a useful metric for subsequent analysis, the results you uncover may surprise you.
- *Number of Positions.* This statistic can be measured in terms of long positions or short positions or in aggregate across the portfolio. The number of positions on your sheets is a crude but useful measure of the level of diversification in your portfolio; and by comparing this to the profitability in your account, you stand to learn a great deal about how well this diversification program is working.

As you may very well surmise, it is in your power to combine these core data sets with other position attributes in order to obtain an even clearer and deeper understanding of portfolio dynamics. For example, you may wish to see how each of the listed metrics operates at the sector level or asset group level (e.g., grains versus meats) for commodities. Similarly, you may wish to beta adjust the totals in order to obtain some idea of how volatility and market correlation factors play into your investment decision-making process. I highly encourage these types of second order analyses and believe that they can only expand your knowledge base in ways that are conducive to the objective of increased portfolio efficiency.

CORE TRANSACTIONS-LEVEL STATISTICS

Now that you have set up your transactions-level database, you will find that there is a virtually unlimited set of statistical analyses that are available to you. I don't intend to cover all such analytics in this book. I will focus very directly on a few key themes in order to provide the broadest possible idea of how this data can be processed and interpreted with an eye toward improving performance. We will start with some basic calculations that in and of themselves may not be particularly fascinating but that will serve as the basis for evaluating performance in a manner that cannot be simulated absent this information set. With these basics in place, we will then move toward more complex concepts that hone in on specific aspects of trading performance that might lend themselves to efficiency improvement.

Let's begin at the beginning then, shall we? The first set of statistics you need to gather will not give you great insight on its own, but rather will serve as the basis for subsequent analysis on a more detailed level:

Trade Level P/L

Although we've discussed the P/L time series concept in great detail, we now want to turn to the equally valid methodology of evaluating your relative profitability across individual transactions. The idea here is simply to calculate the profitability of the individual trade, which can be done by either matching up buys and sells of equal quantity or calculating average entry/liquidation prices. This will be a key unit of account for your overall transactions-level analysis.

Holding Period

Also for reasons of subsequent analysis (which will become more apparent later in this chapter), it is important to calculate the time duration of your transactions. This figure can be derived in several different ways, but to me the most accurate approach is one that mirrors our approach to defining an individual transaction, where the holding period is defined as the time interval between the beginning of the initiation of a trade and such time as you have fully liquidated it or reversed its direction from long to short or short to long. The ideal unit of account for this statistic is the number of days; however, for day traders it may be possible to express the holding period in terms of hours or even minutes. This level of specificity is in most cases inefficient, though, as it becomes very difficult to accurately report the precise length of time that a given position is held intraday in your account; the associated statistics are often skewed by such factors as the interval between the time the trade is executed and when it is reported back to you, and even the lags that may exist in terms of recording the transaction in your books and records. For these reasons, I suggest that you express holding periods for your intraday trading in daily units, using either 0 or 1, as appropriate.

These "derived" statistics, along with the transactions attributes that I asked you to collect at the beginning of this chapter, place you on a path toward improved understanding of the trade-level characteristics of the portfolio. The first such bits of information that I recommend you analyze are the following:

Average P/L

This statistic is your total P/L divided by your total number of transactions. While admittedly limited in scope, average P/L can actually have somewhat important implications for understanding overall success levels. First of all, at the risk of stating the obvious, this number can only be positive if your overall P/L is positive; so in this sense, average P/L becomes an absolute indicator of your overall performance. However, beyond this, the evaluation/comparison of your average profitability across different periods of analysis enables you to explore the finer points of your performance more deeply than was possible with tools previously discussed in this book.

Significantly, when comparing results across two periods, you can look independently at both the numerator (total P/L) and the denominator (number of trades) of the equation. Are they moving in a consistent fashion? Does it appear that you are more profitable when you execute more individual trades or fewer trades? If you are more profitable, why? If not, why not? These issues will become increasingly interesting when we add more components to the transactions-level tool kit. However, there is no reason not to look at this data in isolation because it begins to enable you to understand the power of information available to you at the level of the individual trade.

Once you are able to calculate average P/L across the entire portfolio, it may be useful to subdivide the individual observations into various category classifications in order to determine whether there are wide discrepancies across them. It could be extremely edifying, for example, to calculate your average P/L on trades initiated on the long side versus those on the short side in order to determine whether you have a more finely tuned edge based on a specific market direction. You may also want to undertake this exercise across market sectors (e.g., technology versus financials), specific instruments (soy beans versus live cattle), counter parties, modes of execution, and so on. Indeed, there are as many ways of comparing average P/Ls as there are of characterizing individual trades; and later in this chapter, I will introduce the comparison I feel to be the one of single greatest importance: P/L on winning versus losing trades. In the meantime, please take some time out to think about the various ways you might want to parse out the average P/L statistic, as this alone will get you thinking about the subcomponents of your portfolio management process for which greater mastery can often lead to increased portfolio efficiency and, in turn, to greater profits.

Finally, it is important to note that you can calculate average P/L both gross and net of commissions; and by comparing these two results, you begin to determine how much commission costs are cutting into your overall profitability.

P/L per Dollar Invested (Weighted Average P/L)

This is simply the calculation described prior with the denominator weighted by the dollars invested in each transaction. For example, if your transactions history contains nothing more than two transactions—a $50,000 investment in Security A and a $100,000 investment in Security B— your weighted average P/L would differ from your average P/L in that the latter would equally weight the two transactions, whereas the former would assign twice the weight to the trade in Security B.

By calculating a weighted average, we obtain a sense of the relative return on investment associated with the portfolio at the transactions level. This offers a slightly different perspective than the simple average P/L calculation. For example, if you make $10,000 on both Securities A and B, your average P/L would be $10,000, but your weighted average P/L would only be two-thirds of this amount—a reflection of the fact that a dollar invested in Security B only generated half the returns associated with your Security A investment. It's important to compare and contrast these figures. If, for instance, the weighted average is lower than the simple average, it may be an indication of inefficient sizing of positions. Needless to say, you can also play around as much as you want with these statistics by grouping your transactions data into subcategories and comparing and contrasting weighted and simple averages across these narrower information sets and by other similar tactics.

Average Holding Period

Just as you can translate P/L figures on individual trades into portfolio-wide averages, so too can you apply the same concept to holding periods. Here, however, weighting each observation by transaction size takes on added importance. Also similar to average P/L, it is very instructive to break down your portfolio into various categories in order to determine whether there is a broad disparity in your approach as defined in these terms.

An equity trader may find, for example, that his or her holding periods are significantly longer for short positions than for longs; and in my opinion, such a discovery might very well be worth further evaluation and analysis. You may learn, by way of further illustration, that this is attributable to the fact that most of the short positions in the portfolio are hedges, having a more generic quality, and are used specifically to guard against the event risk of an abrupt, marketwide downturn. These may not be tied to specific catalysts and, in fact, may remain on a more consistent basis in your portfolio thereby creating a condition of extended holding periods on the short side. Or it may be that the short positions in a given portfolio simply tend to carry hypotheses that require longer time intervals to play themselves out. Finally, the pattern could indicate an entirely unintended bias. In any case, it is worthwhile to understand these things with an eye toward ensuring that you are actively managing all controllable elements of the investment process and making adjustments whenever they are most likely to add efficiency to the entire mechanism.

P/L by Security (P/L Attribution)

Professional and part-time traders must try to understand where they made and lost money on an individual names basis. Typically, professionals will receive this information from their firms on a routine (e.g., monthly) basis. Most brokerage firms supply this information to individual investors if not in the form of monthly brokerage statements then certainly by request. I think it is important to scrutinize this information for insights that it may provide into where you can allocate your trading capital for maximum efficiency. For example, securities traders may find themselves trading a certain set of names more efficiently than others, and these trends will become apparent through a basic but comprehensive P/L attribution analysis. The same pattern may emerge for futures traders. Take a close look at these figures. Does anything in particular jump out at you? Are there similarities across the names where you are making the most money? What about the big losers? The results may tell you a great deal about which parts of the market offer better money-making opportunities than others.

Equity traders often operate more effectively in certain sectors than others. Certainly, when we review the big technology run-up of the late 1990s, it is common knowledge that most individual investors who were generating great returns were doing so in technology names such as Yahoo! and Amazon.com rather than in more earthbound parts of the market, such as auto manufacturers and real estate investment trusts. Similarly, futures traders may demonstrate a big edge in trading, say, interest-rate products such as bonds and eurodollars, while performing much less effectively in agricultural products, foreign exchange instruments, or equity indexes. If such a pattern is discernible in your own trading, it is useful to examine the range of potential underlying causes. Are you performing better or worse in markets that you understand better from a fundamental perspective? In markets that are rallying or breaking badly? In markets experiencing certain volatility patterns (e.g., highly volatile versus relatively stable)? Whenever you can form such hypotheses, it may be worth your while to test them by deploying additional incremental capital where you are operating effectively, perhaps at the expense of areas of the market where you are not.

In addition, it makes sense to compare your P/L attribution across periods of varying performance. Take a look at returns in individual names during periods of maximum success and compare them to your returns on a security-level basis during more difficult market intervals. Is your underperformance concentrated in what are traditionally your most profitable names, or did large losses in other tickers reduce your profitability? By keeping track of these patterns, you should be in a stronger position to efficiently allocate your capital, manage your exposures, and do all of those other things that I have argued are essential to maximizing profits.

Long Side P/L versus Short Side P/L

It is equally important, in my view, to examine your performance on transactions where you have bought into the market presumably expecting it to go up versus transactions where you have established a short position, presumably anticipating the market to go down. As we have discussed, I believe that trading on both sides of the market is important, from both a risk-management and a market-opportunity perspective.

There are multiple methodologies for two-sided trading; and factors such as the nature of the markets in which you are participating as well as your own biases and orientations will determine the manner in which you attack this challenge. One common approach is to allow your directional market bias to show itself unencumbered and to then use positions on the other side of the market to provide a hedge. This is often the way that participants in the equity market operate: hoping to make most of their money by identifying securities they expect to go up in value, and using the short side of the market by and large as a means of hedging out their exposures.

Other methodologies, including the so-called relative value trading, involve identifying two similar market instruments that appear to be mispriced in relation to one another and buying the one that is undervalued while selling the one that is overvalued. Finally, there is a highly effective methodology that involves bona fide position selection on both sides of the market and that seeks to capture revenues not on a relative basis but rather on an absolute, position-by-position basis. This methodology is common among hedge funds that seek to be uncorrelated to the underlying markets.

The manner in which you interpret your long-side versus short-side performance statistics should, of course, depend entirely on the methodologies you are using for dual-orientation trading. For example, if you are an equity trader who buys stocks and uses the short side purely for hedging purposes, you would expect the overwhelming majority of your P/L to derive from the long side of the market. In fact, I would argue that if, using this methodology, you saw most of your profitability tied to short-side positions that are intended primarily to dampen exposures, it would provide a strong indication that something in your model is not working correctly. By contrast, if you are a relative-value trader or if your methodology involves pure two-sided position selection for absolute return, you would have reason to hope that your profitability would be balanced across both sides of the market.

However, as with other elements of our statistical tool kit, the purpose of quantifying and comparing your long-side P/L with your short-side P/L is not to determine how well you fit into some textbook template of portfolio strategies, but rather to offer yourself the ability to ask subsequent questions that will enable you to better understand the workings of your portfolio management system as a whole. Once you have calculated the basic statistic, you may find it useful to delve more deeply into your analysis, perhaps grouping your results into the following two-by-two matrix:

Winners	Losers
Long-side	Short-side
Short-side	Long-side

Take a look at the individual names that fall into each of these boxes. Is there a common, identifiable thread within each of them? Is there something similar about winning/losing trades in general (long or short)? How about long/short trades (winners or losers)? Perhaps they fall into a specific sector or asset class. Perhaps there is something common about their modes of execution, holding periods, market conditions at the time of position entry, or other factors. If so, you can then ask yourself a number of additional questions, including: Are these patterns consistent with your core portfolio management strategies (as you understand them)? Do they highlight inefficiencies that you can perhaps improve in, say, the execution or risk-control processes? Only when you begin to solve these mysteries (and I am betting that even if they don't lead to magnificent paradigm shifts in your methodologies, they will take you on a discovery process that is bound to be beneficial to your efforts as a whole) are you ready to unleash the full power of diagnostic portfolio analysis on your trading prowess.

In addition, it may be very useful to mix and match this statistic with other elements of your statistical analysis for even deeper insight into portfolio dynamics. For example, you may want to look at your long/short P/L by market sector, by length of holding periods, and by other transactions components. There is a virtually unlimited number of combinations you can examine in this regard, and I believe you'll find the results to be instructive.

Finally, as is the case with other statistical tools, it is useful to compare long/short performance across periods of relative success. Oftentimes, I have found that these types of exercises help identify concentrated areas of underperformance within a portfolio. You may find that during difficult periods any one of the four boxes in the matrix shown on page 167 may represent a disproportionate percentage of the underperformance; and in each case this would provide an opportunity to answer additional important questions regarding your results. You may wish to ask yourself why your long-side winners are not producing the gains that they once generated. By the same token, you may discover that your short-side losses are deeper than they were during periods of peak accuracy. Can you tie these trends back to conditions in the market; perhaps to some change in your selection, execution, and risk management methodologies; perhaps to some combination of the foregoing?

CORRELATION ANALYSIS

In preceding sections, I have described a data collection methodology that will enable users to analyze many aspects of their portfolio activity as it is measured in terms of both individual transactions and the investment profiles that are created by these trades. We will now review some of these statistics in combination with the time series tools that we covered earlier to unleash a truly mind-blowing analytical cocktail that ties portfolio construction to performance efficiency.

While it is possible to apply complex statistical tools to this task, for our purposes we will focus on correlation analysis as a proxy for the types of predictive modeling that can be accomplished with more complex statistical methodologies. Recall the correlation analysis from the previous chapters in which we used it to compare profitability patterns with external phenomena such as the returns to equity benchmarks, including the S&P 500 and others. While that type of analysis is essential to an understanding of portfolio dynamics, it is only broadly descriptive in nature. For instance, you can always try to adjust your correlation patterns to the indicative benchmark indexes you have identified. However, you can only accomplish this indirectly, by changing the decision-making components of your portfolio management activities that you suspect are causing you to exhibit these patterns; and this is a path that is fraught with the potential for error.

Let's look at an illustration: As a net buyer of equity securities, you might find that your correlation to the S&P 500 index is higher than you would view as ideal and, in response, might try to dampen this correlation by running a more balanced portfolio, reducing the market sensitivity of the securities you are trading and other similar matters. This may reduce your correlation to the broader equity markets (on the other hand, it may not), but perhaps at the expense of a portion of your profitability.

By contrast, the correlation analysis I recommend in this chapter is one that compares your performance to the actual decisions you make in the portfolio management process. Correcting a portfolio management correlation pattern that appears to be suboptimal will not necessarily lead to unilateral increases in success (more about this shortly). Targeted intervention based on the type of correlation analysis featured here, rather than that associated with standard portfolio correlation statistics such as beta calculations and the like, will in all probability give you a better chance for success.

Because the concept of correlation can be confusing, it is important both to review its basic premise and to establish a useful framework for analyzing its results. *Correlation* is a measure of similarity between two variables—across a series of independent data points. Typically in financial analysis, these data points fall across points in time, and this will be the core but not exclusive focus of our discussions here. Financial variables that display consistently similar patterns across time or other factors can reasonably be thought of as being interrelated in some manner. Either one is a predictor of the other, or both are driven by a similar set of independent dynamics. However, please note that correlations can also be negative, indicating that although the behaviors of the variables are interconnected, the factors that drive them tend to have opposite impacts on their paths across time.

For example, one might expect the price of wheat and the price of corn to be highly correlated, due not only to the fact that both are consumable grains but also to their common reliance on everything from weather conditions to the cost of farm raw materials to the global demand for food products. In a similar sense, the correlation between gold prices and the level of the Dow Jones Industrial Average has, over broad periods of history, been strongly negative because investors have typically driven up the price of gold as a safe haven for their capital when equity market prices are declining or are expected to do so shortly. Finally, there are wide ranges of financial variables that are wholly uncorrelated, suggesting a complete absence of a relationship among the variables. For example, there's no reason to believe that there are any statistical commonalities between, say, the Swedish rate of inflation and the price of silkworms in Malaysia; and over time we would expect a correlation between these two variables to be roughly zero.

In terms of magnitudes, the *correlation coefficient* has a maximum value of 1.0, or 100%, indicating perfect correlation (e.g., the temperature in Toronto as measured in Fahrenheit and Celsius), and a minimum value of −1.0, or −100%, indicating perfect negative correlation (e.g., the price of a zero-coupon bond and its yield). All values in between are valid, and the process lends itself to all the subjectivity that the human mind can muster. However, you may find the following (admittedly simplistic) rules of thumb to be useful:

Value of Correlation Coefficient	Interpretation
Less than −50%	High negative correlation—merits full investigation.
Between −50% and −10%	Material negative correlation—take a look.
Between −10% and +10%	Statistically insignificant—ignore.
Between +10% and +50%	Material correlation—take a look.
Greater than +50%	High correlation—merits full investigation.

The following topics constitute a subset of the types of correlation analyses that you can calculate between your own portfolio patterns and your profitability.

Number of Daily Transactions

This analysis will give you some idea as to whether your profitability increases or decreases with your level of trading activity. In my experience, the outcome will vary from account to account and across such factors as basic trading strategy and external market conditions. If the number is materially positive, it suggests that for the period of analysis your active engagement in the markets (as we have argued earlier can only be fully manifested through actual trading) is a positive contributor to your overall success. I suspect that this is true for most market participants who tend to be less active in their actual trading than is absolutely conducive to their maximum success. Thus, I believe that in most cases a sustained, positive, and material correlation between the number of trades you do and your profitability should induce you to trade more. Get active in the markets, act on your instincts when putting your positions on, and be quick to reverse your course when you're wrong. In addition to potentially increasing the number of profitable trades you experience, I'm guessing that the effort will also produce benefits in terms of enhancing your market insight, honing your executions and risk-control edge, and in general improving your portfolio management skills.

However, there are points of diminishing and even negative returns to this process that become apparent through negative correlations between trading activity and P/L. If this applies to your portfolio management activities, it gives rise to the possibility that you are overtrading. Typically, this only happens in the case of truly hyperactive accounts, but it is a condition to guard against nevertheless. Day traders (online or otherwise) might be particularly susceptible to this and should consider performing this analysis in particular when trading at a very high velocity but underperforming in terms of the bottom line. When this happens, I suggest you take the opportunity to slow down a bit (how's that for an intellectually daring recommendation?). Review your activity on a trade-by-trade basis. I'm guessing that a whole bunch of superfluous transactions are staring you right in the face. From there, the next logical step is simply to place a slightly tighter filter on what constitutes an actionable idea. You'll know pretty quickly if the filter program is working by virtue of (1) whether the negative correlations patterns diminish, and, more important, (2) whether your profitability rises.

Capital Invested

This correlation statistic measures the level at which your profitability is either a positive or a negative function of the actual amount of dollars you are putting to work in the marketplace. In many ways, this is among the most important measures of your overall success: While a positive correlation between capital utilization and P/L suggests that you are doing a good job of using your financial resources effectively, based on market opportunities, any other outcome suggests portfolio inefficiencies. At minimum, a nonmaterial correlation indicates that you are not doing as good a job as you might of putting capital to work when opportunities are at their greatest. What is worse, if the correlation is meaningfully negative, it suggests that the more capital you deploy in the markets, the worse your performance. This is plainly a less-than-desirable outcome that bears full-scale examination.

If the results of this analysis are favorable, it should boost your confidence to assume risk in situations where your conviction about your positions is high. One way or another, you are reading the markets with some degree of accuracy, and this is something you can build on. Trust your instincts here by increasing your size in your favorite trades. The data indicates that the outcomes will be favorable on the whole. Similarly, you should take the positive correlation statistic as an indication that if you don't see sufficient opportunity in the markets, it's probably a good idea to be underinvested. Again, the data indicates that your instincts are serving as your ally in this regard.

By contrast, if the correlations are low or negative, then it's time to reevaluate the way in which you are sizing your positions. If this pattern occurs during periods of profitability, it suggests that you are capturing some market inefficiencies and simply not doing a great job of identifying the relative quality of the opportunities you are trading. By definition, it implies that the correct calls you made were ones where you didn't have maximum dollar investments involved and that your biggest winners were in names where you had a good deal of capital invested but the position didn't actually move that much. I suggest that you carefully examine the individual trades that comprise this dichotomy. I'm guessing that you will see patterns that are correctible in terms of the sizing of your bets.

If you are experiencing the worst possible combination of negative returns that are negatively correlated to the amount of capital you are deploying, it's probably an indication that something is fundamentally wrong with your entire trading/investment program. Perhaps the markets have changed, or perhaps your portfolio management dynamics are not conducive to profitability. Take a good, hard look here because, needless to say, this is not a pattern that you will be able to sustain for long periods of time—unless you have infinite amounts of capital at your disposal (which you do not).

Net Market Value (Raw)

In addition to calculating correlations between your P/L and various benchmark indexes, such as the S&P 500, you can determine the extent to which your fortunes are tied to those of the underlying markets by calculating a correlation between your returns and the net market value in your portfolio at any given time. If this correlation is strongly positive, it suggests that you do better when your portfolio has most of its positions on the long side of the market and that your bias is toward the net purchase of securities (as opposed to their net sale). By contrast, if the correlation is strongly negative, it indicates that you have a short bias, preferring to operate with short positions as your key themes. Finally, if this correlation result is statistically insignificant, it means that there are no specific directional biases in your portfolio strategy.

As you may well surmise, the zero/low correlation outcome is probably the one that is most conducive to stable, scalable profitability across full ranges of market conditions. While you should never orient your methodology toward any goal other than risk-adjusted return, obtaining a benign correlation between your P/L and portfolio net market value may be a useful subobjective. If you have high correlations to net market value, understand that your strategy is geared toward directional market bets, which, as a general rule, tend to be more volatile than balanced portfolio strategies. Take a look at the side of the market that is opposite from the one that the analysis suggests is your strong side, and see if there are any opportunities to incorporate positions without damaging your profitability. If you can find these, your largest losses are likely to be lesser in terms of magnitude and frequency. Further, as this phenomenon evolves, it places you in a more confident position to deploy more capital. Remember that portfolio strategies that dampen direct market exposure are almost always more scalable than those that embrace a market bias. Whether it's your own capital or someone else's, the more neutrality you can achieve, the more your business can grow.

Net Market Value (Absolute Value)

As a slight wrinkle to the net market value correlation analysis, I have found it useful to calculate a correlation between P/L and *absolute net market value*, defined as your net position in dollar terms with the sign convention removed. For example, a net market value of $1 million, whether positive or negative, would be expressed in the time series as $1 million.

Your P/L correlation to absolute net market value will give you a slightly different insight into portfolio dynamics than your correlation to raw net market value will. Specifically, rather than telling you whether you do better or worse depending on how bullish or bearish you might be, it tells you the extent to which you perform better or worse depending on the level of balance that exists in your portfolio. If the correlation is high, it suggests that you do better when your entire portfolio is a directional bet (long or short) on the markets. A negative correlation suggests that your performance improves along with its level of market neutrality. A low correlation of either sign indicates that these factors don't have a great impact one way or another.

Because directional bets tend to carry more event risk than portfolios that retain a measure of balance do, it is my view that negative correlation is probably the best outcome. Such a result suggests that your exposures are more targeted to specific ideas you have about the securities you are trading, and these types of edges are the ones that tend to be the most effective of them all. However, beyond this, it also means that you are doing well under portfolio constructs that are likely to minimize your exposure to market crashes or frenzied rallies such as those that drove the

path of the Nasdaq Composite to above 5000 early in the year 2000. You
may still get hurt when the market moves dramatically in one direction or
the other, but the impact is likely to be dampened relative to that of a portfolio that is entirely loaded up on one side or the other. Moreover, if you
put the effort into portfolio construction that features two-sided position
selection (as opposed to one side being primarily comprised of hedging
positions), then the protection you achieve from sharp market corrections
is not likely to come at the expense of portfolio returns. Finally, balanced
portfolios are entirely more scalable than are directional ones because
there is a much more binding constraint to the amount of risk the capital
provider should be willing to take in accounts whose fortunes are so
directly tied to the idiosyncrasies of the market.

The purpose of correlation analysis is to provide insights into dynamics that aren't immediately observable, not to create objectives or to divert
your goals away from risk-adjusted return. If you happen to have a high net
market value correlation statistic and things are working well on a consistent basis, do not be too greatly troubled on this score. Be mindful of the
condition, but don't reorient an approach that is otherwise succeeding to
achieve a different result on a secondary statistic. If things start going
badly for you and the condition persists, perhaps there's an opportunity to
dig deeper into the net market value correlation. Otherwise, don't fix what
ain't broke.

Number of Positions

As one measure of the effectiveness of your diversification program, you
may wish to examine the extent to which your portfolio performs better or
worse as the number of names you have on the sheets increases and
decreases. As follows the pattern observed with other elements of correlation analysis, a high positive correlation implies that you do better with
more investments on the books rather than fewer; a high negative correlation suggests the opposite; and a modest result of either sign indicates that
your portfolio is not impacted by the number of investments you are holding at any given time.

As you may very well surmise, there is no ideal number of positions
other than the one that is most conducive to your own maximum profitability. For this reason, the *number of positions* correlation statistic may
be of most use to you in trying to pinpoint some of the causes for periods
of underperformance. When things are not going well in your account, you
may wish to see if there is a trend away from the equilibrium number of
names in the portfolio, as well as an associated opportunity to apply corrective techniques to help stem the tide of reversals. This could mean
increased portfolio decentralization. Your risks may be concentrated too

dramatically in a handful of positions—particularly during periods of highly volatile pricing conditions where even your best ideas are subject to the whims of the broader market. Or you might discover that a large number of the positions you are holding in your account are doing very little but taking up space on your blotter and using up capital that might be better either held in cash (either earning interest or saved for future opportunities) or used to increase your size in the positions where you bear a higher degree of conviction. Correlation analysis can help uncover these patterns, but the manner in which you react to either take advantage of them or adjust them is the main challenge that confronts you. Try small, controlled experiments when adjusting your portfolio strategies, and use statistics to measure the results. This may cost you a bit of money in the short run, but it will stretch you as a portfolio manager in many invaluable ways over the longer term.

Holding Periods

Another extremely interesting correlation pattern is the one between P/L and holding periods. Do you tend to do better when you are maintaining positions over longer time horizons, or do extended holding periods work against you? Correlation analysis can help you answer this question and perhaps provide opportunities for improved portfolio efficiency. Positive correlation suggests that your performance improves the longer you hold onto positions, while negative correlation indicates the precise opposite relationship.

Because the timing of entry and exit points is perhaps as difficult as any of the portfolio management arts, this is one of the more important correlation statistics to analyze. In fact, in my experience I have found that it is almost impossible to perfectly time the markets on a consistent basis and that even the best traders in the world have to work very hard to approach maximum efficiency in this aspect of their activities. It is very easy to be either too quick or too slow (and sometimes both) with your liquidation, and correlation analysis can help you pinpoint these patterns. For example, day traders often fail to capture the full set of opportunities available to them—due to a desire to take quick profits and use trading velocity to minimize losses. While day trading can be a very effective strategy, those who engage in it may well benefit by an understanding of the magnitudes of their holding periods and of associated impacts on profitability. If you measure your holding period in minutes (as many day traders do), you may not be giving yourself enough time in your positions to capture the price movement you anticipate. This would be consistent with one of a high, positive correlation to your holding periods. If you find this type of pattern in your own account, then I strongly encourage you to seek methodologies for extending the amount of time you maintain key positions. For most, the major obstacle faced is a laudable desire to control exposures by adhering to a discipline that implies position liquidation in the face of adverse price fluctuation of any magnitude. In order to allow for sufficient time to capture positive trends while at the same time maintaining this discipline, I suggest you measure your holding periods in terms of price movement, rather than hours, minutes, or days. Commit to a stop and an objective for each transaction, and try holding on until one or the other price target is breached. By doing so, you will have limited your downside to an amount that you specified beforehand as being the maximum level of pain you are willing to take in the trade. Similarly, if the transaction works out the way you would have hoped, by liquidating when the security reaches your objective price target, you will lock in profits that may elude traders and investors who for whatever reason cannot bring themselves to liquidate positions in a timely fashion.

I highly recommend that you size positions such that the dollar loss associated with an adverse move is an amount that you are comfortable losing. If your position reaches either its objective or its stop level, be very compulsive about liquidating it. Because most rational traders will put positions on where the realistic target gains exceed their stop-associated losses, I'm guessing that if you're right even close to half the time, the overall result will be positive. Finally, it is important to keep track of your performance on transactions to which you have applied this methodology. I suspect that your results will be favorable. But if they're not, then by all means establish an amount you are willing to lose under this modified trading approach; and if you hit this level, go back to what was working best.

While day traders tend to experience positive correlations with their holding periods, most of us who are not engaged perpetually in the markets fall into the opposite prototype. Typically, we hold onto our positions—particularly losers—for too, too long and tend to bleed cash (through inertia) that could be better deployed anywhere else but in positions that are working against us for an extended period. This is even the case with top-tier portfolio managers who may have great portfolio ideas but who, if not careful, run the risk of neglecting longer-term positions for which, best case, the arguments in favor of the original theme have deteriorated. Moreover, even your profitable trades can turn into mediocre ones when you don't find the appropriate exit point.

In general, when your returns have a negative correlation to your holding periods, it is an indication that your positions are no longer subject to the underlying economics that caused you to put the trade on in the first place. In these cases, the appropriate question to ask yourself is not whether the trade has a chance to work as you initially anticipated, but instead whether you would initiate the position at prevailing price levels today with your unutilized capital. If the answer is yes, by all means maintain the position; however, if the answer is no, liquidate it.

The use of the stop/objective methodology for all transactions can be important in the management of the position liquidation process for those who suffer from a negative P/L holding-period correlation. They should establish a target price on the positive side and a stop-out level on the downside for every transaction they execute, just as was the case with the day traders. As previously indicated, the target gains should in every case exceed the maximum allowable loss, or the trade is probably not worth doing (unless, of course, a high probability of success changes this relationship significantly). Stick to the discipline and liquidate positions if either level is breached. Note that you may still believe in the idea in these instances—that you were right either about a loser that you are sure will turn around or about a winner that still has upside beyond your original target. In these cases, it is your prerogative to simply reestablish the position. This will increase your transaction costs, but you stand to recoup these incremental expenses many times over by ensuring that every dime of the capital you are deploying is in positions that apply directly to your investment hypotheses.

Finally, if you are a trader with long-term holding horizons, you may wish to establish an absolute time limit on certain positions to supplement your stop/objective regime. If a position operates inbetween your target pricing band for excessive periods of time, then the likelihood of your hypotheses working as you expected them to is pretty minimal in my view. Over time, the purging of such aged position inventory will allow you to deploy your capital more efficiently.

Volatility/VaR

One very efficient way of determining whether you are effectively reading the ebbs and flows of the market is to measure the correlation between your P/L and the *volatility* in your account. All things being equal, positive correlation would be a desirable outcome because, in the best of circumstances, you will want to have your maximum risk position in place during market intervals that coincide with the greatest opportunities. Therefore, a positive correlation with volatility becomes a barometer of your ability to identify optimal opportunities and to seize on them through activity in your portfolio. However, as long as your account performs well from a risk-adjusted return perspective, you shouldn't be too troubled if your returns are negatively correlated to measures of volatility because, among other things, this may simply reflect a tendency to perform better during externally stable market conditions.

As indicated in previous chapters, there are a number of ways to measure portfolio volatility, with the most precise of these (at least in my view) being the actual standard deviation of daily returns. In order to determine the extent to which higher levels of volatility measured in these terms coincide with intervals of outsized profitability, it may be useful to introduce a lagging component into the mix. *Lagging* is a common statistical technique, which is used extensively in correlation analysis and predictive modeling, under which observations from one time series are not matched directly with data points that correspond in time with the other, but rather are lined up against subsequent points in the data series. For example, when determining the impact of your caloric intake with your weight, you may want to correlate yesterday's calories with today's readings on the scale, and so on. Of course, my weight is positively correlated to virtually every random variable in the universe—lagged or otherwise—so this may not be an ideal example.

In terms of the relationship between volatility and return, it may be useful to calculate a correlation coefficient between yesterday's measure of volatility and today's returns. The argument here is that there is a nominal time lag between the point at which you increase the risk of your portfolio and the time when you can measure corresponding impacts on portfolio return. Stated in an alternative fashion, there's likely to be less of an impact on today's P/L to changes you make in your risk profile than there is on tomorrow's P/L. Apart from applying a time lag to the data, it is also possible to capture the sequential impact of risk adjustments on returns by using not the standard deviation of returns as your benchmark, but rather statistics produced by a Value at Risk (VaR) model.

Recall from the earlier discussion on VaR that its precise intent is to *predict* the volatility of portfolios based on the way that their pricing patterns have shown them to react over historical market intervals. Therefore, today's VaR (assuming the program is performing its core tasks with a minimal competence) is a measure of today's risk, and this eliminates the need for applying a lagging operation on the data series.

Unlike the case with several of the other correlation statistics covered in this chapter, I can't offer very many useful strategies for adjusting your portfolio management activities in order to address a suboptimal correlation pattern between P/L and volatility. Strong, positive correlation results suggest that you are doing a very good job of allocating your risk capital to those situations that offer the best opportunities. However, it's not entirely certain that it implies the need for dramatic adjustments to your portfolio management program. It may simply be that calmer markets and lower risk profiles are just a better proposition for you. The best option, in my view, is to use correlation analysis to increase your understanding of risk and reward as it pertains specifically to your portfolio. If the correlations in this regard are high, perhaps you should use this as a pretext for increasing your confidence (and perhaps your market participation) during highly volatile market intervals where you have strong conviction about your ideas. History shows you are likely to do pretty well here. Conversely, if your correlations are strongly negative (and your P/L is still positive), it argues for capping your risk levels and for adjusting them downward when market conditions cause volatility to drift upward independent of any portfolio activity on your account. Finally, if your correlations are negative along with your P/L, it's probably time to take a critical look at your overall trading program. Be careful here because something very basic is not working, and the worst thing you can do is apply more risk to markets for which the data is giving you clear signals that you don't understand.

Other Correlations

There are many supplementary correlation analyses that you can perform against your trading statistics that will offer insights similar to those available through the analyses we've covered: P/L to average position size, to commission dollars paid, to the value of unrealized P/L in your account at any given point in time, and so on. These and others may offer interesting perspectives not discussed in this chapter, and I hope you'll try a few—just for kicks. Think carefully about the implications of the results as in most cases intuition will be your best guide as to what to make of them.

Final Word on Correlation

I caution you, yet again, against reading too much into the implications of the results. Correlation analysis is a very useful descriptive statistic, but it is an imprecise predictive mechanism. As such, I can't stress strongly enough the age-old adage admonishing us not to confuse correlation with causation. The goal here is to gain insight into those elements of your routine trading program that are most likely to bring you success in your quest for risk adjusted return and into those that are causing inefficiencies that can at least be managed, if not altogether corrected.

Remember that, due to the extraordinary amount of complexity that is involved in the portfolio management process, any change you make to your program designed to address an anomaly uncovered by these types of statistical analyses may very well have implications for other elements of your methodologies that could offset the potential benefits you seek through the change. For example, if you attempt to reduce your holding periods to address a negative correlation with P/L, this reduction may end up impacting your win/loss ratio, your capital usage, and any number of other factors. The end result may be that the very steps you take to improve efficiency in one aspect of your trading may have undeterminable implications for the rest of your routine; and for this reason, you need to be extremely careful in interpreting too literally the outcome of the statistics tools provided in this section.

TANK MANEUVERS

There are guys out there, very smart ones mostly, who know they need discipline in their trading and don't entirely trust themselves to adhere to what's good for them. A guy who falls into this category (call him John) once described to me a system he built, called The Tank, that was designed to save him from, well, himself.

The Tank was a very complicated computer program that performed a lot of functions, but none of them all that efficiently. To borrow further from the military analogy implied in the nomenclature, this Tank was more like a Sherman than a Tiger. One problem with the system was that it was written in its own programming language, which, in turn, was created for the sole and express purpose of running the Tank. To be sure, the system was well-documented, with volumes of operating manuals available for anyone who had the time or inclination to pore through them; but while some in the firm had nothing but time, inclination was in very short supply.

The primary job of the Tank was to identify patterns in markets and in trading activities that had acute P/L implications. It featured a healthy component of the type of correlation analysis described in this chapter. One very interesting analytical measurement that John undertook was a correlation between profitability and the ratio of orders he executed with stops in his account. He had an excellent theory that the more he adhered to the discipline of using stops, the more money he would make; and that the more orders without stops, the more money he was likely to lose. As it happens, he was correct. Correlation statistics showed that he almost always did better when he relied on stops and worse when he went without them.

John then did something unconventional, arguably dramatic. He programmed the Tank to shut down his trading capabilities any time the ratio of orders without stops went about 40%. The system tracked this ratio on a real-time basis, but it did not issue warnings when the threshold was in jeopardy of being violated. What is more, John didn't watch it particularly closely. Once he hit the 40% figure, the Tank simply sent a message with the following general language:

```
Orders without stops exceed 40%. System not accepting new trades.
```

The Tank would continue to fill all orders that had been placed before the threshold was violated, but it would not accept new transactions requests until either (1) the European markets opened the next day or (2) John had added enough stops to bring him back into compliance. Although John could have overridden the rules of the Tank by simply picking up the phone and calling a broker or changing the programming logic, to the best of my knowledge he never did. Instead, he'd accept the portfolio profile that he was left with when the system shut down and work diligently to create the appropriate balance in his order structure, when his trading privileges were restored.

John, who was a Brit, was a disciplined trader; and because of this, he only tripped the boundary condition once or twice a year. However, as you may have guessed, this tended to happen during very volatile market conditions when his portfolio exposure was at the high end of the range. His colleagues were sure that his stubborn adherence to what was certainly a rather arbitrary (and entirely self-imposed) restriction cost him millions of dollars a year in trading revenues. They often called him to the carpet on this; and every time they started in on him, he'd just grin and say, "I know the damned thing costs me a lot of money, but not nearly as much as it would to shut it down." His partners would just walk away frustrated.

For what it's worth, year in and year out, he was the most profitable trader in the firm.

This doesn't mean that there are no appropriate responses to patterns uncovered through correlation analysis. It is useful to compare these types of correlations across periods of relative success to see if the differences in your returns correspond to material changes in the subcomponents of your trading activity. It may very well be the case that during periods of underperformance certain of your core disciplines have deteriorated and that the path to improvement lies not through large scale modification of your methodologies but rather through enhanced enforcement of some of the guidelines to which you had committed, but without rigorous, perpetual follow-through. Correlation analysis can help uncover shortcomings that can be eradicated with tweaks to your methodology. If you believe that deeper strategic changes are merited, I urge you to road test these modifications using specified amounts of financial and risk capital and to apply the statistical tool kit to measure the success of the outcomes, with a willingness to abandon your campaign if you lose an amount equal to this risk-capital threshold. This type of approach will enable you to take the risks associated with attempting new strategies with the confidence that these attempts can be framed as controlled experiments with limited, predetermined downside.

FAMILLE HEUREUSE

As we move toward the denouement of the morality tale that this book has become, it's time to wrap up some unfinished business. We can't possibly take our leave without bidding a fond *adieu et bon chance* to our friends and colleagues across the ocean, whose financial, military, and moral support were so crucial in our efforts to win our independence. I want to say again that I had a great experience working in French banking, met some fantastic people there, and both witnessed and participated in some enormously successful projects. Moreover, Société Générale (Soc Gen), where I worked, was enormously profitable year in and year out (at least when I was there) and seldom failed to achieve any business objective to which it truly committed itself.

I also wish to formally distance myself from any animosity expressed by my government and countrymen over that minor difference of opinion during Gulf War II. "*Vive la différence,*" they are proud of saying, and let me echo those sentiments.

Call me a Francophile, and I will plead guilty as charged. I have one small experience to share with you, a souvenir from my younger days, before we make our final return transatlantic voyage—at least for now. I dedicate it to the only French rock-and-roll band that I have ever been able to stand, Les Negress Vertes (LNV). They were a loose confederation of marginal musicians that formed a hybrid sound: part folk, part punk, part, well, African. The overall effect was a little bit frightening; and this, as anyone who has ever had to endure the banal claptrap that passes for rock and roll in France can attest, is a major accomplishment. Although, as becomes such an eclectic enterprise, LNV's eccentric lead singer died in 1993 (yup, heroin overdose); I'm pretty sure the band is still kicking around somewhere. I hope they come to New York some time; I'd really like to catch their act.

In my work at Soc Gen, I had an opportunity to interact pretty extensively with many of its principal financial engineers; and I want to tell you the story of my dealings with one such individual, a small, wiry, chain-smoking politechnician whose exact name I can't recall, so I'll simply refer to him as Petit. One of my missions in the bank was to negotiate with Petit and his entourage, to entreat, beseech, and otherwise plead with him to temper Justice with Mercy in the setting of certain risk parameters for a pet project of my boss's, the details of which escape me in the fog of the years that have since passed.

I didn't come at Petit all gangbusters, because this way never works with the French, particularly if you are an American, for there's nothing about Americans that the French despise so much as our lack of—how can I put this?—finesse. Instead, I just sort of hung around him the summer he spent in New York working with us, taking him to ballgames, feeding his nicotine frenzy, swapping risk management fish stories (yes, they do exist), and all the while gaining his confidence, in the hopes that he would let his guard down.

As Larry Holmes once said of an opponent (I think it was Marvis Frazier, Joe's son), I was getting him drunk before I mugged him.

Late one night (after he trusted me enough to drop trou, so to speak), I finally got what I was looking for: Petit entrusted me with a peek at the source of his risk calculations. He kept them in a 9.5-by-6-inch spiral notebook, filled front to back with dog-eared, tobacco-stained pages. As you might expect, I didn't get to examine this precious document very closely, but I saw enough to receive a frightening glimpse into the depths to which a man's mathematical depravity can take him. Know that Petit's mathematical rational featured no less than seventh-order integration. In other words, Petit was calculating the antiderivative of the antiderivative of the antiderivative, and so on, seven times over.

On paper, these monstrous equations looked something like this:

$$\int\int\int\int\int\int\int^{\infty} e^x \, dx$$

There is almost nothing that I'm aware of in the known universe that lends itself to this level of mathematical complexity. The solving of Fermat's last theorem did not require it, nor, to the best of my knowledge, did the smashing of the atom. Newton himself, were he alive today (and from this perspective I'm glad he's not), would no doubt be aghast to see his precious calculus so ostentatiously abused. I cannot imagine anything in the realm of human perception that requires anyone to ever use an equation remotely like Petit's—nothing, that is, except the formulas generated by Petit and his team to calculate risk limits for the bank's proprietary traders.

Astonishing as all of this was to me, our friend Petit had one more trick up his sleeve, and this one left me absolutely gobsmacked. As I was flipping through his little book of equations, my curiosity naturally drifted toward the last page, and I held my breath in deep anticipation as to the nature of the final fruits of his efforts. And as I turned the page, there, on the other side, in the middle of the other side, away from everything else on the other side, read the following:

$$= 5\%$$

5%!!!!!!!!!!!? *Mon Dieu et Sacre Bleu!!!!* What has become of you, Petit? Wherefore hast thou been led astray? Methinks that even the politechnicians would feel themselves violated by such travesty, committed by one of their own. One hundred godforsaken pages of the most mind-numbing calculus ever imagined, and you end up with a lame number like 5%? Couldn't we be a little glib here and make it, say, 5.14954534%? Our traders, I think, would've gladly lived with this larger number in the name of human decency and good taste.

What happened next is not very clear in my mind. I may very well have followed my first inclination, grabbed Petit by his scruffy, Frenchified collar and demanded that he either add at least 8 decimal places or immediately destroy at least 80 pages of his spiral notebook—all before pitching him right out of the window no matter what his response. Again, I just don't know, as my last memory of the encounter involved falling off a barstool, into a pool of my own sick, at a grimy place on Seventh Avenue, not far from the bank's offices.

I never again laid eyes on my good friend Petit, nor did I ever hear anything further as to his fate. I suspect, though, that he continues to thrive—at least professionally, because guys like Petit always do. The risk management industry grinds them out like link sausages, and firms ranging from banks to broker dealers to institutional money managers gobble them up insatiably. Somehow, I managed to escape to the hedge fund industry, which of course has morality tales of its own. Here, at least, I am confident in stating that we use our calculus with more discretion—a factor that I hope adds a measure of comfort to Newton's slumbers on the banks of the Thames.

PERFORMANCE SUCCESS METRICS

We now turn to a set of statistics that critically defines the success or failure of any portfolio, no matter what its orientation: the percentage of times your transactions generate a profit and the ratio of gains extracted on profitable trades to losses remitted on unprofitable transactions. Indisputably, it is necessary to perform well in terms of at least one of these factors because, to operate profitably, it is mathematically impossible to (1) have a majority of your trades generate losses and (2) on average, lose more when you are wrong than you make when you are right. In light of this inevitability, I have often used these statistics as a first-order diagnostic to determine what is going wrong with a portfolio that is performing suboptimally. The simplicity and the elegance of this exercise will become clear once we have set down the following definitions:

Accuracy Ratio (Win/Loss Ratio).   This statistic simply measures the percent of transactions that liquidate profitably as measured against the total number of transactions for the period. Note that there are several ways to calculate this percentage, including those based on raw number of trades and the amount of dollars invested. It is also possible, and indeed can be very useful, to calculate your win/loss ratio across various subcomponents of your portfolio, including counterparty, industry/sector, and instrument class.

If you are like most portfolio managers, your percentages will vary over time across these subcomponents. I strongly encourage you to identify and analyze these trends, as you can harness them in a number of ways to bring about significant improvements in the overall portfolio management process. High accuracy percentages indicate a strong fundamental or technical edge, and it behooves the portfolio manager to understand as much as possible about this market advantage. A number of specific questions come to mind, including: Does the advantage tend to cycle out across time? If so, it certainly would be interesting to compare and contrast the up cycles with the down cycles. And if you can pinpoint these with any degree of consistent accuracy, the path to higher profits may involve nothing more than being aggressive when you suspect your selection accuracy performance is likely to be at its peak and trading more modestly when the opposite condition prevails. Similarly, it may be possible to isolate areas of systemic over- and underperformance in various subcomponents of your portfolio. For example, a futures trader may be very prescient in grains but simply terrible at predicting price trends in meats. If the data point toward one of these patterns, then adjustments needed to bring about improved performance may be entirely intuitive.

The win/loss ratio is important because it is impossible to trade profitably without being right more often than you are wrong or making more money on profitable trades than you give back on losing transactions, or some combination of the two. However, this is not to say that it is necessary to have a win/loss ratio in excess of 50% in order to have a very successful program. Quite the contrary. I know of many portfolios that are so effective in their actual trading/execution and risk-control practices that they make large sums of money in a consistent, risk-adjusted manner with win/loss percentages in the low forties or below. The trick, of course, is to make sure that your winners pay off at higher multiples than those of your losers. In the meantime, as a final note on selection percentage, the win/loss ratio is obviously a variable that you should make every effort to maximize, and my experience indicates that nothing can help you so much in this regard as simply doing your homework. You should try to understand as much fundamental information about the markets you are trading as is feasible—given whatever constraints you face. This includes financial information, industry dynamics, pricing patterns, flow of funds intricacies, and the like. Don't be afraid to explore your key markets from new perspectives. For example, if you are a market technician, it can't hurt you to take a look at a financial statement or to talk to high-quality analysts. By the same token, if your approach is fundamental in nature, fear not the prospect of looking at a chart once in awhile. It won't bite.

If you do trade on the basis of technical indicators, you should make every effort to hone whatever edge you have developed in technical analysis as finely as possible. Here, win/loss statistics and other analytical tools can be of unique and specific assistance. It is possible, for instance, for you to track your win/loss percentages on the basis of different technical factors simply by isolating the specific indicators that have driven your decision-making process. For example, you may choose to initiate a long position in a security when a short-term moving average price (say, the 50-day) has crossed a longer-term average (for example, the 200-day). At other times, you may rely on such technical tools as Relative Strength Indicators (RSI) or Volume-Weighted Average Price (VWAP) signals. Simple statistical analysis will indicate which of these methodologies produces the most consistent stream of profits. That methodology may differ across industry/sector, instrument type, and so on. All of these trends are entirely discoverable, and all offer opportunity for potential improvement. In my experience, most of the difficulties you will face in this regard stem from the psychological obstacles that often accompany any process under which the inefficiencies of natural habits and patterns of behavior are challenged with hard data. However, I strongly urge you to rise above these entirely human constraints. When it comes to the trading markets, remember that knowledge and information are your friends and that ignorance is anything but blissful.

Impact Ratio (Average P/L:Winning Trades/Losers). This statistic, in my estimation, is perhaps the single most important metric in our entire statistical tool kit because the performance measure that most closely correlates with profitability, in both a raw and a risk-adjusted sense, is the extent to which trades that liquidate profitably produce, on a unit basis, a P/L that is larger than the associated losses on unprofitable transactions. If you can maintain this ratio above 1.0 (and the higher the ratio the better), you are more than likely doing a number of things correctly; and, perhaps most important, you are successfully selecting transactions under the critical criteria that the likely payoff is greater than the associated exposures.

In addition, the impact ratio indicates efficient risk management, including a propensity to liquidate losing trades at levels below which they can cause material damage to overall returns, as well as a willingness to take profits on winners at appropriate times. Finally, it is consistent with a very active and diligent approach to trade execution, which is also a cornerstone of successful portfolio management. For active traders in particular, it is my experience that the difference between profitability and loss can often be measured in small fractions, and it is with respect to these portfolios in particular that the impact ratio best measures the quality of the executions process.

Before carrying forward with a broader discussion of the applications of the impact ratio, let's try to define the statistic with some level of precision. There a number of ways to effect this calculation, the simplest of which is to utilize the definition of *trade* provided earlier in this chapter (namely, that a trade is defined as the group of transactions in a single financial instrument that takes the portfolio from zero exposure back to zero exposure as your base unit). From here we would undertake the following steps:

1. Separate trades into a group of winners and a group of losers.
2. Calculate both the number of trades and the total P/L for each group.
3. For each group, divide total P/L by number of trades.
4. Specify the results as the average P/L of winners and the average P/L of losers.
5. Divide the former by the latter.

The resulting figure is your *raw* impact ratio, and it expresses in simple terms the magnitude of your winners and losers in relation to one another. Note that you can also calculate the impact ratio on a *unit* basis by utilizing "dollar values" instead of "number of trades" in Step 2. While the resulting *unit impact ratio* offers a slightly different set of insights from the raw figures, I caution against assuming that the unit calculation is superior to the raw figures. Both are useful, and each provides unique and complimentary insights. In particular, because the unit calculation will offer a clearer picture of your performance success on a dollars-invested basis, it arguably provides a better means of discerning success across your entire portfolio. Conversely, the raw score, which makes no such dollar-invested adjustment, will supply a better measure of the level at which you are sizing your trades according to what represents, ex-post, your best set of market opportunities. Apply both methods across multiple time horizons in order to gain the broadest possible perspective on the subject.

As an alternative means of calculating this ratio (and particularly for those who maybe be unable to execute the formula at the individual transactions level), you can capture much of its intent by calculating the ratio across individual securities (average gain on a winning security versus average loss on a losing one) or trading days (average gain on a profitable day versus average loss on an unprofitable one). While you may lose some precision here, both of these alternative formulas convey the same sorts of messages regarding trade selection, risk control, and the like, as are implicit in the pure-form impact ratio.

The impact ratio is a critical diagnostic of portfolio selection, execution management, and risk control; and it is typically the first statistical measure to which I would turn in order to help isolate a problem within an account. In order to do this, it is necessary to track the statistic over multiple time periods and to use the results as a filter through which to evaluate your trading performance. If you are in the midst of a difficult period, chances are that your impact ratio will have declined contemporaneously. When this is the case, by evaluating the underlying components of the calculation, it is often possible to pinpoint elements of your performance that are displaying material inefficiencies. Break up the numerator and the denominator, and compare the unit performance with respect to each to periods of greater success. Is the performance degradation concentrated in the numerator? It could be a sign that the quality of your themes isn't quite as strong as it was when you were on a roll. Alternatively, it may be that you are simply being impatient and liquidating before your hypotheses are fully playing out.

By contrast, if the denominator in the calculation is edging up, it can be an indication of several things. Most likely, it suggests that you are holding on to positions longer than is optimal, a factor that can be the result of several underlying inefficiencies in the decision-making process, including such common themes of human nature as wishful thinking, stubbornness, and laziness. Beyond this, a larger-than-optimal average P/L on your losers may suggest problems in the markets you are operating, including diminished liquidity and poor performance on the part of counterparties and/or those responsible for your executions.

Finally, your impact ratio can drop as the result of both a decrease in your average positive P/L and an increase in your average P/L on losing transactions. If you see this pattern emerge, it suggests that a number of things may be going wrong simultaneously, among them those that fall into the combined categories of portfolio selection and risk management. If the pattern sustains itself, it's probably time to take some corrective action; and later in this chapter, we will discuss some of the corrective methodologies at your disposal.

Performance Ratio. As it happens, it is possible to combine the accuracy ratio with the impact ratio in a way that provides an overall index of portfolio management efficiency. This index, which we will call the *performance ratio*, is derived by simply multiplying the two component ratios together. For example, if a given portfolio manager has a win/loss percentage of 50% and books $2 of profits for every $1 that he or she gives back on losing trades, the associated performance ratio would simply be the product of the two ratios: $0.5 \times 2.0 = 1.0$.

The performance ratio provides a most comprehensive single assessment of overall portfolio management effectiveness because (1) there is a lower bound to the statistic below which it will be nearly impossible for any account to be profitable; and (2) at higher levels, you can be increasingly confident of your ability to generate sufficient risk-adjusted returns to increase your exposures toward the maximum levels supportable by the working capital you have at your disposal.

The performance ratio also synthesizes all portfolio management into two distinct yet complementary objectives: (1) to be right more than you are wrong and/or (2) to make more on your winners than you give back on your losers. Indeed, it is no exaggeration to suggest that every action you take in your trading/investment activities should be oriented toward one or both of these goals. This includes any market research you conduct (which, if done correctly, impacts both), all the efforts to maximize your execution efficiency, and all risk control activities. Think about it. Each of these is almost by definition geared toward either improving your win/loss percentage or your ratio of performance of winning trades versus losing trades. I often find it is useful to view portfolio management activities through such a filter, perpetually asking the question of what specific part of the performance ratio I intend to influence by each action. If, from this perspective, you are able to reorient your efforts in such a way that either component of the equation increases in value, I'm confident that the associated results will become apparent to your bottom line.

In terms of interpreting your performance ratio score, as previously indicated, I assert that in order to be successful, there is a minimum level of competence that is required in this regard. Specifically, the absolute lower bound that would be compatible with success is somewhere around 0.5. One fairly intuitive way of thinking about this is that a score of 0.5 can be achieved by being correct in your market view exactly half the time, while making precisely as much on winning trades as you give back on losers. Although there are some combinations of performance below this threshold where I could envision at least some transient profitability, for the most part, over the long term, unless you are north of 0.5, it is safe to assume that something is amiss and that unless you take some steps to evaluate and correct the problem, the prospects for a long and prosperous trading career are not overwhelmingly favorable.

By the same token, if your score is consistently above a certain threshold, say, 1.0, it would imply some combination of accuracy above 50% and an impact ratio above 1.0 such that sustaining it almost guarantees an extended, successful run as a portfolio manager. If your performance consistently exceeds this threshold, my best advice to you is to increase your capital usage. Whatever approach you are taking, it is certainly working to your advantage, and you should make every effort to maximize the dollar returns you can generate under these conditions.

METHODS FOR IMPROVING PERFORMANCE RATIOS

Once you have identified a condition of underperformance, the next crucial step toward correcting the situation is to try to isolate the specific causes; and a review of the components of the performance ratio is an excellent place to start.

Performance Ratio Components

If the numerator is low (say, below the 50% threshold), it suggests that you may need to be more careful in your position selection process. Try changing or enhancing the research you conduct before putting on a trade. Make sure you have a detailed plan for each transaction, covering everything from the catalyst you are attempting to monetize, to the time frame in which you expect the catalyst to occur, to the price target you are seeking if you are right, to the level at which you will commit to liquidating if things fail to go your way.

I have argued that unless you have not only (1) a *clear hypothesis* but also (2) *target/objective prices* and (3) *stop-out levels* in mind, you have not, in most cases, done the work necessary to justify putting on the trade. It is also quite useful to keep track of these statistics for all your transactions and to use an independent source (e.g., other traders, a broker, etc.) to check rationality of these parameters. You may even wish to monitor your performance across all three factors, specifically seeking statistical answers to the following questions:

- Irrespective of whether you made money on the trade, are the catalysts you expect actually occurring?
- If so, are they occurring during the time frame you expected?
- Were you invested when the catalyst took hold; and, if you were, at what percent of what you considered as your full position going into the trade?
- If not, what blew you out of it, and what could you have done to avoid this outcome?
- Did the security you traded hit its target price (again irrespective of your P/L on the transaction)?
- If not, did it hit your stop-out level?

As is the case with so much of our tool kit, your performance with respect to all of these factors is likely to vary along with your overall success as an investor. This provides the opportunity to compare intervals of favorable results with those that produce results that are less than optimal across the specific components of the decision-making process. You may find that any deterioration in your win/loss ratio can be specifically attributed to one or more of the named factors and that in each case there is at least a nominal remedy. For example, if the catalysts you are identifying are simply not playing out, then you must very clearly reexamine your selection model in order to determine how and why it diverges from economic reality.

In turn, there may be myriad reasons for this divergence, including internal ones (your views of key events differ from those of the investing public in general) and external ones (the fundamentals of the markets you trade have changed), or some combination of the two. Similarly, if your time frames are off or if the risk/reward ranges you have established are consistently inaccurate, there may be systemic reasons for this as well. In any event, it's useful to know what's breaking down in your model when things that worked previously are now working against you.

One critical factor in the management of your performance ratio that I encounter repeatedly as the cause of sustained breakdown is the inability to effect a timely liquidation of positions that are not working out favorably. Note that a failure to remove positions that may once have been good ideas but no longer hold their original promise can adversely impact both your win/loss ratio and your impact ratio performance. This happens to nearly everybody from time to time and is typically attributable either to a failure to adhere to established stop-loss levels or to inaction on positions that hover in a trading range long beyond the point where any reasonable hope for catalyst either materializing or producing the desired price movement has disappeared.

What happens here is that positions you should have long since liquidated can remain on your books—due to benign neglect or wishful thinking, or some combination of the two. To guard against this, you should frequently review your entire portfolio and make sure that you have a good reason for being in each position. You should also pay close attention to the length of associated holding periods and to your cumulative unrealized P/L. In each case, ask yourself whether the trade you have on is one you would execute at prevailing market prices. If the answer is yes, keep the position. If no, get out of it. No matter how diligent you are in managing your book, my experience is that there will routinely be positions in the account that, at best, are no longer driven by the catalysts originally identified and that, at worst, offer not the foggiest indication of why the trade was made in the first place. The benefits that you will gain by being meticulous about scrubbing these positions out of your portfolio can be substantial, often turning bad years into decent ones, decent ones into good ones, and good ones into outstanding ones.

The process of identifying inefficiencies in the denominator of the performance ratio is much the same as the one that applies to the selection-winning percentage component in the numerator, though the root causes tend to differ substantially. Again, the main culprits typically include elements of the selection process, execution management, and risk control. However, in the case of the impact ratio, which measures unit gains on winning trades versus unit losses on unprofitable ones, we would expect the breakdowns to assume different forms. For example, if your impact ratio is falling, it may very well have to do with the selection process. Rather than focusing on whether your general view of the markets is accurate, in this case I would instead look at the manner in which you are prioritizing and sizing your trades as a function of the quality of the opportunity. At any time there may be a specific number of trades you think will work. However, due to reasons of capital constraints, limited mental bandwidth, and so on, you may only be able to execute a percentage of these trades. Moreover, you will have decisions to make in each case about sizing, timing, modes of execution, et cetera.

Plainly, you will want to both prioritize and parameterize these prospective opportunities on the basis of what you stand to gain if you are right versus what you will lose if you are wrong. If your performance ratio suggests room for improvement—particularly if your winning percentage remains acceptably high—it may be that you need to fine-tune your selection process such that it more efficiently captures not only the price direction you expect in your positions, but also magnitude. If it indeed turns out that you are right most of the time in the markets but are subsequently experiencing only small gains when you are right versus large losses when you happen to be wrong, there are a number of tools at your disposal to assist you in achieving improved unit performance. For example, a better understanding of charts, including such key concepts as support and resistance, may help you to better monetize ideas where your directional call is correct, while minimizing the pain you take when the market moves against you.

Maximizing Your P/L

The other likely root causes of performance ratio degradation are more intuitive and relate to the critical topics of execution management and risk control. In order to maximize the amount of money you make on winners as a multiple of your P/L on losing transactions, you should operate with the following objectives.

Cut Your Losers/Let Your Winners Ride.   As mentioned throughout the book, this concept can be thought of as the key objective of all trading activities. If you are successful in this regard, there are very few external factors that will constrain you from prospering as a trader/investor. Moreover, there's not a great deal of science needed in the management of this effort; instead, you should simply operate under the following premise: *If you're wrong, get out; if you're right, let the market achieve its new equilibrium before you contemplate liquidating.*

Note that by cutting and riding, you will not necessarily capture every single bit of price movement in the names you are playing. Indeed, there will be times when getting out when the market moves against you means you will fail to capture the perfect inflection point. By the same token, letting your winners ride may mean you repeatedly find yourself in a position where you may have held onto a trade beyond the point of maximum profitability. Nevertheless, by consistently adhering to the discipline of cutting your losers at the earliest logical opportunity while resisting the temptation to liquidate a winning trade at the first whiff of profitability but while there is considerable upside according to your original hypothesis, over the long run, you will be much more successful than you would under any other approach. So don't worry about whether, on an individual trade, your strategy didn't follow the precise road map of the pricing action in the instrument you are trading. The approach I recommend will keep you in the game, which is the important thing.

You may accept this logic without great difficulty and still face a formidable challenge with respect to its application. The secret lies in the planning that you do before you first put the trade on. Every rational trade that you do should feature both a target and a stop-out level. In turn, these should be situation specific, tied to everything from your trading style, to overall market conditions, to the specific catalysts you are attempting to monetize in the names you have been trading. If you maintain this discipline in your trading, then your course is clear. Cut your losses when your securities hit your stops, and let your winners ride until the market hits your price target. If there is reason to stay in the trade beyond the thresholds in question, liquidate it anyway and reinstate it with new parameters. This will increase your transactions costs, in all of their unholy forms, but I encourage you to consider these costs as part of the risk management investment.

Diligently Manage Your Executions. Different trading and investment strategies have different sensitivities to the executions process. For example, the results associated with high-velocity trading strategies tend to be more dependent on the executions process than are buy-and-hold investment approaches. Similarly, the executions process will be a much more critical driver of profitability in complex, structured transactions than it might be in plain vanilla markets with ample liquidity. However, portfolio managers should seek to attack the executions process with as much effort and energy as they apply to any other element of their investment program.

There are several reasons that attention to execution is so important. First, there's real money involved; and the difference between an active and aggressive executions program and a passive one involves, at minimum, several percentage points of performance—no matter whether you are managing a small nest egg of a few hundred dollars or a multi-billion-dollar institutional investment program. Second, by managing your portfolio with an objective to capture every single available tick, you develop a level of discipline that positively impacts such critical portfolio mechanism as risk control in a way that can only be beneficial to your overall returns.

"Watch your pennies, and the dollars will take care of themselves," my grandmother used to say; and what's more, she lived by these words. She did not become a great portfolio manager, but she never blew up either. Will your grandchildren be able to write this about you?

Third, by declaring war in the executions portion of your activities, you are, in effect, giving the market its props, demonstrating that healthy sense of respect for the game that is vital to your ultimate success. By contrast, those who treat the executions portions of their portfolio management process as being a secondary or administrative aspect of the overall process place undue faith in the accuracy of their position-selection efforts. Think about it. Are your ideas always so good that they place you in such a profitable position that you can afford not to attack the executions process with every bit of zeal and intelligence you can muster? Not in this world, and perhaps not in the next.

A TALE OF TWO HEDGE FUNDS

It was the best of times, it was the worst of times. It was a quarter that exceeded expectations, it was a quarter that disappointed us all. It was an interval of irrational exuberance, it was a season of lost fortunes and dashed hopes. We were all going to be fabulously wealthy, we were all on our way to destitution. In short, the period was so far like the present period that some of its noisiest authorities thought it would make an interesting and useful case study. I'm talking, of course, about the late 1990s and the associated explosion in long/short equity strategies—particularly among hedge funds. Let's consider the case of two competing participants in the hedge fund arena: Julius and Augustus. Julius is an honorable if ambitious man, and one of the world's most renowned stock pickers. For several decades, his market conquests filled his investors' coffers. His research efforts were legendary, and once he got an investment opportunity in his crosshairs, he seldom missed his target. As one profitable year followed another, Julius soon found that he was managing an enormous amount of capital. Prudently, he redoubled his research efforts, hiring some of the best minds in the industry to help him figure out what things were worth. When he got a good handle on something that was undervalued, he would instruct his minions to grab every share they could get their grubby hands on. Nothing pleased him more than to see the market moving against his position while he was building it up, as he viewed these dynamics as nothing more than an opportunity to improve his average. He did not particularly care about the daily fluctuations in his portfolio; he was always playing for larger themes, and he made or broke his bones on the basis of whether or not his hypotheses played out.

In summary, it was fair to say that he was not particularly price sensitive. If he thought he was right, he didn't care what it cost him to put on a position. Moreover, if his conviction was high enough, he would typically scale his position to a level of market visibility, and past liquidity thresholds, in such a way as to remove any ability to limit losses if his hypothesis somehow failed to materialize.

While Julius's approach was all about being bold and aggressive, Augustus, like the Roman emperor from whom he drew his name, derived his brilliancy more from tactics. He could be as assertive as Julius when he thought the timing was right, but he was much more careful about the details. He relentlessly worked every order to make sure he got the absolute best price he could, given his vast set of resources. He guarded his moves in the market with a military secrecy. He never put a position on that was so big he couldn't liquidate it at what he considered to be acceptable loss levels. When he was wrong, he got out; and when he got out, he squeezed every dime he could out of the liquidation process.

The successes of both Julius and Augustus are a matter of market legend. For my money, I prefer the model namesake of the son to that of the father. Great ideas are elusive to come by and even more difficult to generate consistently over the long haul. Effective execution of strategy is something that is within the grasp of every market participant, every day. Get this part right, and it's a fair bet that like Augustus (and unlike Julius), your portfolio will avoid the indignities of a violent death, suffered at the hands of individuals and entities with whom you worked side by side, for lifetimes.

Note that the concept of effective executions management is a science all its own and worthy of more attention than I can devote to it in these pages. The world's brokerage firms employ hundreds if not thousands of professionals in this task. The exchanges themselves are nothing more than executions and clearing mechanisms for the trades you execute. Moreover, the largest and most effective portfolio managers in the world employ teams of highly trained individuals whose explicit and sole responsibility is to achieve efficient execution of the transactions that comprise their portfolios. However, most traders will have to undertake this task on their own, for which the following general guidelines can be helpful:

- *Watch the screen as actively as possible.* Whether you are actively managing an existing execution, looking for an entry point, or trying to liquidate, I know of no better approach than watching each name on a tick-by-tick basis. Charts are also very useful guideposts, as are certain technical measures like the volume executed at each price. The more active you are in watching the pricing action in your names, the better off you will be.

- *If possible, use multiple execution sources.* While professional traders and portfolio managers are trained to distribute their trades across multiple brokers and counterparties, it is typically easier for the rest of us to simply call our brokers. Subject to constraints involving your level of trading activity and the amount of time and attention you are able to contribute to these tasks, it is beneficial to have multiple outlets for your executions, which will bring competition into the mix. It will also give you a much better understanding of what constitutes quality execution and what does not. You may find it useful to make your execution sources aware that they don't have exclusivity with respect to your account. In addition, particularly for larger accounts, it is often productive to make a habit of liquidating your trades with brokers and counterparties other than those where you originally put the trade on. Specifically, this will protect you against the unfortunate but common practice among the brokerage community of profiting from too close a knowledge of your portfolio management activities.

THE FRONT-RUNNERS

You may be surprised to know that there is a whole segment of investment that has sprung forth from the practice of knowing where the buy and sell orders are in the market and the trading positions that anticipate the filling of these orders. This is nice work if you can get it. Think of the advantages of knowing in advance that, say, a large mutual or pension fund is buying a sizeable block of Stock A and selling an equal quantity of Stock B. In most market conditions, Stock A will go up and Stock B will go down. Moreover, even if this script doesn't play out precisely, Stock A is likely to *outperform* Stock B; and you can make virtually riskless profits by buying the former and selling the latter. My observation is that these types of portfolio rebalancings occur all the time and cannot be done on a large scale without involving many brokers and traders. These people face a significant conflict of interest as their obligations to provide the best professional service to the funds that are their clients must be balanced against the temptations they face through the prospect of trading against their clients' positions.

Strictly speaking, the practice of "front-running" is illegal. Specifically, the pending transactions in the marketplace for a given security fall under the general heading of inside information, and market participants are prohibited from trading on the basis of such information. In addition, almost all financial firms have explicit, written policies against such trading and work very hard to enforce these policies. However, there is a massive "gray area" where the line between the highest levels of ethical behavior and the rights of market participants to capture every legitimate market edge they can unearth is not well-defined. Consider, if you will, those cases where brokers have not specific knowledge but rather strong reason to suspect that trades that are likely to move the market are about to occur. Are they bound not to act on this information? Instead of trading, can they disclose what they know to their other customers so that the benefits they derive are indirect and commission-related? Further, whether told by their brokers directly or not, other market participants who are active traders may surmise that a significant trading or order pattern is underway. What are their obligations? Perhaps they have been shown a large block of securities for sale by a given firm and then go to another brokerage firm to trade ahead of this order.

All of these patterns fall within the mosaic of what sophisticated market participants refer to as front-running. My experience is that while most market-based entities strive not to cross ethical boundaries with respect to issues that fall under the general heading of front-running, some form of this activity almost certainly takes place in many guises every single business day. Brokerage firms live off information flow, which in many cases is as important as commissions. Most large banks and broker/dealers have proprietary trading arms; and though these groups are typically prevented from transacting based on information derived from the trading patterns of their customers, some slippage is inevitable. These firms also have market-making operations whose business it is to provide liquidity to the markets and who cannot provide this essential service unless the associated trading they undertake themselves is consistently profitable.

For all of these reasons, it's pretty safe to assume that as an individual or an institutional investor your trading patterns offer profit opportunities to your counterparties and that these opportunities will, with varying frequency, come at the expense of your P/L. Of course, the magnitude of this problem is a direct, positive function of the size and the visibility of the capital that you are managing. To be sure, front-runners care much more about the activities of the Warren Buffetts of the world than they do about the trading patterns of you or me (well, at least you; these guys tend to watch my every move like a hawk). However, it would be a mistake to assume that this type of conflict doesn't exist even among those providing services to seemingly insignificant accounts of individual investors. If you don't operate in a manner that precludes market professionals from accurately anticipating your every market move, it's a fair bet that there's someone out there who will try to take advantage of you in this regard.

Guard the privacy of your book as jealously as other aspects of your personal life that are nobody's damned business.

- *Evaluate the quality of your executions relationships in a holistic manner.* If you are able to utilize multiple execution sources, you need to be aware that there are many criteria across which you should evaluate these service providers. One very important measuring stick is commissions charged; and while I would be the last guy to tell you that you should actively seek to pay higher commissions, I would nevertheless point out that the lowest commission rate does not always translate into the cheapest execution cost. In particular, it is important to also take into account the extent to which your orders get executed at the best available prices. Traders refer to anything inferior to best execution, rather quaintly, as "slippage"—a factor that can be a major drain on your P/L, irrespective of whether you are an active trader managing large pools of capital or not. However, for reasons that should by now be obvious to the careful reader, the larger and the more active you are in the markets, the larger the potential impact of slippage, and the more carefully you will need to watch it.

    Unfortunately, slippage is not the easiest factor to track for anyone not positively flush with resources to apply to the task of trading analysis. One very straightforward way of evaluating noncommission executions costs involves splitting individual orders across multiple transactions agents and recording executions performance for subsequent statistical analysis. This can be a very useful exercise, but it will be far from costless. It will force you to track and perhaps maintain positions across several brokerage entities, in the process possibly removing otherwise useful opportunities for effecting margin efficiency, cross-collateralization of positions, and so on. Moreover, it is my experience that you need to collect a good deal of data across disparate sets of market conditions in order to get a true feel for executions quality differences across transactions agents; so if you do decide to go down the analytical path (and if you have the time, energy, and resources, I think you should), you'll have to keep at it for awhile if you expect it to confer any benefit. There is, however, a happy medium between using approaches involving costly statistical evaluation and ignoring the issue altogether. My advice is to keep your ear to the ground, talk to your friends and colleagues, and watch your fills on an anecdotal basis. If you sense you are getting your "face ripped off" (another charming industry epithet), you're probably right; and there's no reason (1) not to complain and (2) to change brokers if the situation doesn't improve.

    Finally, it is important to take into consideration the other services that your brokerage houses provide to you when you evaluate the quality of your executions relationships. Often, you will find that the entities that will lead you most directly to your maximum profitability are those that provide the best research, market flow information, and other nonexecution type benefits. It is very important that you do what is necessary to understand these benefits and that you manage your execution flows accordingly.

- *Don't accept inferior service; if necessary, vote with your feet.* While this may surprise you, the brokerage industry wants every dime out of your pocket that it can possibly extract. This doesn't make them evil or unethical; quite the opposite—it's their responsibility to maximize the profitability of your account from their firm's perspective. As a result, the only way that you can ensure fair treatment is to place yourself in the right position to critically evaluate their performance, to voice your displeasure when you perceive that they could have done a better job for you, and, ultimately, to move business away from them if they fail to respond in an appropriate manner.

  Don't let personal-relationship considerations interfere with this process. Just as your brokers and trading counterparties have an obligation to extract every dollar they can from you, so it is your obligation to maximize the return you get from a dollar invested in your relationship with them. You are on your own in these battles, but you are not unarmed. Your account and those of your peers comprise the entire raison d'être for your brokerage entities. If you are prepared to take the necessary steps to obtain the level of service you deserve, it is in your power to achieve this objective.

Practice Thorough, Sound, and Consistent Risk Control. This is simply a catchall phrase instructing you to pretty much take all of the advice I have offered in these many chapters. However, it is now possible, at long last, to be a little more specific. What I'm really trying to say here is that whatever risk management program you have in place, it is important to apply a measure of discipline in sticking to it. There are many ways to attack the challenge of risk control, and the best programs don't come from textbooks but rather are specifically tailored to the portfolio management conditions under which you operate. As such, your risk control should be based on your experience over the years, with specific consideration given to the markets you trade, the amount of time you are able to devote to the portfolio management process, your own personal (or, if applicable, professional) tolerance for risk, and other factors. Hopefully, it makes use of some of the concepts we have discussed in this book, including volatility management, trading in a wide range of names on both sides of the market, and the disciplined application of stops.

The point is, ultimately, that just as only you can determine what risk management program works best for you, you and only you are in a position to implement the plan. Whatever specific risk control steps you believe make the most sense, you will never achieve maximum profitability unless you faithfully apply the program. If you are undisciplined in this regard, I can almost guarantee that your results in terms of the ratios we discussed in this chapter will be less than they could otherwise be. By definition, this means your overall performance will be suboptimal as well. From time to time, it will be useful to critically review your risk management program (particularly in periods of disappointing performance) to ensure that it is efficiently oriented to your specific trading framework. However, unless you diligently adhere to whatever control regime prevails at the time, you are almost guaranteed to leave significant money on the table.

Profitability Concentration (90/10) Ratio

Some years ago in my observation of P/L patterns, I noticed the following interesting trend: For virtually every account I encountered, the over-whelming majority of profitability was concentrated in a handful of trades. Once this pattern became clear to me, I decided to test the hypothesis across a large sample of portfolio managers for whom transactions-level data was available. Specifically, I took each transaction in every account and ranked them in descending order by profitability. I then went to the top of the list of trades and started adding the profits for each transaction until the total was equal to the overall profitability of the account.

What I found reinforced this hypothesis in surprisingly unambiguous terms. For nearly every account in our sample, the top 10% of all transactions ranked by profitability accounted for 100% or more of the P/L for the account. In many cases, the 100% threshold was crossed at 5% or lower. Moreover, this pattern repeated itself consistently across trading styles, asset classes, instrument classes, and market conditions. This is an important concept that has far-reaching implications for portfolio management, many of which I will attempt to address here.

To begin with, if we accept the notion that the entire profitability of your account will be captured in, say, the top 10% of your trades, then it follows by definition that the other 90% are a break-even proposition. Think about this for a moment: Literally 9 out of every 10 of your trades are likely to aggregate to produce profits of exactly zero. It almost makes you want to pack up your charts and go home, doesn't it? Indeed, the main danger in being aware of this concept is the tendency to misinterpret its implications. For this reason, we want to be very careful about how we use this information in driving the portfolio management process and all of its sub-components.

Most people's first reaction when they see their "90/10" score is to assume that it is a problem that wants correcting. This is simply not so; and if they respond by trading less, concentrating their portfolio exclusively on what they feel to be their best ideas, they are likely to be disappointed by the results. The 90/10 rule is hard to overcome, and so I think the better way of looking at it is that you need the 90 to get the 10. To best understand this, let's use a baseball analogy (why not, everyone else does). Think of the situation faced by a .300 hitter in baseball, who, even though he knows he's going to be unsuccessful 70% of the time cannot simply decline to step up to the plate on the 7 out of 10 occasions where (statistically speaking) he isn't likely to get a hit. Truth is, the 7 outs he makes in 10 at-bats are a *necessary condition* of his .300 batting average, and he can no more expect to be more successful by limiting his at-bats than you can expect to be successful in your trading by reducing your number of transactions. True, just as the batter may know that he does better against certain teams and pitchers and in certain parks than others, so will you as a portfolio manager have some insights into the conditions that are most conducive to maximum profitability—across individual names, market cycles, and other factors. However, in both cases, the individual in question cannot expect to gain any benefit through a lack of participation.

Therefore, the principal lesson you should derive from 90/10 may well be that the lower 90% of your transactions, which are likely to sum up to zero P/L, are a critical component of your success. If properly analyzed, these trades can provide insights into the controllable elements of your portfolio management activities that can be enormously valuable to your bottom line. However, if you fight against this tide, you are likely to fall into a large group of market participants who have very useful skill sets but who inevitably become their own worst enemies.

Once I observed the 90/10 pattern, it made sense to examine what was taking place at the other end of the performance spectrum. Specifically, I wanted to know whether there was some sort of concentration of large losses that had material impacts on overall portfolio performance. In statistical terms, if the answer was yes, it would imply that most individual transactions-level return patterns demonstrated *kurtosis*, or a larger than expected number of observations at each end of the distribution. If the answer was no, then we would characterize these data sets, from a statistical perspective, as being *skewed* to the positive. This would be a positive, if unlikely, outcome (at least for most accounts), indicating a real edge on the high-magnitude trades in their portfolios.

I must admit that I spent less time on this subject than I did on the analysis of the high-profitability transactions. Don't ask me why; I don't rightly know myself. Perhaps I was just tired of looking at losing trades. We risk managers do get tired of wallowing in losses, you know, or did you think we had an infinite appetite for this sort of thing? Anyway, the answer that I came up with is that there is a similar, if less dramatic, concentration of drawdowns in a handful of losing trades. Call it 80/20, or even 70/30, and calculate this statistic by adding up your biggest losers until the dollar value meets that of your largest drawdown. Then calculate the percentage of trades this represents. The number is surprisingly small.

What does all of this mean? Well, for one thing, it's pretty plain that a good deal of your time as a portfolio manager is likely to be spent spinning your wheels, setting the stage, so to speak, for the outcomes associated with that small subset of your trades that is actually driving your performance. Okay, fair enough, but let's take a look at how to apply the information productively across various elements of the portfolio decision-making process:

- *Position Selection.* This one's pretty intuitive, right? If one is aware that 10% or less of one's trades are generating all of one's profitability (and perhaps all of one's drawdown), one ought to take this into account in one's position selection, no? But most people make the mistake of focusing on the nominally bad news that 90% of their trades don't work as planned, ignoring the (factually) good news that all they need, in order to be successful, is to have 1 out of every 10 trades (perhaps fewer) reach their targets at "fully invested" risk levels. As a case in point, let's go back to the ol' ballpark. Just as it's impossible for the allstar batter to know in advance which at-bats are going to produce a hit for him, so it will be impossible for a trader to know in advance which trades are going to work for big returns and which are not. A really great player, say Ted Williams, goes out there thinking, "Hey, this is easy; I can fail 6 or 7 out of 10 times and still be a hero to an entire generation." A little bit of this mindset with respect to your trading probably wouldn't hurt much at all. Just as Ted never grabbed his wood without expecting to get a hit, so should you only put on positions expected to make money (unless, perhaps, they are specifically designated as hedges). However, given that most of these trades won't contribute appreciably to your bottom line, you should orient your position selection toward putting you in the best situation to capitalize maximally on the "impactful" 10%, while ensuring that those that fall into the 90% category are not ones that will cause enormous damage.

  What is required, above all else, is a deep understanding of the prospective risk/reward characteristics of each trade you are contemplating. Awareness of the 90/10 rule provides you with an opportunity to focus on those trades that, if they work, will produce material profits, while if they don't, they won't cripple you from a capital-preservation perspective. What is more, it is very easy to evaluate your performance in this regard, once again by keeping track of your objective and stop levels and comparing them to your trading attribution results. You should feel pretty good about any position that, even if it didn't produce the hoped-for profits, didn't create a big negative revenue outcome. Simply tell yourself that it fit well within the pattern of what is prescribed by the 90/10 rule.

- *Trading Frequency.* Another superficially logical but (in my view) incorrect reaction to the 90/10 rule is a desire to decrease trading frequency. In fact, this is the exact opposite of what I would recommend. Remember, your only goal here is maximizing risk-adjusted profitability; and as long the trades that aren't producing big gains for you are on balance approaching a break-even proposition, my advice would be to participate as much as you can in the markets. Active trading offers a number of important benefits, offering you insights that are unavailable through observation alone.

First, these insights include a better sense of the price sensitivity, liquidity, and other execution characteristics of the names you are trading—factors that can only increase in importance as you evaluate them across different market conditions, position sizes, counterparties, and so on. For example, by executing frequent transactions in a given stock across a long temporal interval, you stand to derive keen understandings of how it will trade around key information dates, such as earnings releases. Over time, you will begin to understand who owns the stock and why, how they manage their position, and what constitutes a material change in their viewpoints. Digging deeper, you will begin to notice how the trading in one name interrelates to activity in the stocks of competitors and other companies that operate closely within a given part of the economy. All of this information offers a critical edge over the average market participant who typically evaluates only a subset of this data when making portfolio decisions, and it can only be mastered in my view through the actual trading process.

Second, active trading elevates your status in the marketplace. To the brokerage community, you become an important source of commission flows. To other market participants, you become a critical outlet for information, insight, and market liquidity. As a result, you will find your information flow improving dramatically with your level of trading activity. People will pick up the phone when you call or return your calls more quickly if they are otherwise engaged. Remember, you are looking for a few big scores a year; and just as is the case with the baseball player who needs the at-bats to produce the results he seeks (or the basketball player who needs the touches), you cannot possibly maximize your returns to trading unless you get in there and mix it up a bit.

Third, the more actively you trade, the more you achieve a connection with the markets that cannot be gained by other means, and the better position you will be in to manage your destiny on each individual transaction. You will learn that no position is priced too high to

buy or too low to sell—particularly on the liquidation side of a transaction. And by being an active trader, you will rise above a condition
that I would term, for lack of a better alternative, "position paralysis."
This typically occurs when you have developed a very strong market
hypothesis that, for one reason or another, has not played out in the
marketplace in the manner you expected. Oftentimes, you still like the
play and will be reluctant to liquidate your position because, invariably, it will seem that your liquidation is the very catalyst the position
needs in order to move in the direction you originally expected.

These things happen much less frequently to active traders than
they do to the buy-and-hold crowd. This is because active traders operate with a mindset that reinforces the notion that both the liquidation
and the reestablishment of a position is just a trade away. They might
have the opportunity to put the trade on and to liquidate it (or at least
to trade around it) a half dozen times before their catalyst monetizes
itself. In the meantime, while they have generated transactions costs,
they have gathered potentially important information with each new
trade. Even if they happen to be out of the position when it starts to
move in a favorable direction, they are in a position to change this in a
heartbeat. While they may not capture every major move that they may
have anticipated in its entirety, in most instances the good ones capture the fat part of the pricing action.

By trading actively in a disciplined manner, you stand to increase
the size of the 10% pool that will determine your trading destiny over
any period you choose to examine. The size of individual gains in these
names may be smaller than those associated with a buy-and-hold strategy, but, by definition, you'll have a lot more of them; and I believe that
on the whole you'll be substantially better off.

I think I'll close this section by invoking the image of Teddy Ball-
game one last time. I know that we should probably let him rest in
peace, but that does not seem to be what the Almighty has in store for
him. On September 28, 1941, the last day of the baseball season and
months before Pearl Harbor compelled Teddy to leave the diamond
and strap himself into fighter planes for the next three odd years, the
Boston Red Sox, 17 games behind the Yankees (who else?), played a
doubleheader in Philadelphia's Shibe Park against the last-place
Athletics. Ted Williams started the day batting .3995—the statistical
equivalent of a .400 season, a feat that had not been achieved in over a
decade and has not been accomplished since. A whole lot of folks (his
agent no doubt among them) encouraged him to sit out these mean-
ingless games, so as to ensure his place in the .400 club. But Teddy was
having none of it. He played both ends of the twin bill, went 6 for 8,
including a homer that gave him the American League championship,

and finished the year at .406. I reckon Teddy understood better than anyone the point I'm trying to get across: Every good swing you can get is probably worth taking.

TELEPHONE TAG

It's often easy to be right conceptually and wrong on timing. I once was acquainted with a situation in which a European Telecom analyst, of Teutonic demeanor and self-assurance, was making a presentation to an active trader about why he should short Nokia (or Nuk-ya, as he liked to pronounce it). Specifically, he showed with mathematical precision and cogency of argument why Nokia would have to sell 1.3 handsets for every man, woman, and child alive on earth in order to justify their prevailing valuation.

The trader in question looked at the analyst and said, "This is a very compelling argument. Unfortunately, Nokia may double before the investment world catches on to the validity of what you are saying." As it turns out, they were both right: Nokia did double from that point, but then it proceeded to crash along with the rest of the global technology sector. Eventually, when the stock came careening back to earthbound levels, the analyst won kudos from his peers for his clearheaded evaluation.

Rumor has it the trader made money buying the stock till it hit its peak and shorting it all the way down.

Risk Control. Awareness of the 90/10 rule offers portfolio managers a partial road map for risk control that represents a significant advantage relative to models that don't contemplate profitability concentration. To fully understand this, consider the rule's following key components:

- Approximately 10% of your trades are going to account for 100% of your profits.
- The other 90% of your trades are likely to be, best-case, revenue neutral.
- The best traders won't have corresponding high-magnitude losses to offset the gains in the top 10% category; those who do are likely to have significant volatility problems in their accounts.
- There are no reliable methods (that I know of) to anticipate in advance which trades will fall into the 10% category.

Given these realities, the ideal risk control program becomes one that preserves capital for maximum effectiveness when the top-tier opportunities do present themselves while at the same time doing everything possible to guard against the big transactions-level losses that can operate like poison on your return stream. In turn, this means pretty much doing everything in your power to ensure minimal slippage on the 90% of your trades that will not fall into the category of big winners.

The best means of accomplishing this is to actively manage every position with an eye toward protecting your downside. Forget about the fact that any given trade may be that big winner that you are forever seeking. Focus on your commitment to liquidate every position that is going against you at predetermined levels of loss. Such a strategy may deny you the opportunity to capture the entire price move that you have anticipated in your selection process; but the savings, in terms of minimizing the magnitude and incidence of big losers, will far outweigh this opportunity cost. You should continually review the reasons you are in each position with a predisposition to liquidate any position where conditions have changed materially. A very simple but underused methodology is to ask yourself on a frequent and routine basis whether you would put the same position on at current prices at the time of the review. Every position that you can't answer in the affirmative should be a strong candidate for liquidation.

Although there are multiple schools of thought on this concept, you should adhere to your liquidation points on the upside with roughly the same discipline you adhere to on the downside. If a position has hit the desired target, it may very well have additional room for continued price movement in a favorable direction. However, it may also reverse itself. Remember, there are others in the market who are thinking the same thoughts that you are. If they bail out of a winner once it has hit what appears to be a new equilibrium price level, you may be left holding the bag (or holding Herman). Again, one way of doing this is to review the positions that have hit your targets and to ask yourself whether you would reestablish the position at the new price level. If the answer is no, it's time to take your profits. In any event, you will never lose money by scaling back your position by a fixed percentage (say, by half) as it hits your price target. The bankable P/L you gain in the process should be of enormous comfort to you, particularly in difficult market conditions where there is little momentum-based follow-through. You may kick yourself for not riding the position for all it was worth; but you'll take much more psychic pain for those instances when your script played out exactly as you anticipated but you failed to take profits and the market subsequently reversed itself. If you adhere to this model, you will gain the confidence that perhaps your entire methodology is scalable across many individual transactions. However, if you repeatedly are on the right side of the market but fail to make money because you didn't liquidate in time, it's hard to envision how you will ever gain the momentum in your account necessary to achieve maximum success.

This all being said, there is a whole school of investing, called *momentum trading*, that calls for portfolio managers to increase their position sizes as the market moves in their favor. Over the years, this has led to spectacular successes for many portfolio managers, but I suspect that they are significantly outnumbered by the incidence of spectacular failures.

In the best of all worlds, momentum investing has been shown to work only under certain market conditions, and under a very specific and complex methodology. My advice is that unless you understand these programs in great detail, you are much better off taking profits when they present themselves.

One final aspect of your risk control program of which you should be mindful is *market liquidity*. You can easily find yourself trading in positions that will require care in the liquidation process and for which the damage associated with unwinding your position under conditions of market duress will cost you more than you would expect them to before the fact. Due to technical factors in the marketplace, multiple market participants often set their specified liquidation points at similar pricing levels. When markets move adversely toward these common points of action, there can be a liquidation momentum that can cause prices to move much farther against you than is justified by the prevailing fundamental information on which market participants are acting.

This problem occurs whether you trade on the long side or on the short side of the market. Many rallies are caused at least in part by squeezes on those with short positions, by participants that have keen insight into the difficulties that short sellers face in maintaining their positions when markets are going up, and many sell-offs are the result of savvy traders seeking to force liquidations at below-market levels. Finally, it is important to be aware that the use of so-called stop-loss orders may not help you much to control these exposures because these types of orders merely instruct your broker to liquidate your position at any price if the market touches a given threshold. Often, investors who think they are protected by stop-loss orders find that their actual liquidation prices are at levels much worse than those implied in the instructions to their brokers. In a common, worst-case scenario, many a trader has confronted a situation where an adverse market move has triggered a stop order, which in turn has caused the broker to liquidate the position at a price that was not only much worse than the trader anticipated, but was actually the worst price of the day—the market subsequently reverted to levels much more favorable to the trader's original position. Very few other events are more frustrating to market participants.

I nevertheless recommend the use of stops for individual investors. The situations where a stop-loss causes problems are reasonably rare and tend to happen most routinely during periods of acute market volatility.

Under most market circumstances, your stop-loss orders ought to work out just fine. Moreover, when you do see the market moving sharply against you, you can always manage the problems associated with stop-loss orders by simply canceling them and replacing them with outright liquidation instructions at prevailing market prices.

The objective is to make sure that the bottom 10% of your trades don't take away from the core benefits you are almost certain to derive at the opposite end of your P/L distribution. A sound risk control program that features active position management is the critical component.

Trading Psychology.   As a final point regarding the 90/10 rule, I encourage you to use this knowledge to fortify your patience. In my experience, the typical portfolio manager may go through weeks, if not months, of difficulties in the markets before he or she ultimately gets paid. In these intervals, your thoughts may lean toward the radical as you assume that the core fundamentals of your model have broken down and that drastic changes are needed. In fact, the 90/10 rule instructs us otherwise. It's useful, during these moments, to remember that even the best traders are subject to profitability concentration and, as such, often have extended periods of underperformance. As long as you are managing your risk properly during these intervals, it is likely that what you are experiencing is not a fundamental, negative shift in your portfolio management prospects, but rather the ebb and flow of the marketplace, which, as a rule, does not award large profit opportunities to market participants on a routine, continuous basis.

Time is on your side here, provided that you can effectively control your exposures. Over the longer haul, the market is likely to offer you ample opportunities to fill that 10% bucket to the brim. By contrast, if you radically change your strategy every time you go through an extended dry spell, it's difficult to imagine how you will ever achieve the type of flow that is conducive to your best trading intervals.

PUTTING IT ALL TOGETHER

The material I have presented in this chapter is a lot to digest. In an effort to help you visualize the overall transactions-level statistical analysis and see how we might interpret the results, please refer to the sample portfolio shown in Figure 7.1.

We have discussed many of these statistics throughout this chapter, and hopefully they make some sense to you. This particular account happens to be one with pretty strong statistical profile, so there's not much for the likes of me to complain about. Over the course of the full year that is

	7/1/02–9/30/02	10/1/02–12/31/02	1/1/02–12/31/02
Capital Invested $	3,000,000	3,000,000	3,000,000

Return Stats

Total P/L $	361,394	19,000	619,000
Average Profit/Trade $	11,293.56	730.77	5,895.24
Average Profit/Trade %	0.38%	0.02%	0.20%
Profit/Loss — Long Side $	234,906	11,210	377,590
Profit/Loss — Short Side $	126,488	7,790	241,410
Average P/L — Long Side	12,363	534	5,721
Average P/L — Short Side	9,730	708	6,190

Transaction Stats

# of Positions Taken	32	26	105
# of Daily Transactions	0.50	0.41	0.42
% Winners	53%	49%	54%
% Winners — Long Side	65%	59%	61%
% Winners — Short Side	35%	41%	39%
Average Holding Period — Days	4	3	3
Average Holding Period — Long Side	3	2	2
Average Holding Period — Short Side	7	5	5

Correlations

Correlation to Account Activity	0.58	0.67	0.63
Correlation to Account Volatility	0.17	0.23	0.21
Correlation to Capital Invested	0.71	0.59	0.65
Correlation to Net Market Value	0.15	0.03	0.09
Correlation to S&P 500	(0.43)	(0.37)	(0.12)
Correlation to Nasdaq Comp	0.17	0.06	0.21
Correlation to Treasury Note	(0.09)	0.21	0.15

Ratios

Accuracy (Win/Loss) Ratio	0.53	0.49	0.54
Impact Ratio	1.77	1.03	1.70
Performance Ratio	0.94	0.50	0.92
% P/L reflected in top 10% of trades	103%	105%	105%
% P/L reflected in bottom 10% of trades	59%	71%	64%

P/L by Security/Asset

Financial	(7,228)	(1,045)	(30,950)
Energy	72,279	3,420	111,420
Industrial	61,437	5,510	120,705
Technology	(25,298)	380	(18,570)
Utilities	126,488	4,370	219,745
Index	89,264	3,648	145,465
Other	44,451	2,717	71,185

FIGURE 7.1 Transactions-level-statistics.

covered by the analysis (I have also provided quarterly statistics for the two most recent quarters), a number of positives present themselves. There is a healthy balance between long- and short-side P/L, a positive correlation to such factors as account activity and capital invested, and the ubiquitous P/L concentration in the top tier of trading activity—all of which I have argued is consistent with a high-quality portfolio management effort.

	7/1/02–9/30/02	10/1/02–12/31/02	1/1/02–12/31/02
Buying Power ($)	3,000,000	3,000,000	3,000,000

Return Stats

Total P/L $	361,394	19,000	619,000
Total Return(% Buy. Pwr.)	12.05%	0.63%	20.63%
Average P/L (Daily $)	5,647	297	2,456
Average P/L (Daily %)	0.16%	0.00%	0.07%
Sharpe Ratio (Daily)	0.20	0.00	0.10

Volatility Stats

Std. Dev. (Daily P/L $)	28,090	32,550	25,349
Std. Dev. (Daily % of Buy. Pwr.)	0.82%	0.91%	0.75%
Maximum (Daily $)	90,962	82,000	90,962
Minimum (Daily $)	(60,587)	(122,000)	(122,000)
Maximum / 1 Std. Dev. P/L	3.24	2.52	3.59
Minimum / 1 Std. Dev. P/L	(2.16)	(3.75)	(4.81)
Downside Deviation ($)	14,130	25,452	17,498

Daily P/L Stats

Number of Days	64	64	252
Percentage of Up Days	50%	50%	54%
Percentage of Down Days	50%	50%	46%
Average Up Day	27,122	24,063	19,439
Average Down Day	(15,828)	(23,469)	(17,139)
Win / Loss Ratio	1.71	1.03	1.13

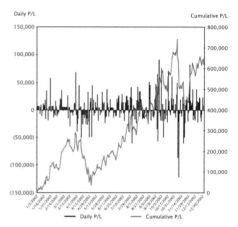

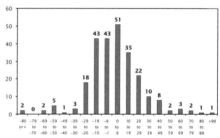

	7/1/02–9/30/02	10/1/02–12/31/02	1/1/02–12/31/02
Capital Invested $	3,000,000	3,000,000	3,000,000

Return Stats

Total P/L $	361,394	19,000	619,000
Average Profit/Trade $	11,293.56	730.77	5,895.24
Average Profit/Trade %	0.38%	0.02%	0.20%
Profit/Loss — Long Side $	234,906	11,210	377,590
Profit/Loss — Short Side $	126,488	7,790	241,410
Average P/L — Long Side	12,363	534	5,721
Average P/L — Short Side	9,730	708	6,190

Transaction Stats

# of Positions Taken	32	26	105
# of Daily Transactions	0.50	0.41	0.42
% Winners	53%	49%	54%
% Winners — Long Side	65%	59%	61%
% Winners — Short Side	35%	41%	39%
Average Holding Period — Days	4	3	3
Average Holding Period — Long Side	3	2	2
Average Holding Period — Short Side	7	5	5

Correlations

Correlation to Account Activity	0.58	0.67	0.63
Correlation to Account Volatility	0.17	0.23	0.21
Correlation to Capital Invested	0.71	0.59	0.65
Correlation to Net Market Value	0.15	0.03	0.09
Correlation to S&P 500	(0.43)	(0.37)	(0.12)
Correlation to Nasdaq Comp	0.17	0.06	0.21
Correlation to Treasury Note	(0.09)	0.21	0.15

Ratios

Accuracy (Win/Loss) Ratio	0.53	0.49	0.54
Impact Ratio	1.77	1.03	1.70
Performance Ratio	0.94	0.50	0.92
% P/L reflected in top 10% of trades	103%	105%	105%
% P/L reflected in bottom 10% of trades	59%	71%	64%

P/L by Security/Asset

Financial	(7,228)	(1,045)	(30,950)
Energy	72,279	3,420	111,420
Industrial	61,437	5,510	120,705
Technology	(25,298)	380	(18,570)
Utilities	126,488	4,370	219,745
Index	89,264	3,648	145,465
Other	44,451	2,717	71,185

FIGURE 7.2 Consolidated report.

In addition, the win/loss ratio hovers at just above 50% over the period in question; and the impact ratio is an impressive 1.77, indicating that while the trades in the account liquidate to winners at little better than 50%, the account takes in $1.77 or so of profit for every $1.00 it gives back in losses. The attendant performance ratio of 0.94 is, according to our measures, a pretty high-quality result—substantially above the 0.5 that we have argued is a benchmark minimum threshold for sustained profitability.

If we really want to be ambitious, we can combine the transactions-level analysis covered in this chapter with the time series review discussed in Chapter 3 in order to evaluate account performance in a truly holistic manner. In fact, let's do it now, for the combined benefit of yuks and erudition (see Figure 7.2).

Paints a nice picture, now, doesn't it? There's nothing like attacking the same problem from two different angles to give perspective, I always say. Are there any areas for improvement? To be perfectly honest, there's not a lot of negativity to hang our hats on here. Probably we'd like a benchmark correlation to the S&P 500 to be a bit lower in absolute value terms because we can't be entirely sure as to how this account will perform on all tapes. He had a nasty little drawdown around Thanksgiving but recovered quite nicely and finished near his highs. Overall, I'd say our friend is doing just fine.

There are virtually unlimited paths to explore in transactions-level analysis, and the ideas presented in this chapter are simply the ones that I find offer the best cross section of being relatively intuitive while also lending themselves to straightforward statistical analysis. Hopefully, at minimum I have convinced you that your market success is less a function of external and uncontrollable forces than you previously may have believed. Performance is the direct result of a number of routine decision-making activities that can be broken down and analyzed from an efficiency perspective. While even the best traders and investors are going to need the markets to smile on them from time to time, my experience has shown that the manner in which they adapt their activities to changing market conditions is a much more critical driver of success than are the evolving dynamics of the markets themselves. Our goal here, minimally speaking, was to open your mind to that concept and, beyond that, to offer you some simple methodologies that will enable you to act on that concept in a constructive fashion.

CHAPTER 8

Bringin' It on Home

Factum est illud, fieri infectum non potest.
(Done is done, it cannot be made undone.)

—Plautus

Improbable as it may seem, we are now entering the last leg of our journey together. It's not that I have run out of interesting insights to share, but rather that I'm certain you've reached the point where you can endure them no longer. Those of you who have hung with me this far should be commended. You are most certainly going places if not because these methods have helped you reach your objectives as a portfolio manager, then, at minimum, because you have demonstrated the stamina and endurance to bear untold hardships in pursuit of a greater good. This is a powerful resource, and I urge you to use it judiciously, as the forces of darkness are ever among us.

The mechanisms and methodologies we have discussed in this book are designed to help you identify the important subtexts of your portfolio management activities so that inefficiencies can be quickly isolated and, if not corrected, at least minimized in terms of their profit/loss (P/L) impact. Most certainly, the metrics I have presented will have varying utility to you. I hope that you will come away from this book with these general concepts:

- Portfolio management success and failure can be viewed as the cumulative result of a large number of decision-making activities that fit broadly into such categories as position selection, execution management, and risk control.
- It is possible to measure your success at these individual decision-making levels in such a way as to obtain a more precise understanding of what is working well in your program and what isn't.

- When things begin to go bad, if you can identify weaknesses in specific areas, they will be much easier to correct than it would be to improve under the (likely erroneous) assumption that either the markets have turned bad on you for all time or that your portfolio management skills have permanently deteriorated.
- These methodologies will enable you to identify the sets of market conditions that are most conducive to your success so that you can maximize your activity during these intervals and reduce it when the conditions that prevail are less ideal.
- For all of these reasons, most traders, investors, and portfolio managers have a much greater ability to master their destinies in the markets than they generally believe they have.

It has been my primary and perhaps exclusive objective throughout this book to help you unleash the power of these concepts from inside you. In the process, I have borrowed a large number of basic principals from the field of statistics and superimposed them on a trading/investing framework. It has not been my intent to turn you into an egghead like me; rather, I simply want to provide you with the means of better understanding why your performance varies across external and decision-based factors under which you operate, such that you can bring out the best in yourself under any given set of external circumstances.

With this in mind, I'd like to use what remaining attention you are willing to devote to these pages to revisit some core concepts of portfolio management of which you can make more precise use through the filter of our statistical tool kit. In many cases you will have heard these notions before. Indeed, some of them are as old as civilization itself (which arguably began and was cultivated for no other purpose than the creation of the market mechanisms in which you are now deeply immersed). I hope to show you that many of them can have new meaning when viewed through the perspective of the analytical approaches I have described. The statistical tools that have been our core focus will both reinforce these concepts and provide you with mechanisms to evaluate the extent to which you have been governed by them, as I believe you should be, whether you choose to take any other elements of my advice or not.

MAKE A PLAN AND STICK TO IT

I come across countless instances (and suspect that the true number is in the millions) where traders and investors are active in the markets but have no clear idea what they are trying to accomplish in them or don't know whether the strategy they are using is even remotely designed to achieve their objectives. Some are in it because they love the action; others because they think it is the thing to do. I occasionally also run into some market types whose main objective is actually to make money in an efficient manner. However, it is my observation that this class of market participants comprises a rather meager minority and doesn't necessarily draw disproportionately from the pool of humankind whose trading activities represent their vocation in life. Indeed, I know many professional portfolio managers who have failed to produce so much as a clue as to what exactly they are attempting to capture through their trading and investment affairs, *despite the fact that they are often managing huge sums of money and are routinely paid millions of dollars for their expertise.*

I'm hard-pressed to comprehend how these folks succeed at the task of capital preservation (much less accumulation) over the long haul. Plainly speaking, unless you have a pretty good idea of what you're doing in the markets to make money, you're unlikely to continue making money for very long. What is worse, without a well-defined strategy, if you happen to enter the markets in a timely fashion with an approach that affords you some initial profitability, you run the risk of gaining a false sense of confidence about your own trading mastery that can be very hazardous to your financial health when the theme that has been working runs out of steam.

It is therefore critical that you design your trading program to capture something very specific in the marketplace that is consistent with your core skill sets, capital availability, risk tolerance, and trading environment. Just as you should avoid trades at sizes that would wipe you out if you're wrong by small amounts, so should you steer away from strategies that are incompatible with your lifestyle, resources, and other factors that may indirectly affect performance.

Doctors with full patient loads and surgical schedules shouldn't try to day trade, for example; they simply don't have time for it. Similarly, traders should stay away from options and complex derivatives unless they have a basic understanding of the pricing dynamics (or, ideally, the underlying mathematics) and unless they have the desktop tools needed to calculate the pricing on the instruments that they hold. I'm constantly amazed at how often and how obscenely basic rudiments of common sense such as these are violated in the markets. Benjamins, sweet Benjamins, fly from us in the process, presumably into the arms of other Lotharios with more foresight, and almost certainly never to return. So wasteful, so unnecessary, and above all, so preventable.

Further, I routinely make the acquaintance of traders and investors of all levels of sophistication who enter into strategies for which they lack the understanding and/or the resources to master. To me, this type of thing is the financial equivalent of scuba diving without the proper equipment or operating a chain saw blindfolded. No matter what your basic skill set, you're bound to get hurt in the end.

Now that I've beat you to death with the notion that you need a strategy, I'd be remiss if I didn't offer some insight as to how to devise one. While there are a number of ways to attack this, you may wish to frame the problem in terms of the following four questions:

1. What markets will I trade?
2. How much capital do I have to work with?
3. How much am I willing to lose before throwing in the towel?
4. What type of infrastructure do I need to operate efficiently?

In terms of the markets you select, a large part of your choice should be driven by the identification of exploitable inefficiencies in some portion of the market economy. I would argue that unless you can pinpoint some systemic inefficiency in the markets and can further devise a trading strategy to capture these inconsistencies, your success as a portfolio manager will be driven almost exclusively by good fortune, which quite clearly is outside the realm of what you can control.

The process of trading with the benefit of an exploitable inefficiency is known in the parlance of the markets as trading with an edge, and we will explore this concept in greater detail shortly. Unless you can convince yourself, with objectivity and conviction, that your trading program has an edge, you shouldn't be risking a great deal of capital, if indeed any at all. However, once you are satisfied that your program does provide you with an opportunity to monetize on a nonrandom basis, the next questions you will want to ask yourself pertain directly to capital:

- How much can I put to work?
- How much am I willing to risk losing?

The answers should be based on considerations very specific to your personal situation (whether the capital is provided by you or an external funding source) but also on the characteristics of the markets you are trading. For example, you don't want to be trading futures contracts if you can barely scrape together the money to post margin. By the same token, you should avoid resorting to indirect funding sources to finance your trading activities, and you don't want to put yourself in a position where there is a meaningful possibility of losing more than you can afford to drop across your entire program. The tools in this book will help you manage the process effectively, but these tools will be of minimal value to you if you don't do some work up front in fitting your program to the financial resources available to you.

Finally, you need to give some thought to the infrastructure aspects of your portfolio management activities. In order to do so, you should have some idea about everything from the way that prices change over time (do they move on a minute-by-minute basis, like technology stocks, or with less frequency, such as private equity investments?), what is required to calculate your portfolio performance on a real-time basis, and what you will need to ensure that you have the information and other resources necessary to adjust your position in a timely and efficient manner when the markets move. In addition, you must make sure that you have an efficient network of brokers and/or counterparties who can assist you in the executions of transactions when adjustment becomes necessary.

Just as you shouldn't trade at financial levels beyond your means, you probably don't want to be trading European equities or Japanese government bonds unless you are prepared to monitor your positions during the off-cycle hours in which they trade. It's also probably a good idea to make sure, if you are trading these markets, that there are brokers at your disposal who are both at their desks and awake enough to be useful should their phone ring and it happens to be you. Again, these points may seem like nothing more than basic common sense, but I am constantly amazed at the multitude of otherwise rational and intelligent individuals I encounter who are happy to dive into markets that are quite unfamiliar to them and that experience the lion's share of price movement when these individuals are either asleep or otherwise engaged. I even know a few people who are successful at this; but for the vast majority of people, this is a path they will want to avoid.

Hopefully, by now, we are in agreement that your trading program should be one that is consistent with your financial resources and objectives, that causes you to operate in markets that you understand and feel you can exploit, and that features the appropriate tools to enable you to efficiently manage your portfolio as market conditions change.

Now comes the tough part: sticking to your program. There are no tricks here. Concentrate your trading exclusively on the group of financial instruments on which you have committed to focus, utilizing the methodology you have chosen to capitalize on the market inefficiencies that you set out to exploit, under the portfolio management plan you have created. The more rigorous you are in these terms, the better off you will be, particularly at the outset of your endeavors. If you have decided to trade in specific dollar or share-size increments, stick to these commitments. If you have promised yourself that you will liquidate any position that moves against you by 10%, don't renege on this promise. If you are willing to buy securities only under certain specified conditions (e.g., the 200-day moving average has crossed the 30-day moving average on the upside, or the company reports three consecutive quarters of improved earnings), then don't put on trades unless these criteria are met. Use statistics to monitor your success in these areas and then fine-tune your strategies accordingly. The alternative is a breakdown of discipline that places you entirely at the mercy of the markets and that will negate any chance you might otherwise have had to become the master of your trading destiny.

IF THE PLAN'S NOT WORKING, CHANGE THE PLAN

I love contradicting myself like this; it's such good fun. What I mean to say here is that you should not feel compelled to adhere to a single methodology for all time, irrespective of market conditions, its level of success, and other factors. Quite the contrary, it is essential for you to adapt your strategies as markets evolve and as your own individual circumstances change. Change is both useful and necessary, but it should be the end result of careful planning and undertaken in an organized fashion that will help maximize the prospects for success. Specifically, you should only consider modifying your strategy when and if you can generate *convincing* answers to the following six questions:

1. What am I trying to accomplish?
2. What strategy most effectively achieves these objectives?
3. How can I efficiently adopt my modes of operation to my new strategy?
4. How will I measure success or failure?
5. What am I willing to risk to determine if my new course of action is the correct one?
6. What parameters do I need to impose on myself to ensure that I will not lose more than this amount over the course of the experiment?

In an ideal world (I've never been there, but they tell me it's nice), it is better to undertake the risk and the effort of modifying strategies at points where you are making money trading so that the project benefits from the confidence and the availability of resources that will contribute to its prospects for success. I encourage consistently profitable traders and portfolio managers to periodically set aside small portions of their capital for experimentation with new strategies. The most successful market participants whom I have encountered have always been proactive in modifying and testing new strategies when they are doing well.

However, there will come a time in many trading careers when a modification of strategy is mandated by poor performance, and, as such, the changes must be undertaken under conditions of weakness rather than strength. In these latter cases, the preparatory efforts captured in the six questions are of the utmost importance. When what you have done in the past is no longer working and you need to change your approach or quit, the worst thing you can do is to carry out changes in a random, idiosyncratic manner. You *must* have some idea of what you hope to gain by the change, and you *must* create a risk control plan that will preserve portions of your capital that may be required to pay your bills (for personal account traders) or allow you to retain your job (for professional traders). Taking these steps can mean the difference between sustained success and catastrophic failure.

SEEK TO TRADE WITH AN "EDGE"

A couple of decades ago while suffering through the indignities of the MBA program at the University of Chicago, I was exposed to a theory known as the Efficient Markets Hypothesis, which, because I believed it (and have, truth be told, been unable to shake this belief in the many years that have since passed), ruined any thoughts I might otherwise have had about embarking on a career in portfolio management. This elegant little theory suggests that all financial instruments are at all times priced on the basis of the decision making of rational individuals, who are equipped with a complete and accurate set of fundamental information.

While many would quibble with the veracity of this notion (I've read four books this year that declare the Efficient Markets Hypothesis to be utter rubbish), there are dramatic implications for those who buy into it: The current price of any instrument you might want to trade is the economically accurate one, and it is unrealistic to expect your investments to move favorably on anything other than a random basis.

Depressing concept? Well, yes and no. It certainly is if you buy into it full stop. However, like so many other notions that find their origins in the ivory towers of academia, what is true in theory falls a bit short in practice. Although you can certainly count me among those who believe that markets tend to price themselves efficiently *at equilibrium*, there are all sorts of nits in the real world that create inefficiencies that can be exploited in a systemic fashion. As we mentioned early, the market term for exploiting a recurring inefficiency is known as trading *with an edge*. Though I blaspheme by doing so, I submit that there are edges all around us and that your primary strategic mission as a trader should be to seek them out. If you can consistently find and exploit edges, there is no limit to the amounts of money you can make; if you trade without an edge, it essentially means that you are trading efficiently priced assets and can only hope to profit by virtue of the fact that new information coming into the marketplace is favorable to your position—a 50/50 proposition at best and not one that lends itself to the risking of either hard-won or even hard-inherited assets.

Structural Inefficiencies

The types of edges that exist in the markets fall broadly into two categories: (1) structural inefficiencies that bestow advantages on certain participants and (2) methodological approaches that are better adapted to market dynamics than the norm. Let's first take a look at several types of structural inefficiencies.

Timing of Information-Based Decision Making.   It is the legal obligation of all those with information that is likely to impact the price of most financial assets to disseminate this information in a way that allows the entire market to receive it and process it in a contemporaneous fashion. Similarly, it is illegal to trade on information not otherwise disclosed to the public at large. These mechanisms on the whole work pretty well. There are few investors or investment groups that I am aware of who trade directly on the basis of insider information. Those that do so risk prosecution at every minute, and for the rest of their lives. If you doubt this, feel free to consult either Martha Stewart or her pal Sam Waksal.

That being said, there are numerous, information-based edges available in the markets. Perhaps the most prevalent of these fall into the category of disparities in terms of the time that it takes investors to process important pieces of data. This, in turn, is due to the following practical realities:

- Although information has to be disseminated to the entire market at once, investors *receive* this information at different times.
- Different investors *analyze* this information over varying time horizons.

If these things are true, it follows that, contrary to what I was taught, it is possible to gain an advantage over other investors in terms of both the precise time at which you receive pertinent information and the speed with which you process it. In both instances, the professional trader has a big advantage over the rest of us; and in general, the success of any investment program is going to be positively correlated with the amount of time you are willing to devote to both scanning the markets for important data points and analyzing these data points as they become available. Professionals get paid to spend their time in this fashion; hence, the advantage.

A word to the wise: Don't cling too tightly to any illusions that this information-processing disparity doesn't exist or isn't important. There are market participants who are relentless in this process; and, very clearly, they have an edge over their peers. The question you should ask yourself is: Are you a potential beneficiary or a victim of this disparity? If you're working constantly at these processes, combing the full universe of available information sources and then pouncing on the data points you gather with a determined abandon, it is likely that with a modicum of intelligence, you can generate and sustain an information-processing edge. However, if you have neither the time nor perhaps the inclination to attack these challenges with all of the energy you can bring to bear, I would say that by definition you are operating at a disadvantage to those who have made this commitment.

Transaction Flow/Market Proximity. As we discussed, the more active you are in the markets, the better you are likely to perform. In addition to the risk management benefits that active trading brings, you will find yourself much closer to the ebbs and flows of the marketplace, and this carries enormous potential benefits. In the first place, you start to see what the actual trading action is all about in your securities, on a minute-by-minute basis. Further, if you're active enough (and operate with sufficient capital), your market status may evolve beyond that of a mere participant into that of a *liquidity provider*—a designation assigned only to those who can be relied on to participate in transactions flow at material trading sizes on a sustained basis.

Those who have achieved this level of critical transactions mass are commonly referred to as *market makers*, and their presence is essential to the efficient functioning of the markets as a whole. Moreover, market makers are routinely rewarded for their willingness to take part in the transactions flow, with the rewards taking the form of being able to buy on the bid and sell on the offer (thereby extracting the "bid/offer spread"). In addition, market makers often have an opportunity to develop a deep understanding of how the securities on which they are focused trade, including such details as who the routine buyers and sellers are, what type of price action they respond to, and how they process fundamental information.

Market makers typically operate most efficiently when they concentrate exclusively on a relatively small number of tradable instruments that they make it their business to understand in extensive detail. For those who can manage this process with any degree of efficiency, the methodology offers a formidable edge, which should deepen over time as the individuals involved gain greater understandings of the nuances of the markets in which they trade. After many cycles of economic/financial data releases, certain patterns start to emerge, often providing road maps for capitalizing on exploitable inefficiencies.

One of the most efficient of these methodologies seeks to reverse engineer the flow of funds in and out of financial instruments generated by large institutions. I've worked for a couple of places that used this methodology, and, boy, did they have edges. Because the big institutions often deal in position sizes that are large multiples of the daily volume of a given security, it can take days and sometimes even weeks for them to establish/liquidate a position and to rebalance their portfolios. The market makers in the securities in question know these patterns, having a pretty accurate picture of which large participants are holding which securities (in the case of mutual funds, the government is kind enough not only to force them to disclose their positions on a routine, periodic basis, but also to establish minimum holding periods for securities in the portfolio), the price levels at which they have executed, and often (at least through inference) even the price levels at which they are likely to adjust their exposures. When the time comes for these institutions to rebalance, market makers may have the opportunity to extract large spreads from the market—either by taking the other side of these trades or by riding along with them and benefiting from the price action that their trading activity creates.

For example, a given large mutual fund may find itself wanting to liquidate a 5-million-share holding of a given midcap stock; but due to liquidity constraints, it can only do so over a period extending more than a week and in increments of 100,000 or 200,000 shares at a time. As these trades hit the tape, market makers may quickly surmise who the seller is, come to a very informed hypothesis that all 5 million shares are for sale, and use this knowledge to their own trading advantage.

Of course, it takes a significant commitment combined with the appropriate market proximity to operate as an effective market maker in a given financial instrument. Professionals who sit on trading desks of major brokerage houses enjoy this edge, as do floor-based market participants, along with a handful of private investors. Much of the price action in the market is simply the end result of transactions between large investors and market makers. Only a few well-placed souls have an edge in this process, but it impacts us all. I think the market is much better off for the presence of market makers, and one thing's for sure: The good ones are well-paid for their efforts.

Being "the House."   One very important group of market makers typically carries an edge into every transaction—those who operate as the designated liquidity provider for all transactions processed through a given market mechanism. Those with this designation include floor brokers on regulated exchanges, those who sit at banks and broker dealerships trading against clients seeking access to specific markets, designated liquidity providers on electronic exchanges, and a small number of others. In exchange for a willingness to act as a buyer for investors wishing to sell and as a seller to investors wishing to buy, these entities typically are able to buy at the bid and/or sell at the offer, thereby creating a sustainable revenue flow that can be very lucrative indeed.

Of course, the responsibilities that house traders assume are almost never riskless, as they are routinely subject to a nasty type of exposure called *event risk*, under which they might theoretically be caught with a large position in a market that has just received dramatic new information that is negative to their position. In order to incentivize market makers to assume event risk, the bid/offer spread has to be sufficiently large so as to compensate them handsomely under the vast majority of market conditions. Here's a little news flash: It usually is.

There are a number of other exploitable inefficiencies of this nature, but these examples should give you the general idea. The common thread across them is that they may be available only to certain types of market participants (mostly professionals) and cannot be manufactured unilaterally by individuals not operating in the specific structures that are the beneficiaries.

Methodological Inefficiencies

There are also certain methodological edges that just about anybody can create through enlightened portfolio management.

Trading Efficiency and Risk Control. As indicated throughout this book, I believe that there is a very specific science that underlies the business of trading and investing. In previous chapters, we have described it as being contained in some combination of being right more than you are wrong and/or making more when your positions work in your favor than you give back when they are against you. While you may not always see the market clearly enough to be successful on the basis of position selection alone, I have argued that it is in your power to control the ratio of what you make on winners to what you remit on losing trades— and this, as I have repeatedly stated, lies at the very core of the science of trading as I find it.

We have gone into great detail in previous chapters about what it takes to maximize the ratio of gains on winners to losses on losers and so will not do more than repeat at the highest conceptual level what we believe to be the critical subtasks:

- Select positions where the gains you realistically expect significantly exceed the losses you are willing to take.

- Rigidly adhere to your objective/loss targets.
- Determine the amount of capital you invest in any one transaction on the basis of its risk/reward characteristics.
- Seek at all times to minimize your transactions costs, particularly in terms of the prices at which you are trading.

This seemingly simple and entirely achievable set of protocols is an edge in itself, and a significant one at that. What is even better, it is available to all market participants. If you are able to master these objectives, you can avoid the disasters that make trading and investing such a frustrating experience for so many. You will also enhance returns during those rare but exquisite moments when the sea appears calm and there isn't a cloud on your portfolio horizon.

Superior Portfolio Construction/Position Selection. It is also possible to derive an edge by being better at analysis than other market participants. In theory, these types of edges can take many forms, the most obvious of which are driven by individuals who try to dig deeper and process fundamental information with a keener eye toward future price movement than the rest of us. Most professional money managers, including those who manage the mutual fund assets in which so much of the wealth of individual investors is entrusted, strive to fall into this group. In a more extreme example, hedge fund managers, whose services are unavailable to a large majority of investors and who typically charge fees that are many multiples of those paid to mutual funds, must have a superior selection methodology in order to justify their very existence. Beyond this, there are quantitative strategies that seek to benefit from such concepts as a superior ability to price options and other derivatives, as well as the ability to identify and benefit from small, nonintuitive discrepancies in the prices of similar instruments (so-called relative value trading), all of which can be categorized as attempts to create superior portfolio construction models.

The bona fide existence of these "better mousetraps" is a matter that is very difficult to dispute. Be that as it may, you need to be careful about aggressively deploying capital in a trading strategy that you feel has a portfolio construction edge. In the first place, don't underestimate the challenges here; and above all, don't let your emotions call the shots here, as this flies in the face of those elements of the efficient markets hypothesis that are most appealing: (1) Everyone is ultimately dealing with the same set of information, and (2) prices are determined by investment agents making rational decisions. If you really have something special, test it out on small capital and scale with your profits. Trust me on this one; you'll feel better about yourself in the morning.

Finally, even if you do find a methodology that anticipates price movement with greater accuracy and consistency than others in the market, my experience is that sustaining such an edge into perpetuity is nearly impossible. As the saying goes, there's nothing new under the sun, and this includes methods for figuring out the future relative worth of economic assets. Others are at least nominally aware of what you are doing; and if it works, they will most certainly try to begin doing it themselves. The more piggybackers there are, the smaller the profit margins that will accrue to your methodology, and the greater the risk you have to take to capture them.

Thus, in order to continue to beat the market by the sheer forces of your insight and intellect, it is necessary not only to spot anomalies that virtually no one else is seeing, but also to successfully sustain this process of discovery and adaptation when the market inevitably figures out what you're doing and removes the conditions that you have heretofore been able to exploit.

There is one very important exception to the dismal dynamics just described: a methodology known as hard work. Most markets lend themselves to fundamental analysis, and it is possible to be more thorough and to capture a more complete picture of the economics of the instruments you are trading than at least a subset of other market participants. If there's a God in heaven, one ought to have a sporting chance at profitably exploiting the associated information advantages. For example, in the equity markets, you can gather a virtually unlimited amount of written information on an individual company, derived from such sources as the documentation provided by that company (financial statements, press releases, proxy statements, etc.) and analysis made available by brokerage houses and research firms. In addition, with a little bit of ingenuity, even amateurs can gain access to critical information sources within and around the company, including investor relations personnel and agents of customers and suppliers for the firm. Finally, the ability to exchange ideas with other investors (particularly in the Internet age) is constrained only by the amount of time you are willing and able to devote to this effort. Your returns should be positively correlated to both the effort and the quality that you bring to the research elements of your trading program. In my experience, the very best traders in the world are the ones that work the hardest. It's as simple as that.

The universe of sustainable edges extends well beyond those I've covered, and I am not suggesting that you need to map your portfolio management strategies into one of these templates. What I am saying is that you should absolutely frame your trading program around a specific, realistic edge, and understand the consequences of being active in a market that is full of participants who are systematically exploiting inefficiencies, while you are not.

PLAY YOUR P/L

As we have discussed in great detail, among the most crucial determinations you will need to make, over and over again, is how much risk you should take in your portfolio at any given time. I have tried to reinforce the notion that these decisions should be based on an analysis that takes into account both internal factors, such as the amount of risk capital you have at your disposal, and external considerations, including the quality of the market opportunities that you believe are available to you at any given time. I am fond of portraying the risk-taking decision set through the following two-by-two Harvard Matrix:

Risk Capital	Opportunity Set	
	Low	**High**
High	Do what you want, but there's no reason to be a hero here.	Go get 'em, Tiger!!!!
Low	Good time for a vacation. Have you thought about visiting Grandma lately? She's not getting any younger, you know.	Here's where we separate the wheat from the chaff. My advice is to use extreme discretion here, as this box has destroyed many trading careers.

This matrix pretty well sums up most of the capital allocation decision making you'll ever have to undertake; and clearly the difficult choices reside in the northwest (High-Low) and southeast (Low-High) quadrants. Life, by contrast, is relatively simple up in Bangor and down in San Diego, but we risk managers actually prefer Seattle and Miami, as they are much more job-secure climates for those of our ilk.

I have argued that no matter what types of opportunities you believe are out there, you should at no point be invested at levels beyond which the associated losses place you in conditions of either financial or professional duress. The volatility analysis and risk prediction tools I have described in various chapters of this book are designed to provide you with the opportunity to size your exposures within parameters of acceptability.

Underlying the principal of loss reduction is the undeniable reality that even for guys like Bill Gates, the ability to sustain losses is finite. Therefore, by definition, an investor's ability to take risk increases with profits and decreases with losses. I cannot overemphasize the importance of placing your recent performance as the primary consideration in your risk-assumption decision-making process. Moreover, in operating under these constraints, the following core principals should guide you:

- Your risk profile should never allow you to lose more than the amount you have specified as your risk capital except under the most extraordinary and unforeseeable of market events (e.g., a stock market crash).
- As markets move against you and you draw closer to your maximum loss amount, it is imperative that you cut your risk so that you don't exceed the economic stop-out level to which you have committed yourself.
- By contrast, as profits accumulate, you move farther away from your economic stop-out and, thus, have the prerogative to either increase your exposures or take on new types of market risks that may expand your trading horizons in the future.

In previous chapters, I have suggested that a fully invested risk position is one where a one-standard-deviation market fluctuation (occurring in roughly one out of every three market days) does not cause you to lose (or gain for that matter) any more than 10% of the sum of your risk capital plus your year-to-date P/L. For example, if you have committed to a program under which you will not lose more than $100,000, then on day one, I would say you are fully invested if the standard deviation of your returns is $10,000 or less. As profits accumulate, this number goes up, such that if you make an additional $100,000, you are then $200,000 away from your stop-out and can be comfortable with standard deviations of up to $20,000. By contrast, if you lose $50,000, you are $50,000 away from your stop-out, and I would recommend that your standard deviation never exceed $5,000.

There are many benefits to operating under this approach, which, perhaps as much as any other topic covered in this book, I'd like to drill into your psyche. With benefits come responsibilities. Above all, portfolio managers have an obligation to dampen their risk profiles during periods of accelerating negative performance. I have alluded to several reasons why it is in your best interest to reduce exposures as return profiles deteriorate, and these reasons are so important in my mind that they bear repeating in the concluding portions of this book.

First and most important, if you are trading professionally (using other people's capital and receiving a percentage of the profits), there is a point of negative P/L beyond which your interests and those of your capital provider begin to diverge. This comes when you start to perceive that your compensation cannot go lower with incremental negative P/L and cannot grow unless you make up your deficit in rapid fashion. The clear expedient for those of this particular mindset is to increase their exposures, because the incremental benefits from being right (at least at a superficial level) far exceed the additional costs of being wrong.

On the one hand (the worse one), you might lose your funding altogether (i.e., you are unceremoniously defrocked); but this is a realistic outcome only for traders who are in significant negative P/L territory anyway. On the other hand, if things work out for you at higher risk levels, you are likely to be back in the black much sooner and thus reap compensation for your efforts in a much more expeditious fashion.

If you are trading in deficit, you will face a great temptation to increase your exposures; but your capital provider is in the exact opposite position. This entity clearly suffers with every incremental dollar you lose—more so if it is funding multiple trading enterprises and bearing the netting risk. This is why your desk manager is all over you to cut your risk when you are dropping cash. I would argue not only that is the capital provider correct in this mindset, but also that its desire to cut exposures serves both its best interest and yours. Seldom have I seen the strategy of ratcheting up risk for those in deficit pay off the way that the trader/investor hoped; and even when it has, it encourages behavior that is likely to be destructive to the portfolio manager in question over the long term.

Drawdowns are as inevitable in trading as fumbles are in football; and those who respond to drawdowns with prudence can have a long, happy life in portfolio management, while those who go the opposite route will eventually flame out—albeit, perhaps, in spectacular fashion.

WHO IS GOING TO MAKE IT? WE'LL FIND OUT, IN THE LONG RUN.

These days, no risk management book is complete without an analysis of the demise of Long-Term Capital Management (LTCM). I'm sure we all agree that the world needs yet another synopsis of these events, in which a handful of traders, operating from an obscure outpost in Greenwich, Connecticut, and managing a few billion dollars of highly levered capital, threw the global financial system into a state so dire that it could only be solved by that most improbable of problem-solving methods: government intervention. What is more, I figure I'm just the guy to provide it. After all, I was managing risk at a hedge fund of similar focus (if more discipline), whose wings also got singed a bit in the cross fire of these events but who rose to much greater heights in their aftermath.

Besides, the topic is simply too juicy to resist. I don't know of anyone I've ever encountered in the financial services industry that did not have great admiration for the LTCM team. Its leader John Meriwether, is responsible for dramatic advancements in the field of relative value fixed income trading—a strategy that many (including this reporter) believe to be both viable and vital to this day. My own personal case of blind devotion, deriving largely from my status as a wanna-be academic, was and still is skewed towards Robert Merton and Myron Scholes, whose contributions to the world of modern financial engineering speak for themselves, and need no particular embellishment from yours truly. Like Newton, their accomplishments will survive them, in my view for as long as the world continues to devote resources to the challenge of efficient asset valuation. And also like Newton, the fact that their undisputed brilliance rendered them in no way immune from financial setbacks caused by the caprices of the marketplace, serves as a (not so) gentle reminder to us all that this here game of trading and portfolio management is a hazardous one indeed.

So let's take another look, shall we? Our cast of characters features an elite trading team, bones made on the vaunted Salomon Brothers fixed-income trading desk, universally regarded as the 1927 Yankees of proprietary investment. Intellectualized by the addition of some of the pioneers of financial engineering, legitimized by a former vice chairman of the United States Federal Reserve, and fawned over by a global financial services community, LTCM was, in every respect, larger than life. Though no one outside the firm knew the extent of their operation until it blew sky-high, after the fact it was plain that their financial ambitions outstripped even their seemingly unsurpassable collective credentials.

The story of how it all came crashing down—how this group managed first to practically corner the market on an unimaginable array of global securities; then to watch helplessly, unable to liquidate, as this portfolio dropped billions in value over a matter of days (in the process nearly taking down a good portion of the world's leading capital markets institutions); and ultimately to create a situation that required government intervention to avert a global market crisis—is a matter of prolific public record. However, there are some mouthwatering tidbits here, so bear with me for a few more paragraphs, and you'll not be sorry.

For the uninitiated, Long-Term Capital Management was a hedge fund concern created by John Meriwether (former vice chairman of Salomon Brothers). LTCM applied the trading techniques that (to give the man his props) JM had pioneered, this time in a private funding vehicle, where he wouldn't have to be bothered by issues like regulatory oversight and shareholder concern about earnings volatility. Their specific strategy was something called "relative value" investment, under which investors seek to identify small discrepancies in the valuation of securities with similar characteristics, buying the cheap one and selling the expensive one, under the expectation that the two will ultimately converge.

In the mid-to-late 1990s, LTCM was ubiquitous in my world, kind of like Michael Jackson a decade earlier. Indeed, even five years after their infamous demise, I find it difficult to escape the shadow they cast. The derivatives group at the bank I once worked at had cut their teeth at JM's desk at Salomon and had sold a potential trading relationship with LTCM to management of the bank as though it was a matter of high honor and privilege. Later on, when I went over to the "dark side" and joined a hedge fund myself, LTCM was held up to be the ideal to which the rest of the industry should aspire. When their day of reckoning came, in early autumn of 1998, I was responsible for the risk management function of portfolios that had similar components but much better construction than the one put together by the Nobel laureates, Fed governors, and market visionaries that are the subject of this study. Suddenly, everyone became very interested in what hedge funds were doing and how we were doing it. Later, when the fallout from the LTCM incident had worked its way through the financial system, we all paid a price, lectured to on risk management topics by those with only the most rudimentary understandings of the concepts discussed in this book. Finally, nearly five years after the original incident, I find myself unable to resist the temptation of featuring the LTCM boys in my final case study.

A full year before the highly publicized collapse, LTCM was managing a then nearly unheard-of $7 billion. They had managed to average for the three prior years of their existence a net return of 40%, near as I can tell, capitalizing, at least in part, on two very discernible trends in the marketplace: European Monetary convergence and the steep decline in U.S. interest rates. As 1997 drew to a close, these trends appeared to be running out of steam. Interest rates not only in France and Germany but indeed in all European Monetary Union nations were moving in lockstep, and the well was running dry in terms of playing these rates against each other. Moreover, the U.S. Federal Reserve, which had been lowering interest rates aggressively since the recession of 1991, was looking like it was ready to stand pat for a while (though, as we now know, not for a very long while).

In short, the practice of capitalizing on relative pricing inefficiencies in the world of global fixed-income arbitrage was looking like a less lucrative one as 1997 drew to a close, and the LTCM boys did something that looked both daring and brilliant at the time: *They decided to give back half of the $7 billion they had under management.*

"Damn, them buzzards are smart!" I remember thinking at the time (when I talk to myself, I often do so with a southern drawl). The spreads in their markets were narrowing, their risk reward curve was shifting inward, and the responsible thing to do was to scale back their program to the lower level of opportunities in the market. Moreover, it was plain to see that the process of returning capital was far from painless. By all accounts, many of their investors took the news of their redemption as a matter of high betrayal. Nevertheless, the process went through as anticipated; and it appeared from my perspective that entering into the fateful year of 1998, LTCM was well positioned to continue to generate solid, if more earthbound, levels of risk-adjusted return.

Then the bottom fell out, and a much different kind of story emerged. It turns out that LTCM hadn't scaled back its exposures at all; in fact, they had by all accounts increased them dramatically. The return of some $3.5 billion of investor capital was not, as subsequent events proved, driven by a desire to operate at lower levels of investment in the face of reduced opportunity set, but was simply a part of a plan on their part to increase the leverage of their proprietary investment program! While I obviously cannot speak with accuracy about their mindset, this appears to be the only logical explanation, because as we learned in the unwind, they were scaling up their position sizes in a sustained fashion, both at the time of their capital reduction and for months after the fact. What was worse, several of the partners in the firm had actually borrowed very aggressively in order to maximize their investments in the partnership. The end result of these confluences was that individuals who were considered among the brightest lights in the whole investment industry had borrowed money to invest in a fund product that was itself trading in a highly levered fashion, financed through credit arrangements with banks and broker dealers. For these partners, every dollar of actual capital that belonged to them appears to have been mapped into literally hundreds of dollars of market investment. Nobel laureates or not, this requires a heady amount of confidence in one's ability to predict the future.

Lesson one of this tragedy is about identifying the appropriate response to changing risk/reward characteristics in the markets in which you are invested. When the risk/reward curve shifts inward on your portfolio management program (as it invariably will over the course of a long career in the markets), your choices boil down to either maintaining current exposure levels and accepting a lower return or increasing your risk to the point where, if things work out in your favor, you can preserve your historical performance. If you choose the former path, you may have periods of modest results; but you are likely to remain solvent and, perhaps more important, to preserve capital to deploy when the risk/reward curve shifts outward again (as it usually will). Conversely if you adjust your risks upward to meet target performance levels, if the gods are smiling on you, this trade may work out. However, by doing so, you are most certainly placing yourself at the mercy of events beyond your control; and as I have argued throughout these many pages, this is precisely the condition you want to avoid. No one understood these trade-offs better than the LTCM crew; yet their failure to adhere to these core principals is one of the main reasons why their ship, widely thought to be unsinkable, hit that iceberg.

Lesson two, which pertains to liquidity management, also became apparent only when sifting through the wreckage. The size of the Long-Term portfolio turned out to be astonishing—not only when compared to the amount of capital available to fund it, but also in terms of its dominance of certain asset and instrument classes. While the combined value of on- and off-balance-sheet instruments was almost incalculable, it was clear that the fund owned, or held short, an alarming percentage of the float of certain financial instruments. This included frightening portions of the entire debt issuance of individual countries. When events beyond their control (most notably the Russian default of August 1998) caused their positions to move against them, they were unable to effect risk reduction through liquidation because, quite simply, no other market participants, not even the global financial institutions that were their trading partners, had the financial or risk capital to take the other side of these trades. Note that this problem occurs in all markets for anyone who takes control of too large a portion of a single set of assets. Think of a real estate speculator who buys up an entire neighborhood and then has to sell lots for reasons of financial duress. Is he going to get a good price for these assets? Not likely.

The critical mistake made by the LTCM brain trust was that their position size went well beyond what the liquidity of the markets would bear. Moreover, they didn't do this just in one or two financial instruments, but rather in dozens and perhaps hundreds of markets. In their own postmortems on the events of the fall of 1998, Meriwether and his partners will tell you that the real problem was that everyone in the market knew their positions and used this information against them. This is only partially true: While many market participants knew what instruments LTCM was trading, almost everyone was stupefied by the size of their positions. Moreover, that information about their specific positions was widely available to market participants was an inevitable result of their overaggressiveness in the market. If you are going to assume positions that represent 50%, 60%, sometimes approaching 100% of the issuance of esoteric securities such as Danish Mortgage Revenue Bonds and the sovereign debt of the Czech Republic, other market participants are bound to notice. To expect them to ignore the fact that you are trying to liquidate positions that you have been accumulating for months is to ask to operate outside of the financial world that made you wealthy beyond measure in the first instance.

Since the debacle, most of the partners of LTCM have moved on to greener pastures. Several of them started a risk management consultancy practice. Some of the academics went back to their ivory towers. As for JM, he started another hedge fund, this time targeting more modest returns at lower leverage factors.

The investors who are funding your portfolio, whether they be the custodians of a money management institution, individuals who have trusted their personal capital to you, or some other profile, will be mindful and appreciative of the care you have taken with their assets and will reward you in the long term by more permanently entrusting you with your portfolio management responsibilities. In my experience, these entities understand the conflicts that arise when you hit a bad stretch (as you are well likely to) and will allocate their discretionary capital to those who manage it prudently, with their interests in mind. A trader who is looking to get fat on other people's risks is a bit like the proverbial and much-maligned used-car salesman. Ultimately, customers see through his angle and deal with him as little as possible. Note that in many cases, it is possible for both to enrich themselves; however, no one rationally mistakes their efforts for high-quality professional service.

Some of the dynamics involved in managing other people's money are also at play for those trading their own capital. Here, instead of coming into conflict with an external funding entity, you will find yourself personally torn between the objectives you have as a manager of your own personal wealth and your desire for success in the markets. Though perhaps more subtle in nature, these conflicts can be every bit as destructive as those between the professional portfolio manager and the source of his or her capital funding. Certainly, the internal strife you may suffer in this regard cannot be constructive to your decision making in the markets, and it can often cloud judgment in ways that are catastrophic to your financial well-being. Of course, if you reduce your exposure in times of difficulty, you obtain multiple benefits, including capital preservation, the ability to continue to participate in the markets, and the confidence that your trading and investment activities are not likely to damage your financial profile beyond repair.

One more thing I'd like to reinforce about the concept of risk reduction in the midst of a drawdown: *If you have hit your loss limit, stop trading.* The breaching of this threshold means one thing and one thing only— the game is over and you have lost. The only question that remains is whether you want to play again in the future. If the answer is yes, then your path is clear. By contrast, if you refuse to capitulate under the rules that have been established at the outset (i.e., your account won't lose more than X), then in addition to any incremental damage you may suffer to your financial or professional well-being, I can state for sure that you are headed down a path where your trading prerogatives will belong to others (e.g., creditors or angry employers), and not to you.

Now let's take a final look at the sunny side of the egg, namely, the additional risk-taking capacity that is available to you during and immediately after intervals of sustained profitability. Just as your losses bring you closer to your economic stop-out, so do gains separate you, in terms of P/L, from your maximum-loss threshold. Thus, one of the many happy implications of positive returns is that it adds, dollar for dollar, to your risk capital as we have defined it throughout this book. While I have described risk reduction during drawdown as being an *imperative*, I would characterize the concept of increased risk taking after a run-up as being a *prerogative*. Specifically, rather than stating *you must* increase exposure as risk capital increases, I would tell you that *you can* accept higher risk levels; and in specific situations, I would more emphatically suggest that *you ought* to.

To review our rationale: Positive P/L creates a risk cushion that allows you to think more expansively about your portfolio management activities and provides the ideal framework for some portfolio experimentation. This may take the form of larger position sizes and/or longer holding periods than you would consider comfortable when you are flat or down. Or it might involve everything from dabbling in new markets or instrument types to testing out new counterparty relationships. I have suggested that the best way of exploring these new horizons is to frame them in the form of a controlled experiment, under which you set aside a specific portion of the revenues you have generated that you are willing to risk in an effort to expand yourself as a portfolio manager. Set up a separate account, if necessary, to capture this activity; and by all means, use the statistical tools I have described in this book as a way of measuring your relative success in these new activities. If you lose an amount equal to what you have established as risk capital for these efforts, discontinue the strategy and go back to the core of what was working for you. If the new stuff juices you and makes you better in the markets, let the fair winds blow you where they may.

The best portfolio managers I know all define their experiences in terms of these types of risk/reward cycles, delevering during drawdown and seeking to expand their horizons when times are good. The payoff you will derive from this ebb and flow takes the form of allowing you to maximize your adaptability to everchanging market conditions: You will have the ability to weather most times of tribulation for your trading activities, and you will find yourself with a much broader set of methodologies to operate successfully as markets evolve.

AVOID SURPRISES—ESPECIALLY TO YOURSELF

If you buy into the methodologies we've discussed, you should be in a position where pretty much everything that happens to your portfolio is within the range of normal expectation. Of course, there will be exceptions to this rule. For example, if you found yourself, on September 11, 2001, with a lot of airline and insurance company exposure, the losses you may have experienced when the markets reopened the following week would have been difficult to anticipate. Don't blame yourself too much if this happens, as you will have clearly been the victim of events beyond your control. If you sized your portfolio exposures appropriately, you should be able to handle the attendant volatility, and my guess is that the next roll of the dice will work in your favor.

More important, absent these types of market events, the risks and rewards you take in the marketplace should be at all times quantifiable. This rule applies both to institutional money managers and to those trading their own capital. In each case, the concept of P/L fluctuations beyond what had been specifically anticipated is one that reduces confidence and inspires smaller, not larger, money management mandates. It is critical to at all times be cognizant of the P/L ranges that are likely to govern your trading. If you find yourself surprised by a given outcome, you should strive to figure out the reason why and to put measures in place to guard against recurrence. If you're trading professionally, you never want the risk control elements of your funding entity to be surprised either. They need to understand your portfolio dynamics and will feel very burned if events occur in your account that neither you nor they had anticipated.

What types of market and portfolio dynamics lend themselves to surprise outcomes? In my experience, the primary culprits are markets with nonlinear pricing patterns. This most prominently includes derivative markets; and generally speaking, it is fair to conclude that the more complicated the derivatives portfolio, the higher the likelihood for unpredictable results. You should, as a matter of core principal, avoid trading any derivative instruments (or combination of derivative instruments) where you don't fully understand not only the range of outcomes, but also the associated causes and effects.

It is not sufficient to understand the boundary conditions of derivative trading; you should avoid these markets unless you understand well what may happen to your portfolio inside these boundaries. For example, portfolio managers of every level of sophistication are comfortable purchasing options because they know that their losses are limited to the amount invested in the options' premium. Is this sufficient? Not in my view. I've seen way too many portfolios that have died a slow death by purchasing option after option that indeed hit that (admittedly identifiable) worst-case scenario. It is necessary to have a much higher degree of understanding of derivative pricing dynamics than worst-case loss prior to having a successful derivatives portfolio model.

Even portfolios that are comprised exclusively of securities that have linear pricing characteristics can offer surprises that serve as red flags to the portfolio management process. More often than not, this occurs when the securities contained in the portfolio move in abrupt and surprising ways—largely due to the unanticipated impact of new information in the market-place. Just as you don't want to trade derivatives if you don't have a very precise handle on how they may react to the full range of likely market conditions, so too is it sinful to be trading cash securities that lend themselves to discrete price movement not contemplated within the portfolio strategy.

What happens, then, when you own a security on which you're willing to risk 5%, hoping it will rise by 10% but instead it drops 20%? If it happens repeatedly, I can only describe it as a breakdown of your portfolio management program. Take a hard look at the factors that caused the correction. Were they anticipatable (e.g., tied to an earnings release or other foreseeable event)? If so, it suggests that you're not doing as much fundamental work as you need to do to understand the contingencies on your portfolio's horizon. If not (i.e., these events are seemingly random), then you are probably trading the wrong markets, as there are pricing dynamics at play that are beyond your ability to comprehend. Effective trading and investing programs are based on causes and effects that lend themselves to scientific evaluation. If these conditions don't exist in your universe of tradable instruments, it's hard to see how you can ever attain, much less sustain, an exploitable edge.

SEEK TO MAXIMIZE YOUR PERFORMANCE AT THE MARGIN

As at least a partially trained economist, I try to look at behavior at the margin as the driving force behind all economic activity—including trading and investing. This means that attention to small details will help reach big goals. Slice your commission costs by a fraction, improve your price execution by a small increment, control your downside exposure in terms of the pennies as well as the dollars—all of these steps can mean the difference between success and failure over the long haul.

It pays to devote close attention to the marginal behavior of the market in general. Success in the marketplace, as in baseball or football, is often a matter, of inches, as opposed to yards. Understand that the pricing of financial instruments is seldom driven by dramatic events but rather by minute shades of perceptional differences between buyers and sellers. A company beats earnings estimates by a fraction, and, bang, the entire equity market moves. Unemployment rates move a couple of tenths of a percent, and the entire interest-rate market can assume a different tenor. A central bank can signal a shift in its perception about the merits of holding gold stocks, and that commodity can change in value by breathtaking amounts.

These are just a few examples of the manner in which seemingly minor changes to the market landscape can have a dramatic impact on prices, which, in turn, will materially impact portfolio performance. If you remain in tune to these patterns and apply them to your trading activities, you stand the best chance for success over the long term.

SEEK NONMONETARY BENEFITS

We all know that we're in this for the money, and I certainly wouldn't recommend any trading strategy that doesn't feature profitability as its primary objective. However, I would submit for your consideration that the rewards that accrue to enlightened market participation can be measured in ways that transcend sheer financial gain. I believe that trading and portfolio management are among the purest and most clinical of intellectual tests, with success requiring perhaps the most diverse set of cognitive skills of any activity you are likely to undertake. The successful portfolio manager must wear many hats, including those of quantitative and qualitative analyst, prognosticator, personal advocate for fair pricing, risk manager, accountant, and financier. In undertaking this responsibility, you are trying to see into a future where current inefficiencies in the pricing of assets correct themselves and where conceptual trends become economic realities. At the same time, you are engaged in a hypercompetitive, two-way auction, where the agents against whom you are competing for the best price are out for blood and know no mercy.

When viewed from this perspective, I believe it is necessary to either embrace the intellectual/competitive challenge of portfolio management or risk failure on a large scale. The individuals I admire most in the markets (who, not coincidentally, are also the most successful) are those who love the battle for profitability that is the essence of the effort and who attack it with the full measure of energy, creativity, wisdom, and whimsy that they can bring to bear. These traders bring the joy of the contest into all of their market-related activities. They are not always successful, but they appreciate their adversary and know that they are at all times enriched by the journey they have undertaken.

Perhaps more important, they have fun. They thrive on the excitement brought about by the uncertainty of their endeavors; and win or lose, they appreciate the very human aspects of the struggle in which they are engaging. At any success level, there is joy in the effort. Of course, most of these individuals are professional money managers who operate under the happy advantages of knowing that they have an edge as well as a honed methodology through which to exploit that edge. Armed with ability and ambition, they rise each morning eager not only to enhance their financial position but also to relish the new elements of discovery that each new day in the markets brings. Indeed, I know a number of professional managers who have generated hundreds of millions, and in some cases billions, of market revenues who still derive the same type of thrill from the single trade that they did when they first started out, before their fortunes were made and their celebrity established. I envy these people, not only because they are materially successful, but also because they have found a way to spend their professional lives in an activity they love and for which the potential monetary rewards are, for all intents and purposes, limitless.

Like any other endeavor, there is a fine line between focusing on an activity that is your passion and operating under the shackles of a debilitating obsession. Trading and investing, breathtaking in their scope and requiring such intellectual passion to achieve a form of mastery, are precisely the types of activities that can foster obsessive behavior. I have witnessed many a market participant who is consumed with his or her portfolio management responsibilities to such a point that critical elements of a well-balanced existence are shut out, and even programs that are successful from a financial perspective begin to exact an unacceptable cost. This, in my experience, is a very risky condition, one that market participants of all types should seek to avoid. Not only is it unhealthy, but it is probably unsustainable over the long haul. Therefore, if you find yourself doing nothing but trading, analyzing, and thinking about trading, it's probably not a bad idea to take an objective review of the situation with an eye toward making some lifestyle changes. Some of the telltale signs that you have gone overboard with your commitment to the markets are:

- Majority of free time is spent on market-related activities.
- Health is deteriorating (e.g., large, unintended weight gain/loss; changed eating habits and exercise program; inability to sleep; etc.).
- Personal relationships are deteriorating—particularly with spouses, children, and significant others.
- Unable to focus attention on non-market-related topics.

I'm not a doctor, and I don't play one on television; but I believe that these symptoms represent an inner voice telling you to slow down. There's simply no reason to grind yourself down into such a state. If you're doing great in the markets, save some of your energy for tomorrow. The markets will open on time, I promise. If you're struggling, then you probably don't need me to tell you that pressing matters won't help. Recognize that at some point there are diminishing returns to your efforts, and seek to not go beyond this point of energy dissipation. If you can't responsibly risk the amount of capital you've currently committed to trading without this type of all-consuming focus, reduce your capital. To state the matter quite simply, it's not worth ruining your health, ending your marriage, or killing yourself over a few extra dollars in the markets. If the sacrifice you are making for success is too great (and only you are in a position to make this determination), either find a different way to make money, or cut down on your expenses. The price you will pay for redlining it indefinitely is far greater than what you will experience by learning to live on a budget.

While we're on the subject, when the burdens of portfolio management become so onerous as to take all of the joy out of the exercise, it's probably time to stop trading. While one might think of this as a rather obvious point, you'd be surprised at how many traders fail to grasp it. No one but you can make this call; but I submit that when the time is appropriate, it is a call you *must* make. Take a month or a year off. The markets will be here when you get back. More important, you'll be ready to attack them with renewed energy and focus.

Finally, I encourage you to take pride in what you do, not only because it is difficult, but also because it is important. I stand (perhaps in the minority, but firmly so) solidly behind the conviction that traders help make the world a better place by assuming risks that other economic agents don't want and by contributing to the mechanisms by which economic assets are efficiently priced. If you doubt that the impacts of these services are real, I suggest you examine those economies that don't have market mechanisms that are driven by traders competing to buy and sell assets at the best available price. I've seen the effects of this and know that they can be devastating, with sellers having to dump assets at prices below cost and buyers being forced to pay outrageous amounts for needed commodities whose availability and production costs give lie to the amounts at which their controllers make them available.

PURE GRAIN

I have only one more anecdote to share; and when I tell you to skip it if you wish, I do so with a Grateful (yes, Grateful) nod to Ken Kesey. In my former career as director of risk management for the Chicago Mercantile Exchange, I was frequently called on to discuss our methods with financial planners from around the world who sought to establish or to enhance futures markets in their own countries, and thus reap the benefits that we in the United States have enjoyed for so long due to the advanced state of our market mechanisms. By this time, many countries with even the most rudimentary market economies had built functional futures markets, so the discussions tended to center around whether this or that form of risk assessment, financial control, or margin offered the best efficiencies. However, one day, more than 10 years ago, I was asked to meet with about a half dozen market economists from the former Soviet Union. These were hard-boiled men, some brilliant, all well educated, some of them having suffered the evils of Stalin *and* Hitler and lived to tell the tale. They were not Westernized in their mannerisms; but they were polite, appreciative, and supremely focused on bringing about a better tomorrow for their people and their country.

Their task was to help create a market economy out of the ruins of a bureaucratic military dictatorship that had crumbled under the weight of its own ineptitude a very few months earlier, leaving no discernible economic system in its wake. In the interim, a handful of localized market mechanisms had sprung up, but these were mainly outlets for the enrichment of corrupt local officials and the enhanced control of mob organizations. Things were truly up for grabs in Russia; but of all the problems that economic planners faced, none was more pressing than the stabilization of the agricultural economy. This staple of Russian social order had deteriorated to the point where the growers of grain could only sell their output for a fraction of its production costs, while consumers were forced to pay murderous sums for the right to buy these products. Often, a bushel of grain that could not be had for less than $6 at a local market, would not fetch more than a quarter of this price when sold by farmers a scant hundred miles away. As a result, perfectly good farms were going fallow right next to urban areas where widespread hunger ruled the day.

My Russian agro-economist friends had organized a rudimentary futures market (or so they tried to tell me, for they spoke very little English and I understood exactly zero Russian), which stayed open two hours a week for the purposes of fixing a regionwide price for commodities such as wheat and corn. They had all kinds of questions written down in their notebooks, ranging from how futures market financial settlements worked to how the process of delivery could be organized in an efficient manner. Each time they asked a question, I was able to bark out a very elementary answer, which I knew failed to grasp any of the subtlety of the sophisticated U.S. market processes. Nevertheless, I got the impression that they understood. They would then debate loudly (in Russian) among themselves for up to an hour while I sat there trying to keep my wits about me as I waited patiently for their next inquiry.

We spent the whole day together in this manner, during which time I believe my collective comments spanned a total of less than five minutes. In spite of this, we had developed something of a bond. At the end of the session, the leader of the group opened a black satchel and handed me a bottle of Russian vodka, heartily shaking my hand and slapping me on the back. Then they left, happily continuing their heated debate (or so it would seem) down in the elevator and into the street. For all I know, their debate continues to this day.

I remember thinking to myself at the time that the country these men represented was at least a generation away from enjoying the kind of market benefits taken for granted in the United States for most of the twentieth century. I could only hope that I'd done something small to push them further down the right track.

I still have that bottle of vodka, though there's more air inside of it now than there was when I received it as a gift more than 10 years ago. Every now and then, I pour me a glass, which I prefer to drink straight at room temperature when no one else is around. And I think of my buds, and I hope they are well. I also hope that they have made some progress on their mission. I don't hear much about the Moscow Commodities Exchange; and, given the amount of attention I devote to the markets, this isn't a great sign. Perhaps these things take more than a decade; perhaps they require a generation or two.

I'm not much of a drinker, but I sure do enjoy that vodka. I like to think that this is partly due to the fact that it is distilled from the fruit of the soil tilled by my very own ancestors who had departed the motherland around the time of the War to End All Wars.

And I can't help but wonder: If there were a functioning Moscow Commodities Exchange at the time of their departure, maybe they wouldn't have had to go.

The benefits of risk transference provided by traders are inestimable. Most of us have been schooled on examples of this, such as the wheat farmer who is able to use futures markets to lock in today's prices for next spring's harvest, and the makers of Swiss watches sold in the United States who are able to guard against the declining value of Swiss francs. These are real and meaningful instances of traders taking on the burden of specific types of risk that exist in the economy but are unwanted by those who would assume them in the normal course of their business. Absent the willingness of market participants to accept these risks, the outcome is clear: Farmers produce less wheat, and fewer Swiss watches get shipped across the Atlantic.

The macroeconomic benefits of these market mechanisms have exploded in the past couple of decades and represent no small contribution to the economic prosperity we have enjoyed over this time period. In particular, with the advent of equity- and fixed-income derivatives such as index futures and interest-rate swaps, the rewards of a trading economy extend to the core capital markets. Companies can now use these products to accompany the issuance of new equity and debt, thereby eliminating the fear that their financial costs will increase dramatically by the time the funds are needed. As a result, the economy produces new goods, services, and jobs at a pace unimaginable one short generation ago.

All of these benefits accrue to an economy because traders are there, willing to assume the risks that are inherent in essential economic processes such as capital formation but that, if not transferred to speculators, represent onerous contingent liabilities to the creators of new products and processes. Without traders of all shapes and sizes, the nature and scope of these liabilities can increase prohibitively and can mean the difference between creating a new company, building a new factory, developing a new product or standing pat. Certainly, the potential rewards to the market participant are sizeable and in some cases arguably stand in disproportion to the hazards he or she assumes. However, if you really examine the situation of the trader, asked to bid competitively for the right to assume these exposures and often armed with little beyond his or her wits and intestinal fortitude, perhaps the opportunities that accrue to traders may seem a bit less outrageous. Moreover, every single market participant represents a piece of this gigantic puzzle, and most are hardly earning king's ransoms for their efforts.

Thus, you should take some satisfaction in the vital role you are playing in the market economy as a trader/investor. On a minute-by-minute basis, it may seem that you are in a very personal struggle, with all hazards and associated rewards belonging to you and you alone. However, there is more at stake than the number at the bottom of your account statement. You are contributing in your own fashion to a critical process that benefits everyone, and those who tell you that your efforts have no value are simply flat-out wrong.

APPLY LIBERAL DOSES OF HUMILITY AND HUMOR

The beautiful thing about the markets is the fact that they represent the combined input of all economic agents who act, at least in theory, to protect their own interests, based on a universally available information set, which they are able to process in a rational manner. This is a formidable force that cannot, in my experience, be overcome in a sustained fashion by the efforts and talents of individual humans.

This does not mean that the market always spawns rational outcomes. Particularly when viewed over short time periods, economic assets can be priced at levels that when reviewed from the perspective of time make us stand back in amazement that they could ever have been the product of the collective, rational thoughts of humans guided by their own economic interest. Ironically, these new perspectives often come rather quickly, such that the same parties that contributed directly to the irrationality are the ones that are the most retrospectively dumbfounded when consistent pricing themes return to prevalence. From Dutch tulips in the seventeenth century to U.S. virtual bookstores at the end of the twentieth century, markets have demonstrated their mastery over every individual human attribute. They are governed unilaterally by neither wisdom nor whimsy, but they will give an occasional nod to both.

In order to be successful in light of these realities, it is necessary to be humble. If you attempt to beat the market, the overwhelming odds are that you will lose; so the best thing to do is not to compete with it. Even if you do come up with a formula that allows you to anticipate price movements with greater accuracy than other participants, this edge is at risk every moment of every day as other economic agents travel the same path of discovery that has led you to your happy state of affairs. Therefore, I urge you to avoid underestimating the challenges associated with generating superior risk-adjusted returns in the future, even if you have done so consistently in the past. I know many traders who thought, with some justification, that they had the game licked for good, only to find, slowly or abruptly, that the rules had changed in ways to which they could not successfully adapt.

Avoid taking failure personally. The market often does stupid things—particularly through the filter of either hindsight or self-interest (i.e., because you are positioned the opposite way). When these stupid events occur, there is often a tendency to project your anger onto the markets as though they act in some direct effort to cause your unhappiness.

These dynamics can conspire to cause traders to spiral into irrational portfolio management in an effort to correct what the individual in question views to be a cosmic injustice. Of course, when this happens, the individual projects this negative energy not on the markets, but rather on themselves—with disastrous P/L implications that can turn difficult trading intervals into catastrophic ones. This is often a sign that a given portfolio manager has hit the end of the line in terms of the productive part of his or her trading journey and may need (at least temporarily) to find non-market-related venues to get kicks. Guard against this kind of thinking at all costs lest you become the victim of your own evil schemes.

As a final note, it occurs to me virtually every day that a bit of self-effacing humor is essential to success in the markets. When you begin to think about the confluence of events of your lifetime (as well as those tied to the social evolution of humanity) that have placed you in a position where you are devoting the flower of your time and energies to the odd little task of attempting to buy economic assets at below their value and sell them at levels above this threshold, it's hard not to recognize the note of absurdity of it all. From here, you can layer on everything from the billions and billions that are spent each year to maintain market infrastructures, to the behavior of those with whom you interact on a day-to-day basis in your trading activities; and you soon realize that even the most imaginative fiction writer could never dream up the stuff that happens every day in real life. The whole thing can be pretty hysterical, all the more so because each and every one of us is part of this absurd little pantomime. Perhaps among the most entertaining elements of the entire dynamic is how grimly many market participants—particularly those who count themselves among the most successful—view the process of trading and investing. Some of them view themselves as latter-day Leonardos, others as the second coming of Napoleon. Learn by their examples, maintain your sense of perspective, and you'll likely make out just fine.

BE HEALTHY/CULTIVATE OTHER INTERESTS

I am not your mother, but I am here to tell you that if you really want to nail it in the markets, you should get plenty of rest, drink a lot of fluids, eat all your vegetables, and exercise often. In addition, it certainly wouldn't hurt to read a book every now and then that's not market related (if pressed, I might recommend either Gibbon's *The Decline and Fall of the Roman Empire* or Faulkner's *Absalom, Absalom!*) and do whatever else that successful people do to enrich their lives. Learn to play a musical instrument; or if you already play one, join a band. If you have a band, go out on tour. Volunteer at a soup kitchen. Write a poem to a girl who has never had a poem written to her. Coach your kid's little league team; and if you're already doing that, try pulling a double steal in a tight situation. Tip generously to all service providers who can't live on their nondiscretionary income. If all else fails, play solitaire (preferably with real playing cards), but don't bother to do this if you're going to cheat. There's more to life than trading, so fill your lungs and exhale as often as possible. Roll around in the dirt every once in a while, for this is the stuff of which you are made.

A vigorous (and hopefully routine) roll in the hay can also bestow a world of benefit.

With that, I reckon I've told about everything I know. I hope that like Huck said about Mark in reference to Tom, I mainly told the truth. And now, ladies and gentlemen, I suggest you prepare yourselves, for the bell is about to ring.

Optimal f and Risk of Ruin

I'll bet you thought I was really done this time, didn't you? Well, I thought I was, too; but in the midst of my leave-taking, I found one critical task left undone, namely, the act of paying appropriate tribute to the body of research that laid the groundwork for the approaches I have recommended for the efficient setting of portfolio management risk parameters. Of course, this is one of the cornerstones of *Trading Risk* and is a process that if not handled effectively is likely to cause more damage to a portfolio than just about anything else that I can think of—at least off the top of my head. Specifically, I refer to two concepts: *optimal f* and *risk of ruin*, which point those interested in risk taking toward the sizing of exposures in such a way as to render them consistent with both objectives and constraints. These concepts, which can be thought of as analogues to the Inverted Sharpe Ratio and Percent of Risk Capital methodologies described in Chapter 5, can be used contemporaneously to form a useful (and aesthetically pleasing, for those who like symmetry) upper and lower bound for exposure assumption. Optimal f is designed to identify the level of investment in individual positions that is consistent with maximum profitability, as based on user-defined inputs of prospective transaction profitability. The mathematics of risk of ruin can be applied to manage exposures such that risk takers don't lose more than that they have designated up front as their risk capital, again as typically measured on the level of the individual transaction.

If these concepts sound familiar to the (by now) legions of *Trading Risk* devotees, it is because, as mentioned earlier, they are very similar to the tools laid out for exposure parameterization in the core of the text. If you caught these similarities, you should congratulate yourself. You were indeed paying attention and have latched on successfully to at least some of the critical themes I have tried to impart. Moreover, I believe that anyone who is using either optimal f or risk of ruin mathematics in his or her own portfolio decision making is on the right track. However, as I hope to make clear in this Appendix, they are at least in some ways less applicable to the holistic task of portfolio risk management than the analogous mechanisms we have covered in this book. Let's take a brief look at each concept so that we understand its application to portfolio risk management and how it works vis à vis the methodologies I have recommended to accomplish the same tasks.

OPTIMAL f

In his book *Portfolio Management Formulas: Mathematical Trading Methods for Futures, Options, and Stock Markets* (John Wiley, 1989), Ralph Vince laid out a formula that computes the optimal transaction size for risk takers given specific information regarding the likely range of return outcomes and associated probabilities. I've done my best to avoid an excessive use of equations throughout the body of this text, and I don't mean to break my streak now; so exclude the exact formula from my analysis. Suffice to say that Vince sets f_{opt} (the optimal transaction size) as a function of the ratio of a given transaction's expected return to its associated likely worst-case outcome.

   That the optimal f concept, which added a useful element of mathematical precision to the sizing of transactions, is a worthy advancement in the field of portfolio science is a matter of very little dispute. However, the methodology, as Vince himself points out, is rife with shortcomings. In the first instance, the concept assumes that we understand more than is the lot of mere mortals to know about the return distribution of our transactions. Specifically, in order to calculate optimal f, it is necessary to input actual return information into the equation; and by now, you should understand that if you actually have this data at hand, there's not much point in bothering about concepts such as risk management. Instead, I recommend that you simply plug this information into your f_{opt} machine and let it work its optimization magic.

   Again, Vince recognized this paradox, stating it succinctly in the following few sentences taken directly from a later work, *The Mathematics of Money Management* (John Wiley, 1992): "In other words, it doesn't matter how profitable your trading system is on a one-contract basis, so long as it is profitable, even if marginally so. If you have a system that makes $10 per contract per trade . . . , you can use money management to make it far more profitable than a system that shows a $1,000 average trade. . . . What matters, then, is not how profitable your system has been, but rather how certain is it that the system will show at least a marginal profit in the future. Therefore, the most important preparation a trader can do is to make as certain as possible that he has a positive mathematical expectation in the future."

I completely concur with these observations, which, in fact, point us directly to the second basic problem with a strict reliance on optimal f as our exclusive means of sizing exposures. Of course, our universal inability to predict the future, that ubiquitous stumbling block on the road toward portfolio management nirvana, trips us up yet again. For anyone who does, in fact, have reasonably accurate estimates of distribution of future transactions returns, optimal f will indeed point you toward return maximization. This is one reason why "clinical" risk-taking environments, such as those associated with coin flipping and the purchase of lottery tickets, offer the most elegant examples of its application. However, in our imperfectly constructed trading universe, the mean return to individual transactions is a great imponderable. Of course, the most rational source of predictive information regarding future returns is probably historical data; and if you want to be an optimal f-er, it is my recommendation that you start there.

The other recognized problem with the optimal f calculation is that it views the world from the perspective of a single transaction, exclusively contemplating the issue of appropriate sizing of *individual positions* to achieve the objective of maximum *transactions-level* profitability. The following problem then emerges: What if, even if I have accurately estimated the range of transactions-level returns, I hit a bad streak and hit or approach my worst-case scenario on contemporaneous transactions? This (again the careful reader of the main body of the text will remember) is very close to the concept of *drawdown*, which, if not managed carefully, may exhaust risk capital before the optimal f machine can even begin to confer its advertised benefit. Under a strict adherence to the methodology, as Vince himself recognized, there is virtually no limit to the size of the drawdown that a portfolio can experience if it applies the optimal f methodology without taking into account the possibility that a string of consecutive losses (or, indeed, even losses in close proximity to one another) can exhaust even the largest reserve of risk capital.

Again, optimal f-ers, including Vince himself, understood the limitations of the approach and have offered elegant remedies to address these critical shortcomings. Most notably, they have created a concept called *secure f*, which utilizes the essence of the optimal f calculation but which (1) relies on historical return information to determine return sequences and (2) features a very useful maximum drawdown constraint as an input to the calculation. These are undoubted improvements, which render the methodology, already a useful metric if applied effectively, that much more applicable.

I should point out, before explaining why I prefer the Inverted Sharpe methodology described in Chapter 5, that it suffers from some of the same limitations as optimal f. Most notably, it requires the user to provide some inputs as to what future returns might look like (through the Sustainable Sharpe concept) that are, by definition, somewhat subjective. Moreover, there is nothing inherent in the calculation, when measured in its "static" form, to preclude single-minded individuals from burning through all of their risk capital, and (perhaps) then some. With all of this in mind, here's where I feel the advantages to the Inverted Sharpe methodology lie:

- *It utilizes a "portfolio" approach, as opposed to a transactions-level model, to size exposures.* While optimal f will give you some notion of transaction sizing and its attendant impacts on performance, what happens at the individual transactions level is, in my view, entirely less important than what occurs with respect to the overall portfolio. Very few market participants use a methodology under which their fortunes are tied either to a single transactions or to series of transactions, which take place sequence. This is the implied setting for optimal f research and is another reason why much of the analysis appears to be more applicable to games of chance like coin flips or dice rolls. Portfolio management, by contrast, involves maintaining an inventory of financial instruments, some designed to drive profit/loss (P/L), others to provide some sort of diversification benefit, and still others to act as hedges of other exposures. Optimal f will not assist you in your efforts to size overall exposures at the portfolio level, taking into account these subcomponents; Inverted Sharpe will.
- *The projected return elements of the Inverted Sharpe calculation are based on more realistic inputs than those associated with optimal f.* On the whole, I am troubled by the notion of placing too much credence in the estimation of expected return at the individual transactions level—even when, as is the case with the *secure f*, the inputs are based on historical volatility data. I wonder, for instance, how one goes about selecting the entry and exit points. Moreover, there's still enough of the University of Chicago boy left in me to feel that the expected return on a given, single transaction ought to be somewhere around zero.

By using the Sustainable Sharpe component of the Inverted Sharpe ratio methodology, by contrast, we are basing our return estimates on (1) portfolio-level data (which I have argued in the immediately preceding discussion is more reliable than transactions-level data) and (2) empirical information that derives directly from our own performance. Moreover, as careful readers of Chapter 5 will recall, the Inverted Sharpe methodology does not call for the use of your actual Sharpe ratio in the setting of exposure parameters, but rather suggests you set this input at a comfort level that you can sustain across most, if not all, market conditions. Prudent portfolio managers will set their Sustainable Sharpe ratio inputs at levels below their actual Sharpes so as to render them entirely consistent with an approach that uses past performance data as a means of establishing conservative estimates of future performance

- *The Inverted Sharpe methodology is designed to work hand in hand with the 10% of Trading Capital Rule to ensure that risk taking is neither too high nor too low—given reasonably established objectives and constraints.* If you remember what we covered in Chapter 5, the idea of the Inverted Sharpe/10% Rule is intended to achieve the objective not of optimization but rather of rationalization. The whole idea here is to set your risk levels neither too low to reduce your portfolio management efforts to little more than spinning your wheels, nor too high to impede your ability to manage your risk capital effectively. In this way, the methodology establishes what I believe to be an effective and highly applicable upper bound and lower bound to exposure assumption. The ranges between the two, which for most portfolio managers will be substantial, allow for a healthy dose of that most critical component of most effective portfolio management: judiciously applied discretion. Every situation you face as a trader will be different, and from this perspective two trades are about as likely to be identical as two snowflakes. However, if you set your risk taking at ranges that are consistent with the results of the Inverted Sharpe/10% Rule, you are in a great position if not to maximize returns in every instance, then at least to ensure that scarce resources such as risk capital are never foolishly squandered.

I encourage anyone who uses the Inverted Sharpe methodology to constantly be reviewing the actual Sharpe and aggressively reducing the Sustainable Sharpe in the event that the former falls to levels below the latter. Inverted Sharpe, like every other element of the *Trading Risk* statistical tool kit, is a diagnostic tool designed to characterize the qualitative aspects of your risk taking. Nothing in it implies the need or, in fact, the wisdom of attempting to precisely calibrate exposures on the basis of its results. Again, it is simply there to tell you (1) whether your risk taking is consistent with your objectives and (2) what level of exposure is roughly consistent with the goals you have set for yourself.

The key to using these figures effectively, of course, is to ensure that your Sustainable Sharpe is a number on which you can comfortably bank.

Therefore, in order to use the methodology effectively, it is necessary to take routine periodic checks to ensure that your actual Sharpe doesn't slip materially below the figure you set as your Sustainable Sharpe. If this happens, you must make the appropriate adjustments to your objectives and risk levels or to some combination of the two.

Otherwise, I'd say you're on your way.

Of course, it is not my intention to imply that optimal f and Inverted Sharpe are in competition with one another. Moreover, there's no reason that you can't apply both methodologies contemporaneously, with optimal f applied in the sizing of individual transactions and Inverted Sharpe used as a means of establishing exposure bands at the portfolio level. However, I do caution against the use of optimal f, or even secure f, as your exclusive tool for risk management.

RISK OF RUIN

This is another concept that takes its origins from the universe of gambling. Of course, for centuries, speculators have been trying to determine the probabilities of blowing their whole load, so to speak; but a book by Alan N. Wilson, *The Casino Gamblers Edge*, perhaps best synthesizes these efforts. Wilson, a very cerebral fellow who once worked on the staff of Owen Chamberlain, 1959 Nobel laureate in physics, and later spent 30 years at General Dynamics, as perhaps the defense industry's leading expert in the field of random-number generation, sought to answer the following question: In a game of chance, what is my risk of losing my entire bankroll before doubling it? He ultimately arrived at the following equation, solving specifically for $r(x)$, the probability of losing x:

$$r(x) = A + B(1/S)^x$$

where p = probability of winning on a single play
q = probability of losing on a single play
$S = p/q$
A and B = arbitrary constants that depend on (1) the initial capital of the player, (2) the amount the player is willing to lose, and (3) the amount the player wishes to win
x = the amount of capital the player has at any given time

As is the case with optimal f, the equation simply synthesizes such concepts as (1) how much risk capital the risk taker has and (2) the success-to-failure ratio, into an estimate of what is likely to happen in the tails of a return distribution. Risk of ruin is a very useful means of sizing individual transactions such that there is an upper bound to worst-case outcomes. In order to do so, it is necessary to scale transactions sizes to probability-adjusted return streams, reducing them as remaining risk capital erodes and increasing them when it builds.

Let me say right here and now that I have considerable respect for the risk of ruin approach to portfolio management because it fully contemplates all of the lessons I've tried to impart about increasing risk during times of success while reducing risk during more difficult intervals. However, it does suffer from the same problems that plague optimal f, namely its focus on the individual transaction level and its reliance on very subjective inputs as to what success ratios are likely to be in the future. As indicated earlier, the latter of these challenges is a bit ubiquitous in the portfolio-sizing game, so we don't want to be too explicit in our criticisms here.

About the only direct issue I have with the methodology is that it points at individual transactions rather than at portfolio volatility as a whole. However, it is certainly much easier to convert risk of ruin calculations into portfolio measures than it is for optimal f. In fact, you can think of the 10% Rule covered in Chapter 5 as nothing more than a risk of ruin calculation applied at the portfolio level.

In closing, I'd say that the inclusion of risk of ruin dynamics into the portfolio decision-making process is a good idea. I would only caution that you not get too myopic here. By ensuring that your exposures are sized appropriately at the portfolio level, you stand the best chance of preserving capital for its most effective applications.

Index